Myths and Legends

From around the world

Myths and Legends
From around the world

Re-told by Robin Brockman
Illustrations by Michael McLellan

ARCTURUS

Published by
Arcturus Publishing Limited
for Bookmart Limited
Registered Number 2372865
Trading as Bookmart Limited
Desford Road
Enderby
Leicester
LE9 5AD

This edition published 2000

Copyright © Arcturus Publishing Limited
1–7 Shand Street, London SE1 2ES

ISBN 1-84193-014-8

Text and jacket design: Chris Smith

Printed and bound in Finland

Contents

To Anne and Peter Jousiffe
for their friendship, courage under fire
and the loan of so many
invaluable books.

Introduction

Perhaps a more apt title for this volume might have been 'Favourite Myths and Legends', or better still, 'Selected Myths and Legends From Around the World'. This is above all meant to be an easy to read, accessible book, while being faithful to its subjects. Inclusion has depended entirely on what in my own opinion makes a good, rousing, edifying, amusing, charming or frightening story. References to time, context, location and ethnic origin are contained within the tales so that each one can stand alone, as a short-story, without explanation or elaboration.

It is my hope that this book will encourage many readers to study the original or earlier versions of the stories, as well as other tales from the great wealth of world myth and legend. This volume will best serve as a general overview, perhaps even a primer. Cultural balance of a sort has been easy to achieve because nearly every part of the world and every ethnic strain of man has its gods and heroes, monsters and magicians.

In retelling these tales I have tried to make each one memorable and relevant to the modern reader, whether that reader is new to them entirely or encountering them here reborn. None of the hard information in them has been changed, though. Myth, after all, and even that close relation of it, legend, has far more importance in societies than that of simple entertainment. The very wisdom of the ancients, perhaps the Creator's instructions to humanity, may well be wrapped up in certain of our most universal myths. Memory experts attest that even the most mundane or very practical information is best retained by people if it is presented to them in the form of a story.

Partly for this reason common threads abound in tales from the most widely dispersed cultures. This is the case in even the least cosmic, most un-instructive myths. Just being human, living in these bodies on this earth, provides unlimited universal commonality of experience and imagination. This fact constantly highlights, if not some high-minded message of the brotherhood of man, then at least that the world – which we like to think became so much smaller in modern times – has always been pretty tiny.

There is much that was always pure allegory, of course, or meant to be wondrous explanations to impress the masses, while the ruling class or priest caste were the only ones privy to really important information about the nature of this life on earth. There is, therefore, plenty of magic of a far-fetched and supernatural kind in these stories. This is not restricted to the very early ones of how the universe was formed or how life began, nor is it confined to tales of gods and monsters. Of course, even the beliefs of the *cognoscenti*, the high priests and members of mystery cults, were fantastic by any modern standards. Some people see this as reflecting humankind's greater gullibility in days gone by, during the so-called 'long childhood of man'.

The myths and legends of our own age tend only to exaggerate what we see as reality, and, with a few exceptions, very little of the magical seems to creep into them. We are not even sceptically religious these days. No longer do we accept, for instance, as the Victorians did, so much as the mere tenets of the established faith of the land. And we reject all others with even greater ease. More than any of our predecessors in the recorded and unrecorded history of our species, we demand 'proof' of everything.

However, if pre-history and ancient civilizations constituted the "childhood of man", as some call it, I maintain that our era is surely its adolescence. We believe nothing, doubt everything, and deny all that cannot be seen and measured by the yardstick of our own limited point of view. Nothing exists if science cannot verify it. But science operates in only three dimensions: on this plane, in the present time, among what we call the living, natural world. Human experience tells us repeatedly, and has always told us, that, in reality, there is so very much more.

This takes us into the realm of metaphysics, which all ages have produced. Practical, scientific and intelligent men of logic made as much a study of the unseen and unexplainable in ancient times as they did of the more conventional things many are known for today. Indeed, humanity's greatest minds were more open to such matters in the past than they are now and only a fool would say this was purely out of superstition, naivety or ignorance.

Myth and legend do not grow out of metaphysics, however. They are most often the tools of religion and race or exercises in raising national consciousness. One definition of myth might be the beliefs of defunct or otherwise distant, usually foreign, religions. Legends are notably the stuff of group identity, shining example, nostalgia and folk history. They tell a people who they used to be and what the best of them could achieve. They speak of what a group stands for and what sort of champions they look to see return in times of need, either in the character of their sons and daughters or out of the mists of the world of magic, mystery and divinity. Always these forces favour one's own band, tribe, nation or race over all others.

One of the reasons myths and legends endure, however, is because they are not the true property of any group. This is not only because of their universality, but because they feed on one another, become appropriated by conquerors, immigrants, the oppressed or newly formed groupings. Theft, mixing, regurgitation and incorporation all happen constantly even today.

Along with this process certain parts of history or religion pass into myth and legend. Legend can become myth in this way, though myth seldom becomes legend. The people of a defeated race, who have perhaps been driven into the wilds, develop skills that seem magical, and just in order to survive may become pixies, elves and leprechauns. It happened in Ireland, Scotland and Wales and we can see it happening even now in North America, New Zealand, Australia and elsewhere around the world. Population shifts and the passing of peoples and cultures inevitably invite this transmigration.

We can gain insight, too, from the increasing disappearance of animal species. Because of their absence or loss we find ourselves creating mythical beasts to replace them. Perhaps we an see in this process how our ancestors accepted the existence of rare or supposedly recently extinct animals such as unicorns and dragons.

Many in our society hold that the city of Atlantis existed and some believe it may yet be found under the ice of Antarctica. If such a thing should ever happen, it would not be the first time that myth has become history or reality. It is wise to remember that until very recent times, any suggestion that giant lizards had dominated the earth before mankind would have been regarded as mythological fancy. The existence of dinosaurs is taken for granted now, and most people do not realize we ever doubted it.

Though it is often misused, the term legend can well be applied to many figures in recent history. As the expression has it, these people sometimes achieved this status in their own lifetime, and some became legends for performing one brief act. Myth is another matter but that too is forming constantly. Larger issues, mass opinion, delusion or propaganda fall into the category of myth. Legend, on the other hand, is about a person or individual groups of people. What baby boomer, especially one who has bothered to read history, can deny that the deeds of the generation who fought the Second World War have taken on many of the qualities of myth in our culture? The Old West, too, has long been the subject of myth, and it has also produced its fair share of legends.

All this would have been the case even without Hollywood films accelerating the process. Movies have nevertheless helped propel a higher percentage of subjects, times, heroes and monsters from history into myth and legend than any other medium.

Good cinema, far more than good literature, demands purer, clearer situations; the stereotypical villains or monsters and archetypal heroes and heroines of myth and legend are far easier to portray in a visual medium than half-truths and ambiguities of plot and character. Few mainstream filmmakers can resist the temptation to smooth out the rough edges of a situation and make characters behave better than most of us can hope to. Even when depicting real events of modern times, let alone those of the recent past or a more distant age, the tendency is to dress up the truth, misleading the general, non-history minded viewer and leaving him with false impressions. Movies, though, like myth and legend, are not about trying to tell literal truths. They are about telling higher truths. They are about challenging, inspiring, cautioning and, yes, sometimes tricking us.

Most of all, and again like the movies, they are about entertainment. In common with other art forms, which they most certainly are, they serve that function well.

I hope my retellings of these wonderful tales from around the world has enabled them to speak across time and work their magic on a new generation. If they had not been fun, frightening or exciting to hear or read in the first place, they would have died long ago, despite any other purposes they may have served in society. It is to be hoped that this book will extend their life still further.

During the process of re-writing these tales my imagination and my hand have been guided every step of the way by far greater story-tellers than myself. All of them have been drawn from oral traditions, academic sources or old out-of-print storybooks. These tales belong to all of us, and will continue to belong to us for as long as we are able to look back at the past in wonder, to stare into the future with hope and into our own hearts with honesty and inspiration.

An African Genesis

*This myth from the Makoni tribe of Zimbabwe
is about the development of the world.
Its chief character, Mwuati, symbolizes both primeval man and the moon,
and the magical ngona oil which makes so much happen in the story
represents the spark of life.
Its echoes of science, which agrees that life
originated under the seas,
is interesting.*

When God created the first man he called him Mwuetsi, meaning 'Moon'. He supplied him with a magical horn filled with ngona oil and then plopped him at the bottom of a lake. This was existence, it was consciousness. After a while Mwuetsi asked God if he could go somewhere else, up onto the earth perhaps, for although no one had told him about this place somehow he knew it was there. God told him this was not advisable, but Mwuetsi grew insistent and eventually God allowed him to go.

When Mwuetsi arrived on the earth he found a cold, stark land devoid of plants and animals. Bewildered, he walked first in one direction, then in another, and eventually he despaired. Praying to God, he asked how he was to live in such a place.

"I told you so," God said smugly from above. "But it is too late to go back now."

Mwuetsi groaned.

"You have really started something," God continued. "You have set off on a journey that can only end in death, but I will give you great comfort on your way."

"What is it?"

"A companion of your own kind."

And with that a fine young woman materialized before him. She was called Massassi, which means 'Morning Star'. Instinctively the couple went into a cave, made a fire, and lay down on either side of the cheerful flames. In the night, however, Mwuetsi awoke and his mind began to dwell upon his situation. Why, he asked himself, had God sent this maiden to be his friend. What exactly was she for, or rather, what was to be done with her? Inspired, he withdrew the stopper from his ngona horn and wet one of his fingers with the oil. Then, jumping over the campfire, he touched Massassi's body with his slippery finger and then hopped back quickly to his own side of the fire. This action seemed to calm him and he settled down to sleep gain.

When dawn broke, Mwuetsi woke up, stretched, yawned and glanced over at Massassi. He was shocked to see that her belly was massively swollen. As the rays of the sun flooded into the cave, Massassi stirred, moaning softly then groaning loudly. Within moments she was giving birth. Her first children were grasses, bushes and trees and these took root in the barren landscape. The earth became more bountiful as the trees spread their branches and grew high into the sky, bringing down rain.

Two years went by with Mwuetsi and Massassi living happily, gathering fruits and even starting a small farm. Then one day God took away Mwuetsi's gentle companion, putting her at the bottom of the lake where he could not find her.

Shouting and crying out to God, Mwuetsi wept tears of loneliness and grief. Again God spoke to him.

"Didn't I warn you about death? But now I shall give you a different friend."

Even as God spoke, Morongo, the Evening Star, appeared beside Mwuetsi. She took his hand in her own and led him into the cave. Here, as was his habit of old, Mwuetsi wanted to bed down in his place on the far side of the fire.

"Come on now," smiled Morongo. "Don't be so distant. Lay yourself down over here beside me."

Shyly and a touch awkwardly Mwuetsi looked round, wondering where he had put his ngona horn, but Morongo stopped him.

"You don't need that," she told him. "I am not like Massassi." She patted the place beside her and he went and joined her. "There is another horn which nature has suited for a purpose, that you always have about you." She showed him this purpose, teaching him to make love to her, and when these lessons were done he fell fast asleep.

In the morning, as the light crept into the cave, Mwuetsi discovered Morongo with an enormous belly, sweating and gritting her teeth as she bore new kinds of young. This first morning she gave birth to chickens, sheep and goats. When Mwuetsi lay with her that night, the next day it was eland, ostrich and cattle. They made love again the following night too. At dawn boys and girls were born to them, and by nightfall had become fully grown adults like themselves.

Morongo and Mwuetsi derived much fun and pleasure from their couplings, aside from the wonderful things that also sprang from them. When on the fourth night the couple embraced, lightning flashed outside the cave entrance and there were roars of thunder. Mwuetsi interpreted this untimely interruption as a message from God who was telling him to stop making love with Morongo. Reluctant to desist though he surely was, he was afraid.

Morongo was unperturbed. "Roll a boulder across the cave mouth," she whispered, "and God will not be able to see what we are doing."

The next morning, lions, leopards and scorpions sprang from between Morongo's legs, then snakes, the last of which was a huge black mamba. Desperately, as these things ran, leapt, scurried and slithered around the cave, Mwuetsi rolled the boulder away from the entrance and let them escape into the world.

"I told you so," murmured the voice of God from on high.

After that Mwuetsi coupled with his grown daughters, whose

offspring populated the earth further, until Mwuetsi became the king of a great nation. Nevertheless, it was Morongo he still longed for and thought of daily, but she had become the mate of the black mamba and was content, although she had no more children of any kind.

Wanting for nothing, lord of creation, surrounded by his progeny and their progeny, Mwuetsi was satisfied in every way but one. Even as years had passed, as the world had flourished and found ways to regenerate itself, he had never lost his desire for Morongo, the Evening Star. Indeed, his lust, fascination, gratitude and desperate longing for her had only increased with time.

One night, he went to see her, perhaps after imbibing some recently perfected brew, his heart bursting. Pouring out his emotions and eager for the touch of her once again, he took her in his arms and bore her down upon the bed.

"Please don't," she said, but in his excitement and hunger for her, he would not be stopped.

Now, beneath the bed, coiled up and enjoying a nap, lay Morongo's husband, the black mamba. Wakening to the commotion above him, he understood at once and sprang at Mwuetsi, biting him on the thigh. Shocked and quickly growing sick, Mwuetsi limped away, but he was still a very strong man, despite his advancing years, and he did not die at once.

While he lingered the rain stopped falling, so the streams dried up, crops withered, animals began to perish and in time people started dying too.

The eldest children of Mwuetsi called the others together and they formed a great circle in which they cast magical dice, for they did not know how to talk directly with God as their father had done. The dice would have to tell them the will of God.

"Your father and king, Mwuetsi, is ill and will not recover," the dice informed them. "You must return him to the lake."

Whether by the will of God, a throw of the dice or the plan of his heirs, the outcome was inevitable. They went to where the sick man lay and strangled him, then chose another king to serve in his place.

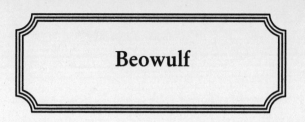

Beowulf

The Anglo-Saxon epic 'Beowulf' is thought to have been written around the eighth century by a Northumbrian minstrel, and is the oldest in the English language. The original tale drew much of its inspiration from pagan Scandinavian folk history and also includes Christian elements. The principal enemy of the hero Beowulf is the original creature from the black lagoon.

Warrior, conqueror and King of the Danes, Hrothgar was famed far and wide for the glory he had won in battle. Many noble fighting men were his kinsmen and countless warriors served loyally in his bodyguard. His power was immense and his courage a byword among men.

Hrothgar was a descendant of the legendary Scyld, who had arrived on the shores of Denmark as an infant in a boat loaded with gold and jewels. When Scyld had grown up and become king, his conquests for his adoptive land were great. On his death, he was put into a boat again, with treasure surrounding him, and set adrift towards the westward setting sun, from whence he had come.

Hrothgar was duly proud of his lineage and of his own considerable accomplishments. He longed for a symbol of them to stand after he had gone, as well as to enjoy while he lived. Summoning the help of all his people, he determined that they build an enormous hall where he might hold feasts and banquets, receive distinguished visitors from abroad and entertain his warriors and thanes. It would be a meeting place for men and a monument to his reign.

Everyone laboured enthusiastically and the vast hall was quickly completed. Glorious were its adornments and lavish its decorations and manly comforts. Towering high and majestic, the walls ended in pinnacles resembling the antlers of a stag, and so the hall was named 'Heorot', or The Hart.

On its completion, Hrothgar, his warriors and people were justly proud of the magnificent structure. The first great feast they held in it was like no other in their history. Hrothgar's heart swelled as he sat on the high seat on the dais and watched his brave thanes and warriors at the long tables eating and drinking merrily beneath the hall's lofty rafters.

So proud were the Danes of their great hall that the feasting went on for days and the noise of their revels floated far from the hill upon which the mighty building stood, set apart from all others. Perhaps it seemed the loud carousing and tumult would never end, or perhaps the disturbance merely reminded the fen-monster Grendel of his old enmity and bitter resentment of men.

Roused and angry, the creature conceived a particular hatred for Heorot itself. The great hall became a symbol of his grievance against humanity. The feasting may also have reminded the horrible half-man half-fiend of its fondness for human flesh. It went quickly from pounding its fists in rage to licking its chops in anticipation of savouring this delicacy. Grendel decided to set out from the deep swamp to take his revenge and his dinner.

Born of a race of giants, sea-monsters and goblins, with the hearts of evil demons, Grendel was of enormous stature, covered in slimy green horn-hard skin on which a sword could not bite. He had unnatural strength even for his great size and no mercy for any creature, not even of his own nearly extinct kind.

On a night when Heorot was less than a week old, Grendel left the fen by moonlight and stalked the entrance to the now quiet hall. Inside all were now asleep after their revels, outside a guard of thirty men stood, no more alert than peaceful times demanded.

By stealth, he picked them off in ones and twos and then charged into the midst of the main body, catching everyone by surprise. Before they could call for help from their drunken comrades within, or act with unity, Grendel had dispatched them all. He spent the next few hours carrying back the bodies to his swampy lair and larder.

In the early morning the men inside the hall staggered out and saw the grizzly evidence of the struggle. Everywhere blood and arms and armour were scattered, and the remains of not a single man could be found. The monster's bloody tracks were plain and none doubted the reality of the danger or suspected human enemies as responsible for the tragedy.

Hrothgar grieved for his men and kinsmen, lost in this horrible way, and he grieved too for the fact that he himself was too old to track and kill such a monster. The lamentation of all the families of the slain grew as night after night Grendel returned. All their valiant efforts to vanquish the monster were in vain and many good men perished in the attempt and in trying to defend the hall.

Eventually champions stopped coming forward and, despairing, the Danes deserted the glorious hall they had been so proud of. Heorot stood unused for its original purpose. None now dared to sleep within its walls. For twelve years this went on, with no one going near the hall after darkness, for by night the fiend haunted its spaces and shadows in search of prey. Neither his appetite nor his enmity could be appeased, and careless sleepers paid with their lives.

As word spread, from far and wide foreign champions arrived to offer King Hrothgar their assistance, but none of them was sufficiently powerful or cunning enough to kill the monster. Many fine heroes were lost in this fashion until finally even the brave adventurers from afar stopped coming. Grendel remained master of the halls. Hrothgar and the Danes, in misery and shame, tried to reconcile themselves to their bondage, while their king grew old in helpless longing for the arrival of someone with the strength to relieve them of this awful oppression.

As these sad events unfolded, far away in the realm of the Geats, of Gotaland, in the south of Sweden, a remarkable boy was growing up and coming to man's estate. Nephew of Hygelac (a mighty monarch with ambitions to extend his sway into the mainland of Germany), his name was Beowulf. This boy was the son of Hrethal's only daughter and a great nobleman, Ecgtheow, and had from the age of seven been brought up at court. A gentle, even-tempered lad, he seemed out of place at this warlike apex of a warlike race. While King Hrethel had lived he had been disappointed in the boy's lack of aggression, his slowness to anger and his kind-heartedness.

By the time Hygelac had succeeded to the throne Beowulf was growing ever bigger and stronger and the king began to see the true qualities of his sister's son. For a time he was still sneered at by smaller boys because of his good nature, but Beowulf nevertheless demonstrated imperterbability, resolve and patience. On the rare occasions when he was roused to anger, he fought fiercely and skilfully but never blindly.

Soon Beowulf's cool head and great strength, particularly his mighty hand-grip, which was said to be equal to that of thirty men, were watchwords among his peers and elders. When all saw his potential greatness he blossomed, excelling at feats of endurance and courage. In an arduous swimming contest he bested the famous champion Breca, and enjoyed the glory it brought him.

For this and many other victories, he was already widely renowned when he requested of Hygelac permission to offer help to the Danish king against the ravages of Grendel. It was a thing he had secretly dreamt of doing for some time. Selecting fourteen loyal comrades and kinsmen, he took leave of the Geatish royal family and sailed for Denmark.

So it was that one afternoon the Warden of the Coast, doing his rounds along the Danish shore, spotted in a small stream running between the mountainous cliffs a foreign war-vessel whose banners he did not recognize. A party of fifteen men, all arrayed for battle, disembarked, secured their ship to a large rock with strong cables, and then made ready to march.

The Warden unhesitatingly rode down into their midst and loudly demanded to know their business on his coast.

"What are such warlike men doing landing here? I am the appointed warden of this coast and hold watch here that no enemy land troops to endanger our folk and property. None has ever landed here more boldly, obviously being no kinsmen of ours and giving no password, than this fair company of yours."

Beowulf stepped forward, a broad smile on his open, honest face, strength and strength of character written all over him. The Warden took the big warrior's measure in a glance, and returned the smile. It had been a while since a man such as this had come among them, and none had been the equal of this one. Beowulf's lordly bearing, air of authority, fine armour and weapons singled him out as the chief of the company.

"Never have I beheld a mightier warrior than this man I perceive as your leader. He is no common man, no common hero, if looks belie him not."

Though Beowulf may have thought this compliment only his due, he had the grace to bow his head a little modestly.

"Now tell me what you're doing here, for we can't have spies running about. Who are your kindred and where is your country?" The old Warden sat on his horse studying the strangers' faces, but especially watched their leader.

"We are warriors of the Geats, members of King Hygelac's bodyguard. My father was named Ecgtheow, a wise councillor who died full of years and famous for his wisdom. We come in friendship to meet your noble king, and we place ourselves in your care. Our purpose is to perform an errand for the great Danish King Hrothgar, son of Healfdene, if it still be needful."

"I see," nodded the Warden.

"Does the monster Grendel yet haunt your great hall by night?"

"He does."

"We have come to help your king to be rid of him, to assure Hrothgar that his troubles are over and that peace and happiness shall be restored."

"I have learned to distinguish between talk and action," the old Warden sighed, "and you look a likely enough band. As I say, you yourself have the look of a most unusual champion. You have my leave to proceed in war-array, and I will see you safely to our king. May your mission be successful."

Turning his horse he led them up the steep cliff paths, while the Geats followed resplendent in their shining armour, with boar-crests on their helmets, shields and spears in their hands and mighty swords on their belts. They marched with confidence behind the Warden, eventually coming onto a rough trodden path, which in a while turned into a stone-paved road. This led on to the great hall of Heorot, which they soon saw towering aloft, gleaming white in the sun.

As they drew nearer, the Geats admired the pinnacled gables and carved beams and rafters. The Warden drew rein and addressed them once more.

"There stands our king's hall. You can find your way from here. May the All-Father keep you safe in your coming struggle. I must return to my duties on the coast."

He turned his horse and rode away as the Geats continued to stare at the great hall. Then Beowulf led the way to the building and up to the enormous doors, where they removed their helmets, lay down their shields and spears and prepared to enter as peaceful guests.

A nobleman named Wulfgar met them at the entrance and asked them where such a splendid body of well armed and equipped warriors had came from.

"Your heroic bearing betokens some noble endeavour," he said, with a twinkle in his eye and a slight quickening in his heart.

"We are the chosen friends and companions to King Hygelac of Geatland. I am Beowulf. We would like to speak to your master, King Hrothgar, of our mission, if the son of Healfdene will hear us."

"I will advise my lord of your presence." Wulfgar withdrew and went in search of his king. Hrothgar was in his high seat, surrounded by his bodyguard of champions.

"Sire," Wulfgar said, bowing respectfully as he approached the dais, "some heroes from far across the sea have come."

"From where?" asked Hrothgar, barely stirring from his depression.

"From Geatland. Beowulf is their leader and it is their prayer to speak with you personally."

The king grunted disconsolately.

"Do not refuse them hastily, Sire. They are worthy, respectable, well equipped men and their chief, Beowulf, is of unusually noble and heroic appearance."

"Beowulf?" Hrothgar brightened slightly. "Why, I knew him as a small boy. His father Ecgtheow, who married the sister of the great King Hrethel, was my friend."

"Ah yes, Sire," said Wulfgar, glad to see the change coming over the king.

Hrothgar, his interest now fully engaged, went on. "His fame has proceeded him. Seafarers report to me that he has the strength of thirty men in his hand-grip alone. Oh, I tell you, Wulfgar, this young man's coming brings me hope, for he may be the one to save us from the horror and oppression of Grendel." Hrothgar's eyes shone and he stared into space, lapsing into a reverie for a moment. "If it was just the hall it would not matter, though it shames us all. But it blights my old age, harms the nation ... So many lives unavenged ... If he can kill Grendel I will heap such treasure on him! Hurry, bid Beowulf and his comrades approach and welcome them in the name of the Danish folk."

Wulfgar went swiftly back to the entrance of the hall and smiled broadly at the brave little band of Geats before conducting them into the presence of the king.

Standing before the high seat the well accoutred foreigners were an impressive sight, their leader especially cutting an inspiring figure in his gleaming ring-mail, with his mighty sword at his side. It did the king good just to look upon such a hero. The truth was that though Grendel was not a human enemy, against whom the Danes were fearless, he had undermined the confidence of even the bravest champion in the realm. Danish manhood secretly held itself cheap and it could not but outwardly show.

The young Geats bowed and Beowulf cleared his throat in preparation for the speech he had rehearsed for this long-dreamt of occasion.

"Hail to thee, Hrothgar, king of the Danes. I am Beowulf, Hygelac's kinsman and loyal companion. Though still in my youth, I have done great deeds of valour. At home we have heard of your troubles at Grendel's monstrous hand. It is said that this bright hall, noblest of buildings, is idle and useless after the evening light has gone. Therefore Hrothgar, ancient and noble king, my friends, warriors and prudent thanes, having seen my might in battle, have agreed to let me seek you out. I beg of you but one boon, lord of the glorious Danes, Prince of the Scylding race, folk-lord most friendly, Warden of warriors. Please do no deny me, for I have come far. I, with my men alone, asking no other assistance, would cleanse this great hall."

The king stared hard at Beowulf, trying to see into his heart. So many had died already.

"I have often heard," the young man went on, "that the monster Grendel, in his recklessness, scorns to use weapons. I will forego to bear my sword, my broad yellow shield, armour or spear and with my hand-grip alone strive and struggle for my life."

Seeing the pale expression that came over the king's features, Beowulf hurried on with his address.

"And if he would carry me off, all gory and torn, to eat me in his den, as he has many a good man of Denmark, well, let him try. Should he succeed, then it will save the expense and labour of burying me. Just send my sword home to my uncle and tell him I did my best."

"Beowulf, you have sought my court for honour's sake," old King Hrothgar replied after listening attentively to all the young man had to say, "and for friendship. You have remembered the ancient alliance between Ecgtheow, your father, and myself. You know that I shielded him from the wrath of his enemies, the Wilfings, paid them the due wergild for his crime, and accepted his oath of loyalty to myself."

"Yes, Sire," Beowulf said with bowed head.

"That time is long ago. Ecgtheow is dead, and I am old and in misery. It would take too long to tell of all the woe that Grendel has brought on this kingdom, or to say how many heroes have stood here and boasted of the great valour they would display in combat with the monster. So often in the past brave men have awaited his coming in this hall with confidence and courage in their hearts and in the morning there has been no trace of these heroes but for the dark bloodstains on the benches and tables. Nevertheless, let us sit down to the banquet and you may tell me of your plans in greater detail."

The room was quickly made ready for feasting. The Geat warriors were seated on the long benches, close to where Beowulf was given place of honour opposite the king. Great respect was shown them all, but particularly to Beowulf, who was looked at in wonder for his apparent willingness to hazard unarmed combat with the terrible Grendel. Huge carved horns brimming with ale were brought to Beowulf and his men and savoury meat placed before them. While they ate and drank, minstrels sang of the deeds of men of old. A rare sense of joy animated the feast, hope renewed by the arrival of the Geat hero and his warriors.

There was one Dane however, who did not quite share the rejoicing over Beowulf's coming. Indeed, his heart was sad and his brow gloomy, for this thane was urged by jealousy to hate any man more distinguished than himself. Hunferth was his name, King Hrothgar's orator and speechmaker, who with his dramatic and often satirical style, quick wit, and sharp tongue made a bad enemy.

From his position at Hrothgar's feet he watched Beowulf with scornful and jealous eyes. He bided his time and waited until a lull in the merry-making before speaking. Someone mentioned in passing the famous swimming match between Beowulf and Breca.

"Why yes," Hunferth remarked in a cold, contemptuous tone, "it was you who strove against Breca, the son of Beanstan, when you two so rashly risked your lives in the deep water, ignoring the urgings of your friends against such rashness. You would go on the hazardous journey no matter what and plunge in, braving the wintry waves despite a rising storm. Was it not seven days and nights you toiled?"

"Yes." Beowulf smiled thinly, not liking the man's tone.

"Then Breca overcame you, having greater strength and courage. The ocean bore him to shore, and he returned happily to his native land, the fair city where he ruled as lord and chieftain. He fully made good his boast against you, didn't he? And now you seem to want to risk an even worse defeat, for you'll find Grendel far fiercer in battle than was Breca, if you dare await him tonight."

Around the two men conversation ceased.

"Friend Hunferth," Beowulf replied haughtily, his brow flushed with anger, "you seem much fascinated by the swimming contest between Breca and me; but you must be drunk, for you have told the tale wrongly. It was, admittedly, a youthful folly of ours, when we two boasted and challenged each other to risk our lives in the ocean that day."

Aware that most ears in the hall were straining to hear this interchange, Beowulf raised his voice.

"We bore our naked swords in our hands as we swam, for it was necessary to defend ourselves against sea-monsters. For five days we floated together, neither out-distancing the other, when a storm drove us apart. The surging waves were cold and the north wind bitter. The swelling flood was rough, especially under the darkening shades of night. Yet this was not the worst, for the sea-monsters, excited by the raging tempest, rushed at me with their deadly tusks and bore me to the abyss. It was just as well that I wore my well-woven ring-mail, and had my keen sword in hand, for these enabled me to fight and kill the deadly beasts. Many a time the host of monsters pulled me to the ocean-bottom, but I fought and dispatched great numbers among them. We battled all night long until the morning light. I could see the windy cliffs along the shore and all around me the bodies of the slain sea-beasts floating on the surf, nine of them in total. The gods are gracious to the man who is valiant and unafraid. Never has there been a sterner conflict, nor a more unhappy warrior lost in the waters. I saved my life and landed on the shores of Finland, but Breca fought not so mightily and did not fare so well." Beowulf paused, and looked hard at his antagonist. "I never heard of such warlike deeds on your part, Hunferth, only that you murdered your brothers and nearest kinsmen."

A ripple of shock ran round the great hall.

"And I'll tell you another thing, son of the bold Ecglafs. The grisly hand of Grendel would not have caused such misery, shame and anguish for your king in his palace, if you, Hunferth, were valiant and battle-fierce."

Hunferth was furious over the reminder of his former wrongdoing and the implied accusation of cowardice, but his belittling of Beowulf had not been received well by either the Geats or the Danes, who were now enthusiastically applauding Beowulf's address. He dared make no further attack on the champion and let pass without comment Beowulf's declaration that he and his friends would await Grendel that night in the hall. The fiend had ceased to expect any resistance from the Danes, and all agreed that the presence of this newly arrived band of warriors would indeed come as a shock to it.

The feast resumed and continued in high spirits until a door at the upper end of the hall opened to admit a woman of noble bearing. This was Hrothgar's wife, the fair and gracious Queen Wealhtheow. The company ceased their merriment and watched as she filled a goblet of mead and presented it to her husband, who joyfully received it and drank it down. Then she poured mead or ale for each man in turn, in due course coming to Beowulf. Wealhtheow greeted the lordly hero gratefully, and thanked him for the friendship that had brought him to Denmark to risk his life against Grendel. Beowulf, rising respectfully, took the cup from the queen's hand.

"I considered the risks well," he replied with dignity, "when I sailed with my brave warriors, believing I alone might win your people's deliverance or perish in the demon's grip. Yes, I accept the challenge. I must perform this knightly deed or meet my doom here in your fine hall in the dark of night."

Well pleased by Beowulf's words, Queen Wealhtheow went to sit beside her lord, where her gracious smile cheered the assembly. The clamour of the feast continued until Hrothgar gave the signal for retiring. With night almost blanketing the sky, it was time to leave Heorot.

The assembly broke up with a chorus of 'Good nights' and the Danes went to their lodgings. Hrothgar, the last to leave, addressed Beowulf half joyfully, half sadly.

"Not since I first held a spear and shield have I fully given over this mighty Danish hall to any man. Keep well and defend this most wonderful of places. Bring forth all your heroic strength, call up you bravery, watch for the enemy and stay alert. You will be marvellously rewarded, I assure you, if you survive this night and triumph in the coming battle."

The king then departed to pass a restless night in a safer dwelling, gripped by nervous expectation, torn between hope and fear. In the meantime, Beowulf and his men prepared themselves for the dangers of the coming night.

"I will strive against this fiend weaponless," Beowulf swore again to his friends, "and with no armour, as he wears none. I will wrestle with him, and try to overcome him. I will conquer, if I win, by my hand-grip alone. Let the All-Father judge between us, and grant the victory to whom He will."

Beowulf divested himself of his mail, sword and helmet, and put them in the care of a Danish thane who bore them away. The fourteen champions of the Geats then settled down to a light sleep, with one eye open as it were, wearing their armour and with their weapons close to hand. Deep down inside, none of these brave men expected to see the light of day again or to revisit their native land. They had heard far too much during the feast about the slaughter of which Grendel was capable, but none was troubled by thoughts of what the night held and soon all were slumbering peacefully

When everything was still, Grendel came. From the fen-fastness, by way of marshy tracts, through mists of acid swamp-born fogs, the hideous monster came once again to the house he hated. Grendel behaved no differently on this night than any other. He strode fiercely up to the door and tried to open it. The fiend's anger was instantly aroused when he found that he could not because it was locked and bolted. He grasped the door with his mighty hands and slowly tore it open.

As Grendel stalked through the hall he seemed to fill it with his monstrous shadow. The green and uncanny light that shone from his eyes illuminated the troop of sleeping warriors. The sight of the men delighted the creature, even as it angered him further. It seemed that all the fools slept, but the fiend did not notice one man, leaning on his elbow and peering keenly into the gloom.

Grendel thrust out a terrible scaly hand, seized one hapless sleeper and tore him to pieces before the poor man could utter a cry. Gleefully, Grendel drank the warm blood and devoured the flesh. So excited was he by this hideous starter that he reached out carelessly for another similarly tasty morsel. To Grendel's utter amazement his hand was seized and held in a grip the like of which he had never felt before. Instinctively he knew that here was an antagonist he must fight with caution and cunning.

Beowulf, who had sprung from his couch as soon as the terrible claws of the monster had fallen upon him, now wrestled desperately with Grendel. It was an awesome struggle, as the combatants swayed and grappled the length of the vast, unlit hall, overturning tables and benches, trampling underfoot dishes and goblets.

The other Geat warriors were now wide awake and with weapons in hand were trying to follow the progress of the struggle and discern how they might help their leader. But they were unable to see the combatants distinctly in the darkness, and ran about the hall ineffectually, occasionally landing blows on the beast when the gleam from its eyes was turned in their direction. Whenever they struck however, their weapons glanced harmlessly off Grendel's scaly hide.

The combat seemed to go on for hours and everything in the hall was utterly wrecked by the time Grendel made to break away. Bested and aware that the gloom was lifting as a new day pushed away the veil of night, Grendel put every ounce of his strength into escaping Beowulf. But the Geat champion held him fast in a grip no man on earth could equal or endure. The monster writhed in anguish as he vainly strove to free himself.

The struggle grew more intense and frenzied, until, with a terrible cry, Grendel wrenched himself free, staggered to the door, and fled, wailing, over the moors to his home in the gloomy swamp. In the grasp of the exhausted victor he left his arm and shoulder, and in his wake a trail of glistening blood. Beowulf sank down, panting, on a shattered seat, still holding his grisly trophy, hardly able to credit what had happened. His men gathered round with a lighted torch and by the sputtering glare, they all beheld the scaly arm of Grendel, ghastly and, even now, threatening. But the monster was gone, and with a wound so terrible that he must surely die.

Realizing this, the Geats raised a shout of triumph, and then took the hateful trophy and fastened it high up on the roof of the hall. Now, all who entered would see the token of victory and recognize that the

Geat hero, Beowulf, had fulfilled his boast – he had conquered with no weapon and by the strength of his hands alone.

In the morning many warriors came to Heorot to learn the events of the night, and all saw the trophy and praised Beowulf's might and courage. Together they followed with eager curiosity the bloodstained track of the fleeing demon till it came to the edge of the gloomy lake. Here the trail disappeared into the waters, which were stained with gore, and boiled and surged noiselessly. There, on the shore, the Danes rejoiced over the death of their enemy, and returned to Heorot carefree and with gladness in their hearts.

Beowulf and his Geats stayed on in Heorot for some days. Hrothgar had to be given a full account of the struggle and there were celebrations to be enjoyed; horse races were run, and wrestling matches and every other manly contest of skill and endurance held.

When King Hrothgar himself came, with his queen and her maiden train, to see the dreadful trophy, he turned with gratitude to the hero who had delivered them from this evil, and cried:

"Thanks be to the All-Father for this happy sight! I have endured so much sorrow at the hands of Grendel, and lost so many warriors, all these uncounted years of misery. But my woe is at an end. Now, a youth has performed, with his unaided strength, what none of the rest of us could accomplish with all our power or craft. Well might your father, O Beowulf, have rejoiced in your great fame and well may your mother, if she yet lives, praise the All-Father for the noble son she bore. You shall always be a son indeed to me, both in love and honour, and you shall never lack anything you desire that I can give. I have often rewarded less heroic deeds than this with great gifts, so I can happily deny you nothing."

"We have performed our boast, O King," Beowulf answered, "and have driven away the enemy. I intended to force him down and to deprive him of his life by mere strength of my hand-grip, but in this I did not succeed. Alas, Grendel escaped from the hall, but he did leave me his hand, arm and shoulder as a token of his presence, and as a ransom for the rest of his loathsome body. I am certain that he can live no longer with so deadly a wound."

The hall was cleared of the traces of the conflict and preparations were made for a splendid banquet. There in Heorot the Danes assembled once again free from fear in their splendid hall, and the walls were hung with gold-wrought embroideries and hangings of costly stuffs. Richly chased goblets shone on the long tables, and men's tongues waxed loud as they discussed and described the heroic struggle of the night before.

Beowulf and King Hrothgar sat on the high seats opposite each other, their men, Danes and Geats, sitting side by side. All shouted and cheered and drank deeply to the fame of Beowulf. The minstrels sang of the Fight in Finnsburg and the deeds of Finn and Hnoef, of Hengest and Queen Hildeburh. The song was good and long, and hearing of the victory of their Danish forefathers over Finn of the Frisians roused the national pride of the Danes. Merrily the banquet proceeded, graced and gladdened still more by the presence of Queen Wealhtheow.

With the gifts which he loaded on Beowulf and every member of the Geat troop, Hrothgar showed the extent of his generosity and his gratitude. Beowulf received a gold-embroidered banner, a magnificent sword, helmet, and corslet, a goblet of gold, and swift horses. On the back of the best of these steeds was strapped a magnificent saddle, Hrothgar's own, with gold ornaments. When the Geat hero had thanked the king fittingly, Queen Wealhtheow arose from her seat, and lifting the great drinking-cup, offered it to her lord.

"Take the goblet, my lord and ruler," she said, "Be happy as a man can be and lavish praise and reward on the young Geats for the peace they have won us. I know that this mighty warrior who has cleansed this banquet hall will be as a son to us. Now may we enjoy the many pleasures of this place and, in security, leave our kinsmen, our lands and lordships when we must journey forth to meet death."

"Just so," said Hrothgar.

"Beowulf," the queen said, turning to him. "Enjoy your reward while you are young, and live a noble and blessed life. Keep well your widespread fame, and be a friend to my sons in time to come, should they ever need a protector."

Then she gave him two golden armlets, set with jewels, costly rings, a corslet of chain-mail and a wonderful jewelled collar of exquisite ancient workmanship. Then, bidding the men continue their feasting, she left the hall with her maidens.

The feast went on until Hrothgar too departed to his dwelling, and left the Danes, now secure and careless, to prepared their beds. The warriors who guarded the hall of Heorot settled down in their armour, and placed their shields by their heads, as was their custom. Meanwhile, Beowulf and the Geats were shown to a very comfortable lodging, where they slept soundly and without disturbance.

But in the darkness of that night an avenger came to Heorot. It came in silence and mystery, as Grendel had done, with thoughts of murder just as terrible and even greater hatred raging in its heart.

Grendel had gone home to die, but his mother, a fiend nearly as terrible as her son, lived to avenge him. She rose from her dwelling in the gloomy lake, followed the fen paths and moorland ways to Hrothgar's mightly palace. When she opened the door of Hearot, a sudden horrible panic filled the Danes inside. Men ran hither and thither, vainly seeking to attack the monstrous intruder. The figure of this horrible woman, though, cast less terror in their hearts than had Grendel. They were confident of overcoming her. But despite their brave attacks, they could not prevent her seizing Aschere, one of King Hrothgar's thanes, and carrying him away to the fens. Again, Heorot became a house of lamentation where only a few hours before men had feasted and laughed so joyously.

When the news was brought to King Hrothgar, he bitterly lamented the loss of his wisest and dearest counsellor. He sent at once for Beowulf, certain that he alone could help in this extremity. Beowulf was unaware of what had passed in the night, and when he came into the presence of the king, he inquired courteously if Hrothgar's rest had been peaceful.

"Do not ask me about peace. My best adviser and friend Aschere is dead. The truest comrade in fight or council, slain by a monster last night in Heorot and I don't know where she has taken his body. This is undoubtedly revenge for your killing Grendel. Yes, his kinswoman has come to avenge him."

"There is another...?"

"I have heard my people say that they have seen two such unearthly creatures. Huge bodied marsh-striders, one in the shape of a female, the other of a male, the one they came to call Grendel."

Beowulf nodded.

"I beg you, my son," Hrothgar suddenly burst out in uncontrollable emotion, "help us if you will, for help is only to be found in you."

"I will, O King."

"But you know not the horror of the place you must go to if you are to corner the fiend in her den. It is a foul and strange place within the swamp. Even a hunted stag will not venture into it and would rather face death at the hunter's hands than hide there. But I will reward you beyond measure if you return alive from such a journey."

"Sire," said Beowulf softly, touched by the old king's sorrow, made worse for having thought himself delivered only the day before. "Do not grieve. It is best for each of us rather to avenge our friend than mourn him over much. Everyone dies at the end of this life. Let us win war-like glory in the world while we can. That is best for a slain warrior after death. Arise, my lord, and let's follow the track of the monster. I promise you, I will never lose it, wherever it may lead."

Hrothgar sprang from his bed with near-youthful energy, and ordered his horse to be saddled. With Beowulf beside him, and a mixed party of Geats and Danes following, he rode towards the home of the monsters, the dread lake so shunned by men and beasts. The bloodstained tracks were easy to follow, and the avengers moved swiftly till they came to the edge of the swamp. There they found the head of Aschere lying on the bank. The Danes looked at in grief and horror. The Geats turned their gaze towards the lake, which was boiling with blood and hot, welling gore. As if to give comfort and to raise their spirits, one man in the party blew a horn, which loudly sang out a fierce, eager defiance. On the water were wrathful and venomous snakes, monstrous beasts and weird creatures which madly shot away when the blast of the war-horn was sounded again. Soon, however, they gathered once more.

Beowulf stood on the shore watching these creatures. Then, suddenly, he drew his bow and shot one of them through the heart. The rest darted furiously away, enabling the thanes to drag the carcass of the slain beast onto the bank where all surveyed it with wonder.

Beowulf began making ready for his task. He decided to trust to his well-woven mail, the close-fitting corslet which protected his breast, the shining helmet, bright with the boar image on the crest, and to a mighty sword which Hunferth, his jealousy forgotten in admiration of Beowulf's bravery, had earlier pressed on the hero.

"This sword is called Hrunting," he had said, presenting the weapon to him. "It is of an ancient heritage. The steel of the blade itself was tempered with poison-twigs and hardened with battle-blood. It has never failed in battle any who wielded it."

Now Beowulf stood ready. He surveyed his surroundings and looked at the sky, the sun and the green earth, which he might never see again. With naked sword in hand he turned to his loyal followers, his friendly hosts and King Hrothgar. There was no trace of weakness or fear in him when, finally, he spoke.

"Do not forget, noble kinsman of Healfdene, illustrious ruler, good friend of warriors, what we two settled when we spoke together. If I, for your safety's sake, should end my life-days here, though I am dead, be as a father to me still. Be to my kindred thanes, my battle-comrades, a worthy protector. Do you hear, Hrothgar? Send all these treasures which you have given me, to my king, Hygelac, so the Geat king, brave son of dead Hrethel, may see by the gold and gems and treasures that I found a generous lord, whom I loved. Give back to Hunferth, too, this wondrous weapon, the sword with its graven blade. I will win fame with it, with Hrunting, or death will claim me."

Beowulf then dived headlong into the swamp. No sooner did he enter those sinister waters than the sea-beasts came at him with tusk and horn and strove to break the protective ring-mail. He fought them off, all the while continuing his descent into the murky depths. As Beowulf neared the bottom, he felt himself being clasped in long, scaly arms of gigantic strength as his heart was torn at by steely claws. A creature both awful and loathsome was pulling him deeper into the cauldron, down through clusters of yet more slimy and horrible sea-beasts, to deliver him to the abode of the hate-filled sea-woman who wanted his blood.

She was waiting for him in the vast cavern, an underwater hall where Beowulf found himself at the end of the dizzying descent. In the water at its mouth he saw the reflection of a strange flickering flame deeper within the cavern, a livid sheen which burnt with the anger of Grendel's mother.

He ventured inside. There the adversaries met and with a cry charged at one another. The sea-woman flung Beowulf down on his back, stabbing at him with the point and edge of her broad knife, but she too was thwarted by the trusty corslet. Beowulf, exerting mighty force, threw her off and jumped to his feet. Brandishing Hrunting, he flashed one great blow at her head, but her scaly hide was invulnerable. Enraged, Beowulf cast aside the useless sword and determined to trust once again to his hand grip.

Grendel's mother now felt all the deadly power of Beowulf's grasp, and was forced to the ground, but still she would not yield. Knowing he needed some weapon to end the struggle, Beowulf looked desperately

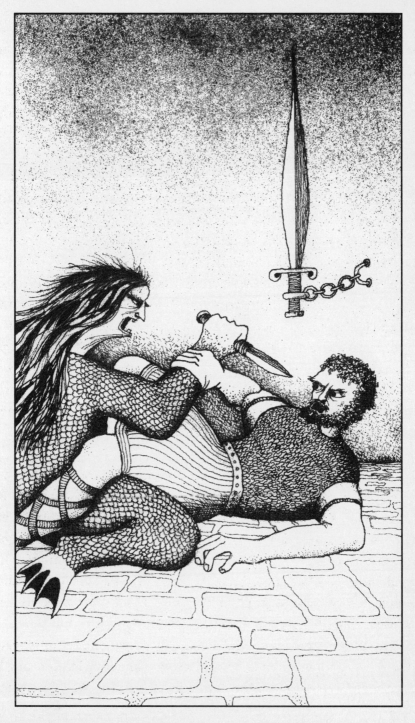

around. There, on one of the walls he saw a magnificent sword, an heirloom of heroes. It was the best of blades, with splendid point and edge, but it had been forged by giants and was larger than any member of the human race could manage to wield in battle – any human that is, other than one with the strength of Beowulf.

The young warrior released the monster and sprang up to snatch this mighty relic of earlier and greater races from the wall. With renewed hope in his heart, Beowulf swung the sword fiercely round his head and struck hard.

The blow fell with such crushing force on the neck of the sea-woman that it broke all the bones therein, killing her instantly. Beowulf, breathing hard, looked down at the lifeless carcass of his foe. Keeping the sword in his hand, he looked warily along the walls of the dwelling and peered into the recesses, in case some other enemy should emerge. As he stared around him, Beowulf saw the body of Grendel, lying on a bed in an inner hall. He entered the chamber and, seizing the corpse by the hideous coiled locks, cut off the head as a trophy. A stream of hissing, scalding, poisonous blood spat at him, melting the blade of the mighty sword until nothing remained of it but the curiously ornamented hilt. Beowulf carried away this hilt and Grendel's head and swam up with them through the now clear sparkling waters.

Only Beowulf's loyal Geats awaited his re-emergence from the lake. The Danes had departed in late afternoon, lamenting the hero's death, for they had concluded that no man could have survived so long beneath the waters. The Geats had stayed on, still gazing sadly at the waves, hoping against all hope that Beowulf would reappear. Their faith was encouraged by a remarkable sequence of changes to the lake. First they saw blood boiling upwards, followed by the quenching of the unholy light deep within it, then the sea-monsters fled its depths and there was a gradual clearing of the waters. Finally, Beowulf rose to the surface.

Their joy at seeing him return to them unharmed was matched by their awe and wonder at his dreadful booty, the ghastly head of Grendel and the massive hilt of the gigantic sword. Eagerly they listened to his story, and vied with one another for the glory of bearing his armour, his spoils, and his weapons back across the moorlands to Heorot. It was a proud and happy troop that followed Beowulf into the hall, through the startled Danish throng to the throne of Hrothgar, where the hideous head of Grendel was laid. Beowulf, raising his voice so that everyone could hear him above the buzz and hum, addressed the king.

"Lo, we have brought for your pleasure, this sea-booty, O wise son of Healfdene, Lord of the Scyldings, in token of triumph, though the conflict was almost decided against me, if the gods had not guarded me! Nought could I conquer with Hrunting in battle, belike it was only proof against human enemies. But the gods granted me another great weapon hanging high in the hall of my foe. So I seized and swung it and thus won through. The blade did later melt in the hot boiling blood when taking off Grendel's head. But I have the hilt here and I have avenged the crime. Now can I promise you that you may slumber carefree in Heorot with all your warrior-troop and all your kindred thanes, the young and the aged. You need not fear for them, a death from mortal foes just as you, Sire, made them safe of yore."

King Hrothgar was now more delighted than ever at the return of his friend and the slaughter of his foes. He gazed in delight and wonder at the gory head of the monster, and the gigantic hilt of the weapon that had struck it off. Then, taking the glorious hilt, and scanning eagerly the runes which showed its history, he held up his hand to still the tumult in the hall.

"I declare that this hero is the greatest I have ever seen. Your glory, Beowulf my friend, will be widespread, both among your own and many other peoples. You have fulfilled everything by patience and prudence and I will surely give all that I promised you. I also foretell that you will long be a help and protection to your people."

King Hrothgar spoke long and eloquently while all around him men listened. He reminded them of men of old who had not won such fame as Beowulf and warned them against pride and lack of generosity. He ended with thanks and fresh gifts to Beowulf, and bade them all make merry.

The rejoicing lasted until darkness settled on the land and long after. When it ended, all retired to rest free from fear. No fiendish monsters would break in upon their slumbers now. Gladly and peacefully the night passed, and in the morning Beowulf became resolved to return to his king and his native land. After arriving at this decision, he went to Hrothgar.

"Sire, we sea-voyagers who have come from so far away must announce our intent to seek out King Hygelac and home. Your hospitality and generosity have been magnificent and if ever I can do more to win your love, O prince of warriors, then I stand ready. Gladly will I wield my weapons for you and if ever your people is threatened by its neighbours, I will swiftly bring to your aid thousands of noble thanes and heroes. I know that, Hygelac, king of the Geat folk, will strengthen me in words and warlike deeds, speeding me to bear my spear over the ocean if our arms should serve your need. And if your son, young Hrethric, comes to the Geat court to gain skill at arms, as it is best for the valiant to learn by journeying to distant lands, then he shall find many friends."

Hrothgar was deeply moved by these words and appreciated Beowulf's promise of future help. He also marvelled at finding so much wisdom in such a young warrior, and felt that if battle should cut off the son of Hygelac, then the Geats could never choose a better king than Beowulf. He renewed his own assurance of continual friendship between the two lands and of his enduring personal affection. Then, with still more gifts of treasure and some tears of regret, Hrothgar embraced Beowulf and bade him go quickly to his ship.

"A friend's yearning cannot retain you longer from your native land."

The troop of Geats then marched proudly to their vessel carrying their many gifts and treasures, and leading fine steeds.

Glad-hearted were the voyagers as they sailed their dragon-prowed ship home to Geatland. The vessel danced over the waves, and in time the Geats strained their eyes towards the cliffs of their native land and its lovingly recalled shores. As the vessel approached the land, the Geatish coast-warden hastened to greet them, having watched the ocean day and night for their return. He welcomed each of them, and told his subordinates to help to carry the heroes' spoils to the royal palace, where King Hygelac and his beautiful queen, Hygd, awaited them. News of the success of Beowulf's expedition had been sent ahead and a banquet was being arranged in his honour. Proudly Beowulf entered the royal residence, where he was seated beside his royal kinsman for the coming festivities.

The celebrations were tremendous. Again a queen's hand poured out the first bowl with which they rejoiced at the safe return of the heroes and toasted their victory. Then the tale was told of how the fen-fiends were slain, and several times Beowulf was prevailed upon to describe his trials and his triumphs. He spoke stirring words of the horrible monsters and the desperate struggles. He waxed lyrical in his description of the undying gratitude and lavish generosity of King Hrothgar. He also prophesied a lasting friendship between Danes and Geats.

"The great Danish king lives in all noble deeds and has given me much treasure," Beowulf said, "great gifts to meet my heart's desire. These I lovingly bring to you. I have few kinsmen but yourself, O Hygelac. My loyalty and service are your due, my own uncle and my hero-king."

Beowulf showed the treasures Hrothgar had given him as reward for his courage, and distributed them generously among his friends and kinsmen, giving his priceless jewelled collar to Queen Hygd and his best steed to King Hygelac.

Beowulf now resumed his position as Hygelac's chief warrior and champion, and settled down once more among his own people. Time went by and naturally, when half a century had passed away, great and often sorrowful changes had taken place in the kingdoms of both Denmark and Geatland.

In that time Hrothgar had died to be succeeded by his son, Hrethric. Hygelac was killed in a military expedition against the Hetware, though Beowulf had done all a warrior could to save his kinsman and king. Beowulf nearly died in the fighting himself but managed to make his way to the coast after cutting through the encircling enemy. Though badly wounded, he dived into the sea and swam back to Geatland, where he sadly told Queen Hygd of the death of her husband.

Beowulf urged her to assume the regency of the kingdom while her young son, Heardred, came to manhood. Queen Hygd, however, called an assembly of the Geats, and there, with the full consent of the people, offered the crown to Beowulf, the wisest counsellor and bravest hero among them.

Beowulf refused it and so swayed the people with his eloquence and unswerving loyalty that unanimously they raised Heardred to the throne, with Beowulf as his guardian and protector. When in later years Heardred, yet childless, fell in battle, Beowulf was again beseeched by the Geats to become king.

He was in any case next in line to the throne, and reluctantly he accepted. The vengeance he swiftly exacted for his kinsman's death fulfilled every ideal of family and feudal duty, and quieted all external enemies. Indeed his fame as a warrior kept his country safe from foreign invasion, just as his wisdom as a statesman also made such an event less likely and increased the wealth and happiness of the Geats

Beowulf was an ideal king, the perfect warrior and hero, and his life ended in an act of selfless devotion and sacrifice for the good of his people. It was in the fifth decade of Beowulf's reign that terror suddenly afflicted the land, a terror brought down by a monstrous fire-dragon.

This beast flew nightly from its den in the rocky cliffs by the sea, scattering the darkness with its blazing breath. Its fiery scales shone so fiercely in the sky that it looked like the glow of dawn but alas, when sunrise did come, it would reveal a scene of destruction, of smouldering buildings and fields, and the charred remains of people and animals.

The dragon's anger was not without justification, for it had been robbed. Unable to find the thief, it had taken its revenge on the people of the region in general.

Centuries earlier its treasure had been gathered by feats of arms, and added to with care and by long inheritance. The family of warriors that had won this immense booty of gold cups and goblets, necklaces and rings, ornate swords and armour, was increasingly given to greed and miserliness, spending little and guarding the treasure jealously. The last of the clan had personally carried the hoard to the cliffs, trusting no servants, and, cunningly devising entrances and recesses within a cave, had hid the riches where only he could find them.

When this soul survivor died, knowledge of the whereabouts of the treasure died with him. The bounty remained undisturbed until the dragon, seeking shelter on the rocky cliff-side, found its way into the cave and discovered the inner chamber. For three hundred years he guarded the magnificent load unchallenged, until one day a fugitive, fleeing from the wrath of an irate chieftain, came across the cave and found the dragon sleeping on its gold.

Though frightened nearly to death by the sight of the dragon, the fugitive stealthily lifted a beautifully made chalice and took it away, as an offering that he hoped would appease his lord's anger and atone for his offence. When the dragon awoke, it discovered the theft and, using its keen scent, discerned that the felon was a human.

The dragon sniffed around the outside of the lair hoping to find traces of the thief but it was too late. Furious at being unable to find the guilty man, it flew over the surrounding countryside, raining down fiery death and destruction on everyone and everything in its path.

News soon reached Beowulf that his people were suffering and dying, and that no warrior felt equal to the task of delivering the land from this nightly devastation. Beowulf, although now an old man, determined that he must confront the dragon himself. He realized that he would not be able to come to handgrips with this enemy, the way he had with Grendel and his mother long before. The fiery breath of the dragon was far too deadly. More than ever he must trust to arms and armour for protection.

At his command, a shield was made entirely of iron, for it was certain that the usual shield of linden-wood would be quickly burned up by the dragon's flaming breath. Next he carefully hand-picked eleven warriors of his bodyguard to accompany him. The identity of the fugitive whose theft had started the horrible business was then discovered and he was forced to act as their guide.

The small party of men soon reached the lofty crags where the dragon's lair was to be found, and there they halted for a rest. Beowulf sat down and meditated sadly upon his past life, and his chances in the coming conflict. Back when he had defeated Grendel, and when he had done battle with the Hetware, he had been confident of victory and full of joyous self-reliance. Now things were changed. He was an old man and there hung over him a dark premonition. This would be his last fight, and after it he would rid the land of no more monsters.

Gloom seemed to beset him and a sense of impending woe.

"I had many great fights in my youth," he mused to his warriors, almost dreamily. "I well remember them all. I was only seven years old when King Hrethel brought me to court to bring up, and loved me as dearly as his own sons. And like brothers to me were Herebeald, Hathcyn, and my own dear lord, Hygelac. You cannot imagine our grief when Hathcyn, hunting in the forest, accidentally killed his elder brother. To the grief was added a greater than ordinary sorrow, because of course we could not avenge him on the killer. It would have been an added horror for King Hrethel to see his second son killed in disgrace as a murderer! Soon after that King Hrethel died, borne down by his bitter loss. How we wept for my protector, my kinsman. Then was slain Hathcyn by the Swedes and my dear lord Hygelac came to the throne. He was so gracious to me, such a giver of weapons, such a generous distributor of treasure. I always did my best to repay him in battle against his enemies. I sent Daghrefn, the Frankish warrior, to his doom with my deadly hand-grip when he killed my king, so he could not show my lord's armour as testimony to his prowess." Beowulf paused, then addressed his men directly, the dreamy look in his eyes having been replaced by steely determination. "But this fight is going to be different. This time I must use both point and edge, which was not my wont in my youth. Here too will I, old though I am, work deeds of valour. I will not retreat so much as one foot but will meet this monster on his own ground. Stay here you fine young warriors, for this is not your fight, nor the work of any man but me alone. And wait until you know which of us wins, me or the dragon, before you do anything. I will both claim the gold for my people, and save them from the dragon, or death may take me. One or the other."

With that, the old warrior raised his huge shield and alone approached the dark entrance of the cavern. A stream boiling with strange heat flowed towards him and hot air which could be felt at some distance. When he reached the cave mouth Beowulf stopped, unable to advance farther for the suffocating steam and smoke belching out at him. Furious at his own impotence, Beowulf shouted an angry defiance at the terrible creature within.

The dragon leapt up, roaring hideously, flapping its glowing wings and sending a gush of fiery breath towards the interloper as it rushed out, its scales of burnished blue and green raised and glowing with inner heat.

True to his word, the hero did not retreat a single step. Meeting the onslaught with his bright sword, he wounded the dragon but not mortally. He struck the beast again mightily, this time on its scaly head, stunning it for a moment. It sprang again at Beowulf, gushing out so dense a stream of flames that the hero was surrounded by a mist of fire.

The heat was so terrible that his iron shield glowed red-hot and the ring-mail on his limbs seared his flesh. Despite the keen pain he was now feeling, desperately Beowulf endured. The fiery cloud was so terrible that the Geats, watching from some distance away, turned and ran, bound for the cool shelter of the neighbouring woods.

Among the fleeing Geats was young Wiglaf, son of Weohstan, a brave warrior whom Beowulf had showered with gifts, for he was a kinsman and had, until now, proved himself worthy of the king's honour. The young warrior had not retreated far before he thought better of his action.

Angry and ashamed for leaving Beowulf to his fate, he took possession of himself, and shouting after his cowardly comrades, he reproached them bitterly.

"Remember how we all boasted as we sat around the mead hall and drank the foaming ale? We gladly took the gold and jewels our king lavished upon us then, and swore that we would repay him for his gifts, if ever he should need us. Well, he does need us and yet we cower. Beowulf chose us especially from the whole bodyguard to help him in this great struggle, and we have deserted him, left him to face alone this most terrible foe. We must show our valour and go to his side. By the gods, I would rather risk my body in the flames than stay here while my king fights for his life. I will not show such disloyalty to Beowulf. No, he and I will die together, or side by side we'll conquer."

His efforts to stir his comrades were in vain, for they simply trembled and would not move. And so, alone among them, Wiglaf seized his shield of yellow linden-wood, took up his sword and plunged into the flaming mist, where his lord was fighting for his life. Moving towards Beowulf, he shouted encouragement.

"Beowulf, my dear lord, take heart and never let your glory fade. Accomplish this last deed of valour just as you did in days of yore. Only allow me the honour of aiding you."

Hearing another voice, the dragon's rage increased and once more it issued a fiery flare, burning to a cinder young Wiglaf's shield. The two warriors now huddled together behind the iron shield, the dragon fairly roasting them in their armour. Still they resisted and Beowulf, gathering up all his strength, struck such a blow on the dragon's head that his sword was shattered to fragments. Infuriated, the dragon flew at Beowulf in a frenzy and grabbed him by the neck with its poisonous fangs. The blood spurted out in streams, running down his corslet.

Grief seized Wiglaf and filled him with horror and grim fury at this dreadful sight. Leaving the protection of Beowulf's iron shield, he dashed screaming at the dragon, thrusting his sword deep into a vulnerable part. Immediately the stifling, searing fire began to subside.

Overcoming his agony, Beowulf drew the broad knife from his belt, and with a last effort cut the hideous reptile from gut to gullet. The venomous blood poured out of the dragon's wound as it died and fell upon him. Now Beowulf's limbs burnt and ached with intolerable pain. Weakening rapidly, he staggered to a rough seat carved out of the rock near the entrance to the cave and sank down upon it. Wiglaf dipped a cloth in the now cooling waters of the stream running from the cave and gently wiped the brow of his lord.

Partially recovering, Beowulf gripped Wiglaf's arm and looked at him steadily.

"Son," he said, "I bequeath to you the armour which I inherited. I have ruled this people in peace for fifty years because none of our neighbours dared attack us. I have endured many trials and toiled much on this earth and held my own justly. I have never pursued anyone with crafty hatred, nor have I sworn unjust oaths. I rejoice now in all this as I sit here dying of this mortal wound."

The young warrior held his king and swallowed hard, fighting back his tears.

"Dear Wiglaf, bring out from the cave some of the treasures I have lost my life for, so that I might see them before I die, and be glad of my nation's wealth."

Wiglaf was dazzled by the bewildering hoard of priceless treasures he found in the cave. Grabbing up as big a load as he could carry, he hurried back to his king and laid the treasures at his feet.

Beowulf was so near death that he had swooned away before the young warrior's return. In despair, Wiglaf splashed water over his face again. The old champion revived one last time to grasp his kinsman's hand and gaze at the glittering pile before him.

"I thank the All-Father that I have won these treasures I gaze upon, that by my passing, my people should gain such great wealth. I have given my life, and you must now look to the needs of our land. I will dwell in this realm no longer, for Destiny calls me yonder. After my funeral have my warriors build me a burial-cairn high on the sea-cliffs head, up on Hronesness, as a memory tower for me. Let it be called Beowulf's Barrow." Beowulf paused to summon his last ounce of strength. "You, Wiglaf, are the last of the kindred of Wagmund, for death has swept all my other brave kin away. Now I must follow them."

With these words Beowulf fell back, and his soul passed away. Drifting upwards he went to meet the bliss reserved for all true and steadfast spirits.

Wiglaf took a moment to collect himself and control his grief, then he remembered that the monster too lay dead. The people were delivered from the terrible suffering it had caused, though at a high price. As he mourned over his dead king, Wiglaf swore that no man should take joy in the treasures for which so great a sacrifice had been made. The cowards who deserted their king must help him seal up the treasures in Beowulf's grave, to keep them from human use and profit.

When these men came out from the shelter of the wood, and ashamedly approached the place where Wiglaf sat, sorrowing beside the dead Beowulf, he stilled their lamentations with an abrupt wave of his hand and a scornful look.

"It would be true to say, seeing you here, all safe and handsome in the war-gear and ornaments Beowulf gave you, that his generosity was wasted. All you gave him in return was betrayal and cowardice on the day of battle. Remember how Beowulf used to boast of his warriors and how brave they would be in time of danger? Yet he alone avenged his people and conquered the fiend. I did what I could to help him, though it was little enough. Too few champions rallied around our hero when his need was gravest. All the joys of love and loyalty are ended now, as is all prosperity. Our nation is in peril, for foreign princes will hear of your flight and the shameless deed of this day. Would not death have been better than a life of shame?"

The others stood silent, knowing the young hero was right, and they grieved all day long. None of them left their king's body but someone riding nearby saw the mournful group, saw Beowulf dead and galloped away to tell the people.

The word went out that the lord of the Geats lay dead, stricken by the dragon lying dead beside him. At his head sat Wiglaf, son of Weohstan, mourning over his royal kinsman. All realized that the joy and prosperity they had enjoyed would vanish now. They hurried to the spot to mourn their king and also to view the monster and its treasure. All harboured hopes for distribution of this booty, but all agreed, too, that leadership had fallen to Wiglaf.

The Geats followed Wiglaf's commands and, while grieving for Beowulf, gathered wood for the funeral pyre, which they piled high on the cliff-head. Eight chosen men then carried the treasures in, while others pushed the dragon's body over the cliff into the sea. A cart hung with shields was brought to bear Beowulf's body to Hronesness, where his people solemnly laid it on the pyre and watched as a torch was put to it.

All the Geat chiefs, and especially Beowulf's bodyguard, then wept for their leader's passing. As they grieved they sang of the best of earthly kings, the mildest of all men, the gentlest and most gracious, and the most keen to win glory.

The Spider Grandmother

*This Hopi story is one of the several versions of how The Spider
Grandmother, also known as the Spider Woman among the
Navajo, created, or helped to create, the world. The Hopi are desert
dwellers of what is today the south-western United States.
The Spider Woman's use of sound or song in prayer and for
carrying messages is a key element in this myth,
as is the destruction of wrong-doers.*

In all the vastness of space there was nothing and this was called, in the
Hopi language, Tokpela. Out of this came at last a tiny flash of
consciousness that grew into Tawa, the Sun Spirit, who made the first
world. He was greatly disappointed by his creation, which amounted to
little more than a great cave in which nothing lived except little bugs,
and so he decided to dispatch Spider Grandmother to go down among
them with a message.

"The Sun Spirit," she told them, "is not satisfied with things as they
are. You do not know the meaning of life. I am instructed to lead you
from this first world to another one. Come."

It was a long and difficult climb to the second world and on the
way countless insects changed into animals. Even in the second world,
however, they did not seem to understand the meaning of life and Tawa
had the Spider Grandmother go to them once more. Again she bid the
animals follow her, this time upwards into a third world. Here there was
more light and the land was not as frightening. On the way, a few of the
animals had become people.

Spider Grandmother proceeded to teach these people how to
weave and how to make clay jars. With this knowledge they could make
clothes to keep themselves warm and store food and water. At last, tiny

insights into the meaning of life began to occur to some of the men and women. There were others, though, called powaka, false medicine men, who twisted this instinctive learning and guided people along the wrong path.

Everywhere people spent all their time having sex with anyone and everyone, betting and taking foolish risks with their property. Hardly anybody looked after the children, who wandered around squealing, dirty and ignorant. By far the biggest outrage, however, was that it was now popularly believed that humanity owed its existence only to itself. Wearily, Spider Grandmother came to them and talked to the few people who knew enough to listen.

"Tawa, The Sun Spirit, is still unhappy with his creation. The powaka and other wizards have taught people to forget the most important things. They are destroying you all. You must escape them."

"How?" they asked. "Where shall we go?" they cried. "Lead us and we will follow."

"You must find the way yourselves," she told them.

After a long time lost in thought, a very old, wise man spoke up and posed this question: "Are there not the sounds of footsteps in the sky above us?"

Other people allowed that they too had heard such sounds, as if somebody was walking around up there. After conferring together the people decided to send birds to find out what things were like above. The first of these emissaries, a swallow, flew up towards Sipapuni – which means The Hole In The Sky in Hopi – but was not strong enough to pass through the opening and had to turn back. A dove was sent next and it passed through Sipapuni and came back at once to tell of what it had seen.

"There is," it told the few believers, "a different world up there."

Next they sent a hawk, and he explored a large area above, coming back to inform them that this other world seemed to be empty of inhabitants. Lastly, they sent the wise and loyal catbird, who flew through the hole in the sky and then far and wide in the new world until finally it saw a hut in the middle of a vast rocky desert. This stone dwelling stood beside a cultivated field where melons, squash and maize were planted, and watered by irrigation. Beside the field a man sat sleeping, his head resting on his knees. Alighting a few feet away, the catbird watched this person who soon awoke and looked up.

On his cheekbones were painted two black lines running to the bridge of his nose. Scars, dried blood and burns marked his face, and strung together around his neck he wore turquoise and bones. His eyes were deeply sunken, almost invisible but for the faint glimmer in them, shadowed by the heavy brow. This, the catbird knew at once, was Death himself.

Somehow unafraid, which surprised Death, the catbird explained its mission.

"The people below would like to come up here and live with you in this world. Is that all right with you? Is it possible?"

Masuwu, as the Hopi call Death, thought for a moment, then sighed and shrugged his shoulders.

"You see what it's like here. But if they want to come and dwell here with me, tell them they can come."

Following Spider Grandmother's instructions, a chipmunk planted a sunflower seed in a village square below the hole in the sky, then the people were shown how to sing it into rapid growth, using the power of music to make it soar upwards. Whenever they stopped singing the sunflower stopped growing, but eventually it was within reach of the Sipapuni. At this point, however, it began to sag under the weight of its large bloom and suddenly drooped halfway to the ground again.

Then the Chipmunk planted a fine young pine tree. This looked promising until, just short of its goal, the pine stopped growing, no matter how much they sang. Finally, a bamboo was planted and it too grew great and tall. This time, however, each time they stopped to draw breath, rest or change the verses of the song a strong growth appeared,

By sunset the Spider Grandmother declared: "It has passed through the Sipapuni."

As the people started on the long climb the Spider Grandmother warned them against taking anything with them and insisted they leave the wizards or powaka behind. Yawpa, the mockingbird, flew about the people as they climbed, crying "Pashumayni, Pashumayni" – "Be careful, be careful." Before long, as the bird could see, the whole bamboo was covered with struggling bodies.

At the top, as people began setting foot in the new world, Yawpa greeted them individually. She also sang out instructions, to some saying "You will be a Hopi and speak the Hopi tongue", and to others, "You will be a Navaho and speak the Navaho tongue." In this way she designated people for all the various tribes.

As people arrived they camped around Sipapuni. Finally, the only people still climbing up were the disbelieving powaka. This was a matter for concern.

"Stop, you people yet climbing," shouted the chief of the village from which the bamboo had grown. "Go back. It was to get way from you and your ways and ideas that we came up here. You mustn't follow us. We don't want you here."

They did not listen to him, of course, and only showed they had heard by gasping the odd insult as they scrambled breathlessly upwards. At last, the Spider Grandmother's escapees from the world below grasped the top of the bamboo stalk, bending and stretching it, pulling together and with a great effort ripping it out of the distant ground beneath. Then they shook the bamboo mightily before letting it plummet back down to the third world they had left. As the enchanted bamboo plant shattered, thousands of misguided people tumbled to their doom on the dark surface of the land below.

Gilgamesh and Enkidu

Gilgamesh is the most famous of all the Assyro-Babylonian heroes.
His exploits have been immortalized in a vast poem,
considered the masterpiece of Babylonian literature, based on the
myths that had existed for centuries in Sumer.
The name Gilgamesh means, according to how it is translated,
'He who discoverd the source' or, alternatively, 'He who saw all'.
This part of his legend is one of the great 'buddy'
stories of all time.

Two-thirds god and one-third man, Gilgamesh the hero-king of Uruk, was without peer in all of ancient Sumer. Heaven had excelled itself in creating him, endowing him with beauty, strength and valour. In form he was absolutely perfect, in height eleven cubits, with a chest width of nine spans of the hand. His body was as powerful as that of a bull, and nothing could stand up to the might of the weapons he wielded in battle.

All this was very well, except that Gilgamesh was restless and forever fighting with or drilling the young men of Uruk, or putting them to work with him on the magnificent walls of his famous city. It was his constant beating of his drum to assemble them that irritated everyone, as he called men out to play or to work or to train for war or for wrestling matches. That and his drumming just for the sake of drumming, for fun and to work off excess energy, which kept so many citizens of Uruk awake at night.

What was even worse, in some eyes, was that he would not leave the women alone. It was not simply the eligible women he showered his attentions on, but virtually all women. He was not content to leave a virgin to her mother, or pass by even a warrior's daughter or a hero's betrothed. He must have them all, and though the girls themselves did not mind over much, the rest of the population was very upset about it.

Now, despite his irritating aspects, Gilgamesh was well loved, as well he might be. He was the great protector of Uruk and its wise, strong shepherd, a unifying force in a city ruled by a council of elders. His tyrannies were those of the spoiled child or playful bully or over-enthusiastic, undisciplined, careless and uncontrollable friend. The people and elders were too afraid, embarrassed, shamed and kind to do much about his antics and outrages. In the end, those who wished his worst excesses could be curbed resorted to prayer.

With such a deluge of complaints and laments coming heavenwards, the gods began to take note of his disturbances and misdeeds, and finally decided that something should be done about them.

The divine Anu was the first to realize the extent of the problem. He summoned the other gods, who took the glorious goddess Aruru to task.

"Aruru," they said. "You are chiefly responsible for creating this man, so it is up to you to do something about him."

"What do you suggest?" she asked, smiling.

"Create something to distract him," Anu advised. "A rival, perhaps, someone just as strong in body and will, someone just as wise. A counter-weight, if you like. Contending with him will keep Gilgamesh occupied and give the much put upon citizens of Uruk some peace and quiet."

Aruru liked the idea and went to work on it at once. If Gilgamesh had been a creative masterpiece, her next work was to be very different but of equal stature. She relished the artistic challenge. In her mind, as a starting place, she conceived the image of the great god Anu himself. Then, after washing her hands, she scooped up some clay and threw it into the wilderness. There she created the valiant Enkidu.

His very essence was that of a god of war but on his head were the long tresses of a woman. His body was hairy, too. He was covered from head to foot with thick hair and wore no garments of any kind. He knew nothing of people but ate grass with the gazelles and ran with the wild beasts, who became his friends. In return, with his mind and hands and his great strength, he became their protector.

One day a hunter spotted Enkidu at a water-hole. Terrified and yet fascinated, the man watched this strange creature, at one with the animals, trusted by them and alert to any danger to them. It was this man-like thing, the hunter realized, who had been filling in his traps lately, tripping his snares and frightening game out of the range of his arrows.

The hunter saw the creature at the water-hole the next day and the next and on the third day it even warned the animals of his presence before chasing him away. The hunter went to his wise father for advice.

"The thing is horrifying," he explained, "and I can take no game while it's around."

"Can you not kill it or trap it?" his father asked.

"It's too clever to trap and it would be death to try and kill it," the hunter replied. He was not a timid man, his father knew, and yet at the very thought of the creature his face went pale.

"I see that it is so, my son."

"This thing is the strongest beast in the country, and of great fortitude, and its courage matches that of Anu," the hunter went on anxiously.

"You must go to Gilgamesh, king of Uruk, and tell him of the might of this man, for man he is, though wild and unusual. Gilgamesh, too, is of incredible strength and courage. He is also full of wisdom." The old man then outlined a plan of action to put to Gilgamesh.

"A wild man has come down from the hills," the hunter explained again, as he stood before Gilgamesh. "He is terrifying and of immense strength such as only you can equal."

He went on to describe the wild man's habit of siding with the beasts, who regarded him as one of their own.

"He is spoiling my hunting and threatening my livelihood."

"Tell me about him again," Gilgamesh requested, curious and impressed with the reported size, strength and wiliness of the wild man."

The hunter waxed lyrical about the strange creature's attributes, none of which was exaggerated, Gilgamesh was certain, despite the hunter's agitated state of mind. Though curious, Gilgamesh had no great interest in the matter and it did not really require his personal attention. With a smile he thought of an excellent ploy.

"Has he a mate?"

"Not that I've seen. I don't believe there could be such a woman."

"Then, as he is a man, a man alone …" Gilgamesh grinned at everyone around them. "Let's get him laid."

"What?" cried the hunter, astounded on two counts. This, more or less, was what his father had outlined, though personally he had believed the old man had taken leave of his senses and he had not been disposed to suggest it to Gilgamesh.

"Yes," Gilgamesh affirmed. "At my expense, find a whore in the city and take her with you to this water-hole where the wild man drinks with the animals. When he sees her, let her remove all her clothes, let her display all the charms of her body to him. He will approach her and be attracted to her and the animals that have lived with him in the wild will see that he's human and disown him."

The hunter accepted the money Gilgamesh now handed him and went in search of a woman who would agree to his terms. The woman he found was attractive, even to him, but bold and greedy enough to take on the challenge. The pay was commensurate with the nature of the work and the potential danger and she deemed the venture well worth her while. The deal struck, they set off together for the wilderness.

On the third day of their journey they reached their destination, and at a short distance from the water-hole they set up camp. Two days passed before the animals came to drink, accompanied by the wild man. The whore stared in disbelief at him, and was sorely tempted to try to re-negotiate her agreement with the hunter.

"There he is, whore," whispered the hunter, preparing to withdraw a discreet distance. "Reveal your breasts to him and your nakedness, let him enjoy the charms of your body."

The woman continued staring, her usual boldness and quick tongue dulled by the surprise appearance of this new client.

"Do not recoil," the hunter urged, sensing her lack of enthusiasm. "Tempt him, enchant him. When he sees you he will surely be attracted to you. Let him fall on you and then teach him the arts of lovemaking."

The whore duly uncovered her breasts and thrust them in the direction of Enkidu. Soon they had his full attention. He came closer and sniffed the air. As he came still closer he touched her. Drawn inextricably, but perplexed, he studied her. Experienced professional that she was, the woman did not recoil and, indeed, began to warm to her task. Soon desire was racing through Enkidu's body, stoked by the provocative way she discarded the last of her clothing. He fell upon her and took her as only a green, sex-starved creature can. He was like all the other beginners who had come to her. After he had worn himself out, slowly and patiently she began to teach him her arts.

For six days and seven nights Enkidu coupled with the whore, and then, satiated on her charms, he returned to his friends, the desert animals. When he came back early that morning, the gazelles were the first to sense his approach. They had seen him with the woman, and now, smelling her upon him, recognized the man scent. None of the gazelles would let him come near, and fled. The other animals of the desert did the same. Afraid and feeling that his strength had diminished, Enkidu found he could not run as swiftly as before, and, try as he might, he failed to keep up with the fleeing animals.

He returned to the water-hole, where the whore was still waiting, and sat at her feet. For the first time he used the power of speech with which he had been born. Looking up into her face, he told her of his utter bewilderment.

"You have become wise, Enkidu," she said. "You are now like a god, so why roam the desert with the animals? Let me take you to Uruk, city of the great walls, to the holy sanctuary, the abode of Anu and Ishtar, where Gilgamesh, who is perfect in strength and might, lives. Here," she added, "he controls the people like a wild bull."

Nodding, he accepted her advice and decided to go with her, for he needed a friend. This was not the first time she had spoken of Uruk and of Gilgamesh. The latter's doings were on everyone's lips then, and due to divine inspiration she was often to complain to Enkidu of Gilgamesh while praising his strength.

"Let's go then to this place you describe, where Gilgamesh rules like a wild bull," Enkidu said, and to please her, he added. "I will challenge and provoke him. I'll cry out in the very heart of Uruk that I am the strongest."

"Ah, now Enkidu ..." the whore laughed, impressed in spite of herself.

"Yes. I am the one who changes destinies," Enkidu shouted at the sky. He too was inspired. "The one born in the desert is harsher and more powerful."

"We will go now to Uruk and let him see your face. I'll point him out to you because I know where to find him, and you can see our wonderful city. You will like it, I'm sure. People wear the most beautiful gems and there are celebrations every day. The boys are brave and the girls are pretty and fragrant. Am I not pretty and fragrant? We can make even the most prominent citizens leave their beds for ours," she laughed.

"What are beds, exactly?" Enkidu asked.

"I will show you," the whore laughed again, "Enkidu, who cries out for life. I will also show Gilgamesh, who is delighted with life, for you must look at him and study him. You'll see that he is all puffed up with virility and might. He wears splendid objects on his body, but he is stronger than you," the whore went on, now a little worried about Enkidu, or perhaps trying to egg him on. "He never rests, day or night.

You'd better forget your exaggeration and bragging. Gilgamesh is protected by the gods Anu, Enlil and Ea, who favour him with understanding."

"We will see," Enkidu shrugged. He was not simply confident, and in his soul he could not fear Gilgamesh. Perhaps the goddess Aruru could not bring herself to cause the two great beings she created to hate one another. Certainly, the prospect of meeting Gilgamesh filled Enkidu with excitement and joy, even though he supposed they must fight, perhaps to the death when they came together.

Suddenly the whore looked into Enkidu's eyes and a shiver ran through her. Goose flesh covered her bare skin and she knew something absolutely without being told, without thinking it or learning it in any ordinary way, but in an instant from somewhere outside herself.

"Before you even leave the desert, Gilgamesh will see you in a dream," she said, gazing at Enkidu in amazement.

And so it was that at that moment, Gilgamesh had woken from a dream and rising had gone to his mother who had also just come down from bed. Sitting with her over their morning meal he seemed puzzled and she asked the reason, so he told her of his dream, hoping she might interpret it.

"I dreamt I was walking among great heroes, when the stars appeared and one of them fell upon me like the luminous meteor, Anu. I tried to lift him but he was too heavy. I tried to move him but couldn't. The people of Uruk gathered around him, they congregated and pushed with the heroes around him and my friends kissed his feet … Then, strangest of all, I knew I loved him. I bent over him as I would over a woman and embraced him, though not in a carnal way, and I lifted him then and laid him at your feet, for suddenly you were there, too. And then, somehow, in the dream, you made him my equal. Oddly, I now recall a similar dream earlier, only there was this axe, discarded in the walls of Uruk. Again the people gathered around, and again I loved the axe and bent over and embraced it like I would a woman. Just as in the other dream, you appeared and I placed the axe at your feet and you made it my equal."

The wise and perceptive Ninsun thought a moment or two about her son's dreams and then smiled at him.

"Gilgamesh, in the first you dreamt of seeing your equal in a meteor from the sky. You could not lift it or move it yet you loved it and I seemed to make it your equal. I see this as the coming of a strong friend, a helper and friend in need. Now, the axe you saw in the other dream was a man. Because you loved it and embraced it as you would a woman and because I again made it your equal, it also means that a strong friend, a helper, will come to you. He would be the strongest in the country, of great might, as strong as Anu in his resolve."

"Perhaps," Gilgamesh grinned, pleased with his mother's explanation but wondering at the possibility of such a thing. "Yes, perhaps this is a good omen, maybe it will come true and by the will of the night there will be a true friend to me and I a loyal friend to him."

Just as Gilgamesh was talking to his mother about his dreams, the harlot and Enkidu had started to walk to civilization, though the poor, wild man had become assailed by doubts. The whore had torn the long hem of her dress off to make a garment of sorts for Enkidu and a very short dress for herself. Now, wearing this loin cloth had made him self-conscious and he sat on the ground, wondering whether he should go on after all.

In some ways his enjoyment of the delights of passion had made it easy for him to forget he was a son of the wilderness, but his doubts about the wisdom of entering the city were profound.

"But Enkidu," the whore whispered, "whenever I look at you, you seem more like a god to me. Wandering with the animals is no place for you. Let me show you Uruk with its great souks and holy sanctuary, as I promised. Arise, Enkidu, and let me take your hand to Eanna where Gilgamesh lives in perfect strength and skill ..." Suddenly she stopped, and was moved to speak as she had not intended. "And ... And you will love him as you love yourself."

Enkidu looked oddly at the whore, who looked oddly back at him. He watched as she shook the confusion out of her head and went on in a more normal tone.

"So, rise from the ground, the bed of the shepherd (for I also promised to show you a real bed), for in a city beds are warm and comfortable and what you do in them is yet more pleasurable as a result. Just look at the state of your elbows and knees," she laughed, leading him by the hand like a child.

After a few more hours walking Enkidu and the whore arrived at the huts of some shepherds where, despite her encouraging words, she thought it best to keep him until he was more accustomed to people and their ways. The curious looks the shepherds cast at him told her it would be ill-advised to introduce him to too much civilization too soon. The shepherds were not exactly sophisticated, urbane types and yet Enkidu both frightened and amused them. Noting the looks they gave her, she also knew a moneymaking opportunity when she saw one, and so it was decided that they should stay awhile.

It was in this company that Enkidu was first given bread to eat. Having been reared on the milk of wild animals and sparse vegetation, he did not know what to do with it.

"Eat the food, Enkidu," prompted the harlot, "for it is the substance of life, as grass is to your gazelles." Then she gave him a cup of strong drink, saying; "And drink this, for it is the custom of the land."

Enkidu ate bread until he was full and drank seven goblets of strong drink, which roused his spirits and made him feel ridiculously happy. Indeed, he was so joyous his face shone brightly. He was also taught how to clean his body and body hair, and how to anoint it with oil. His appearance became less remarkable as a result, and when he put on clothes, he was said to look passsably human.

To earn his keep and help his new friends, he took up his weapons and went out to hunt lions. This very much eased the minds of the shepherds and, as the strongest man among them, he became their guardian and protector.

These were very good times for Enkidu, though his friend, the whore, began to long for gayer company, and the superior comforts and greater profits of the city. Their life together among the rough sheepmen was not to last.

One day a traveller covered in dust, though dressed like a man from town, rushed breathlessly into the encampment, a desperate look on his face. Enkidu, who was unused to strangers and such excited behaviour, was very curious about him and why he was speaking to the shepherds with such animation and growing outrage. It was not them he was angry at, that much was clear to Enkidu, but why was here?

Enkidu asked the whore to investigate: "Please, go and see what that man is saying. Find out why he is here and what his name is."

She did far more than that; she brought the man himself and most of the band of shepherds over to Enkidu. They all seemed anxious to know how he would react to the man's news. Perhaps, Enkidu thought, the fellow had come precisely because word was about that he, Enkidu, was there. Pride mixed with trepidation gripped his heart as he saw that this was indeed true.

"It is dreadful," the man from town said.

"Why are you in such a hurry, fellow?" Enkidu asked "And why have you come here on what must have been an arduous journey?"

"He broke into the meeting house," the man said, wide-eyed with amazement and horror. "The one dedicated to weddings. I tell you the city is defiled and shamed. He has forced on our ill-fated city, cruel and shameful deeds along with his slave labour. They have set up the drum for him, to accompany his voice while he chooses the bride he desires."

"What does all this mean?" Enkidu looked from the whore to the man and to the shepherds in bewilderment. "And who are we talking about?"

"Gilgamesh, the King of Uruk, of the souks and great walls."

"The drum is to assemble the people," the whore explained.

"And Gilgamesh would choose a bride? Is this so bad?" Enkidu asked, nonplussed.

"They set up the drum," the man said, gaining control of himself and now speaking clearly and simply, "so that the people assemble and he can choose the brides before they marry. So that," the man went on with particular emphasis, "so that Gilgamesh can be the first lover before the bridegrooms."

"He would have them all before their new husbands, before ..."

"Any he wants," the whore shrugged. She understood why everyone was so upset, though nothing in the man's story particularly moved her.

Enkidu regarded the act as one of wicked arrogance. Surely, in this world, which he had been told was so much superior to the one he was used to, such an injustice could not happen. A firm resolve swelled within him. If he was to become a part of this world, it mustn't be allowed.

Later that day Enkidu and the harlot set off for Uruk. She planned to show him where he could find Gilgamesh and then leave him to his own devices. The woman was fond of him, no question about it, but she had her career to consider and lately, because of her attachment to him, it had suffered.

People stared at Enkidu as they entered the city and gradually he seemed to draw a crowd of onlookers in his wake. Somehow the people had known of his coming – that is, his existence was known about, and the people believed that one day he would be among them. By means of some unconscious communication from the gods, through their prayers, and their hopes and fears, they recognized Enkidu. There was relief and joy at seeing him, though none could say exactly why, or in what connection.

"He is in form much like Gilgamesh," they said in whispers, when word of where they were going spread from the whore to the people crowding round the couple.

"Yes, like Gilgamesh, but shorter, though bigger boned."

"He is a man of the wilderness," they opined.

"He has suckled the milk of the wild animals of the desert," another surmised.

"The rattle of arms in Uruk," someone at last prophesied, "will not cease."

And then they saw the truth plainly and everyone, especially the hard worked, drilled, wrestled with, and bride-cheated younger men, rejoiced.

"A worthy opponent and rival hero has appeared to match the comely hero-king."

"Yes, there has come to the god-like Gilgamesh his equal."

Throughout the city word spread and a great throng now followed Enkidu as he was guided to his confrontation with Gilgamesh. Everyone wanted to see the battle royal that would surely ensue when the two met.

As it happened, Enkidu came upon the king as he was about to lay with a woman, but she was not some reluctant bride of another man. On the contrary, what the two were in engaged in was part of a religious observance that even the most prudish of the city fathers would not have objected to, though it was a duty the king relished.

It was the rite of the divine and sacred wedding, Hirros Gamos, in which a priestess played the part of the goddess of love, Ishkara, in sexual congress with the king, during a ceremony dedicated to the fertility of the land.

Gilgamesh noted the unusually large crowd as he arrived at the temple, but thought little enough of it, intent as he was on the pleasurable task in hand. However, as he came to the temple door and tried to enter, from out of the crowd stepped a large man, whom he only saw out of the corner of his eye, who, incredibly, was barring his way.

Thinking it a mistake, that the man had stumbled or had been pushed from behind, he did not take offence. There was in the flash of sight he had of the fellow, something suggestive of the county bumpkin, so perhaps he knew no better. Gilgamesh side-stepped and attempted to brush passed, but to his astonishment the man, now beside him and only inches away, shoved him back, and stood his ground, filling the doorway.

Reacting instantly, in a temper and without thought, Gilgamesh half-turned and grabbed the man, and the long-awaited match was on. One was certain he was preventing an immoral abuse of power, the other sure his rights and duties were being violated. Neither had any thought of the recent predictions or presentiments of women.

Bellowing like bulls they threw each other against the door frame and pillars of the building, breaking and cracking them. They heaved, gripped and tumbled one another, neither getting any real advantage until at one point, after turning Gilgamesh on his back and dropping him to the ground, Enkidu saw into the temple for the first time. He saw its furnishings and the bed on which lay the priestess, who was looking daggers at him for causing this unscheduled delay to the ceremony. Holding him entirely culpable, she reached out, picked up a candlestick and tossed it viciously at his head, barely missing.

A split-second later Gilgamesh was on him, getting him in an arm-lock from behind. Enkidu slipped out of it eventually but as he and the king squared off and he looked Gilgamesh in the eye for the first time, he saw the joy and love of life in the man's face. He saw no malice, only wonder and respect. And in truth this was so, for Gilgamesh was not at all a bad man, but surrounded by people who either doted on him or were afraid of him, and would not thwart him in anything. He was like a child, seeking his limitations and, finding none, going farther. To be checked and challenged at last was a revelation and a relief for him. Gilgamesh had also begun, even as they fought, to recognize that Enkidu was the axe, the meteor, the friend in his dream.

As they stood poised for more action while noting the new mirth on the other's face, each now dropped his guard a little. As he saw the other do so, each then eased some of the tension in his muscles and let the wariness in his eyes disappear as he saw it go bit by bit in the other. At last, they smiled and then they began to laugh.

"A drink?" Gilgamesh suggested.

"Why not," Enkidu nodded. "But don't you have business first?"

"Ah yes," Gilgamesh wiggled his eyebrows. "If you've no objection?"

"I have to see a lady, too," Enkidu grinned. "To say farewell, for she has business of her own."

The whore winked at Gilgamesh and he knew that the worker had been worthy of her hire. Soon he would realize it was the best money he had ever spent. The two heroes duly had that restorative beverage, and so began one of the greatest friendships of all times. Many were the battles they would win together, many the women they would woo, though from the day of their first meeting only the fully willing and single.

When the two heroes became bored with their adventures at home the city fathers encouraged them to undertake travels to other lands. Although the influence of Enkidu on Gilgamesh was very good, the two of them were a handful in peacetime. Eventually, the pair decided to embark upon an adventure of truly extraordinary proportions, an awesome task that would test them to the uttermost and put their lives very much at risk.

It had begun when Enkidu fell into a depression, feeling himself weakened by the good life of the city. To be sure he enjoyed it, but he would always be a little torn between civilization and his old home in the wilderness. When Gilgamesh proposed a scheme to occupy their time in an epic manner, even Enkidu baulked at it.

"The demon Humbaba lives in the forest. Let's go and kill him and relieve the world of all evil."

"My friend," Enkidu responded, arching one brow and smiling ruefully at Gilgamesh, "I learned when I was roaming the hills and vast prairies with the animals that the forest extends a distance of ten thousand leagues on every side. Only a madman would dare penetrate it."

Gilgamesh grinned.

"Look," Enkidu said, realizing that Gilgamesh was serious, "the Humbaba's roar is a raging torrent. Fire comes out of his mouth and he is literally the very spirit of violent death."

"I know," Gilgamesh nodded enthusiastically.

"And yet you wish to take on this monster?"

"I have decided to go to the Cedar Mountains and to enter the forest, the dwelling of Humbaba. I shall take an axe to aid me in the encounter." Gilgamesh knew his friend and also that he was often in two minds because he had not come from a background of money and comfort. He did not take such advantages for granted. Even if he were as restless as Gilgamesh, Enkidu did not lightly venture out in bad weather or willingly take on arduous trips and tasks, though when he was actually embarked upon them he coped far better. Gilgamesh was always the instigator, Enkidu always the reluctant one who would never let him down.

"It's fine if you wish to stay behind this time. I'll go alone," he told Enkidu.

Enkidu used various arguments to talk Gilgamesh out of his madcap enterprise.

"And how will we enter the Cedar Forest when its guardian is a warrior that never sleeps?"

"What do you suggest?" Gilgamesh asked, innocently ignoring Enkidu's use of the word 'we'.

"Whatever we do," Enkidu concluded gloomily, "we haven't got a chance. The thing was put there by Enlil to protect the Cedar forest and his appearance strikes terror in everybody. Humbaba's roar is like the waves of a flood."

"It still remains that he is evil and therefore loathsome to Shamash," Gilgamesh said, ever the optimist in these matters.

"We'll die," Enkidu spoke with smug certainty, as if being proved right about it would give him some satisfaction. "Yes, we'll die."

"But who can go up to heaven? The gods alone are the ones who live forever with Shamash. As for humans, their days are numbered and all their deeds are to no avail. They vanish with the wind," Gilgamesh laughed. "For myself, if I die, then my name will be immortal and they will say of me, 'Gilgamesh died in combat with the demon Humbaba'."

"Like a fool, they will add," Enkidu smiled, shaking his head.

"With these words you sadden my heart," Gilgamesh laughed, placing his hand on his chest and sighing. Then he nodded. "I shall make an enduring name for myself."

"Did I say you would not?" asked Enkidu, arching an eyebrow.

"Tomorrow, my friend, I'll give orders to the armourers and they will make the arms in our presence."

Then they fell to the serious business of discussing the weapons they would need, of what type and heft, the various heads of arrows and kinds of sword blades. Leaving nothing to chance, they did indeed oversee the making of each of them, starting the next morning until the armourers were done.

When Gilgamesh and Enkidu emerged armed with the splendid weapons they'd had made, they drew a crowd. The sheaths of their mighty swords were made of gold and the size and weight of their axes were tremendous. People gathered around to admire them and cheer on their enterprise, but the elders, seeing the two men were serious, called a meeting at which they attempted to dissuade them from such a hazardous undertaking. Gilgamesh tried to infuse the old men with some of his enthusiasm, implying that, were they to succeed in their mission, it would enhance the reputation of the city among its neighbours.

"I, Gilgamesh," he told them. "Would see the one the people are talking about, the one whose name has filled the cities with terror. I have resolved to go and overcome him in the Cedar Forest and the world shall hear the tale of the son of Uruk. They shall say; 'How strong was this descendant of Uruk!' "

"Oh, Gilgamesh," exclaimed the chief of the elders and his most senior adviser, "You are still young, your courage has carried you far, but you do not know what you are embarking upon. We have heard that Humbaba is terrifying and strange. So who, confronted by this, can resist?"

He and his fellows went on to rehearse the same arguments that Enkidu had used, to no greater avail.

"No one has yet stood up to Humbaba," all the elders cried. "Why would you two chance this?"

"For that reason," Gilgamesh replied. Turning to Enkidu, who remained silent, he asked if all this sounded familiar, then he laughed. "But how should I answer them, my friend? Shall I say that I am afraid of Humbaba and shall stay at home for the rest of my days?"

In the end, the elders were resigned to their going and gave their blessing.

"May your protecting god grant you victory. May he send you back safely to the harbour of Uruk."

Then Gilgamesh, feeling his responsibilities as king at last, realized that he must do more to put the minds of the elders at rest. For that reason and his own peace of mind, he bowed down in prayer to the god Shamash.

"Return me to my home and may my soul receive blessings and benediction. Spread your shade over me and cover me with your protection."

His devotions over with, he and Enkidu went off to a soothsayer, hoping for some more earthly reassurance, but none came. The fortune-teller was no more optimistic about their chances than the elders had been.

When at last they set off, the people came to see them go and small boys begged to be allowed to carry their weapons for a short way. Again the elders expressed concern for the king's safety. They offered much advice and asked Enkidu to walk before him and be his guardian and guide, because he had been much of the way before. The elders then said many prayers to Shamash for the success of the adventure and the safe, speedy return of the two heroes.

"May Shamash enable you to fulfil your desire," a priestly elder concluded. "And when you have killed Humbaba, as you seek to do, wash your feet. When you camp at night, dig a well and see that your water skin is always filled with pure water. Offer fresh water to Shamash and think of Lugalbanda at all times."

Gilgamesh himself suggested that they visit the temple of Egalmah, which lay directly on their route.

"Let us go to the presence of Ninsun, the wonderful queen, my mother, the astute knower of all. She will give us an honest start and good advice."

So Gilgamesh and Enkidu started walking towards Egalmah, where the king hoped they would be able to enlist her aid with the gods.

"Oh, mother," Gilgamesh said on entering the temple and seeing her, "I have made a decision on a momentous matter. I am to travel far, to the homeland of Humbaba."

Ninsun blanched and fought to control her emotions. She could see how they were equipped and even before he explained what they intended to do, she imagined the danger they would face.

"Intercede for us with Shamash," Gilgamesh said in conclusion, after fully appraising her of their plans. "And pray for us."

Ninsun went into her room and put on a beautiful dress. She

adorned herself with ornaments, put a crown on her head and went up to the roof where she burnt incense and held up her hands to Shamash.

"Why did you give my son a restless and anxious heart? Now you have spurred him on and he is resolved to travel far, to the homeland of Humbaba. He will know great struggle and walk a road that is unknown to him. Aid and protect him and his companion in their sacrifice to kill the giant Humbaba and remove from the face of the earth the evil you loathe."

The queen then extinguished the incense, pronounced an incantation and summoned the priestesses and the sanctified and pious vestal virgins. Next she called Enkidu to her.

"Strong Enkidu, who are not of my womb, I now take you as a son." She then adorned his neck with a jewelled necklace as a pledge. "I entrust Gilgamesh to you, so return him to me safely."

Enkidu, the strangely born, having no family but beasts of the wilderness, was deeply touched and swore to watch over his brother, for his own sake and his mother's.

The two heroes were indeed blessed during the first phase of their great task, perhaps because they did not forget to offer up a sacrifice to the god Shamash regularly. On the first day they walked thirty leagues, and on the second morning fifty leagues. In just three days they covered a distance it would have taken most mortals one and a half months to complete. They pressed on until, after many more days of dogged travelling, they reached the entrance to the forest.

The edge of the forest was dense and dark, the mysteries beyond it too frightening to relate. As dwellers of the plains and deserts, the two heroes would have found this an unimaginably disturbing place. No ordinary forest, it was the very home of the spirit of death. The evil enchantment of the place could particularly be sensed around the entrance, which was twenty-four cubits wide and consisted of a trail passing under an arch of twisted vines and overhanging tree branches.

The trail disappeared into the darkness of the shadows, but under the arch, standing sentinel, stood a demon whom Humbaba had appointed to guard it.

From a distant hill Gilgamesh and Enkidu watched the entrance with growing anxiety. If this hideous creature at the gate was only an underling, what must his mighty lord be like?

"You go get him," Enkidu smiled, "while he is still armed and dangerous, for there's more honour in that."

Gilgamesh appreciated his friend's humour, but only just. "Do you have any constructive ideas?"

"I'm serious," Enkidu replied, a plan suddenly hitting him. "You approach him, slowly and openly. I will move by stealth round the back of him, then, on a signal, we'll attack together."

Both agreed to the plan but neither of them was too keen to be the first to begin the attack. After further prevarication, Enkidu moved off to take up position.

When he was in place, Gilgamesh showed himself and began his leisurely approach, intently watched by the guardian of the forest entrance. Acutely aware of the demon's interest, Gilgamesh would pause to pick a stone out of his boot, to test the edge of his axe or to scratch his backside, all the while hoping that the unseen Enkidu, still in spirit an animal of the wild, was also inching closer.

The nearer they got to the beast the more palpable was its rage, the more overwhelming the suffocating smell emanating from it. Gilgamesh stopped a few yards short of where the beast was standing. He postured a moment, howled his name, beat his chest, and then, elaborately, he charged. This was the signal for Enkidu, who was crouched only feet from the demon's rear, to spring up and join Gilgamesh in the attack. Darting forward with lightning speed, they came together and struck at the demon, who was startled to find himself assailed on two sides.

Swinging their axes with great ferocity the heroes hacked at the demon. Gilgamesh's first blow was blocked as Enkidu's, delivered almost simultaneously, landed on the monster's enormous shoulder. Gilgamesh then aimed a blow at its belly as the demon half turned to confront Enkidu. It screamed and slashed with its claws and snapped with its teeth, even as it bled from its deep wounds, while the heroes darted in to cleave chunks out of its massively thick hide. At last it weakened and fell to the ground, whereupon, knowing they must not hesitate, Gilgamesh and Enkidu leaped upon it and began chopping at its neck in turns until the demon's head rolled free. They collapsed to the ground where they lay for several minutes to catch their breath.

After a brief rest Gilgamesh began to examine their dead enemy, hoping to gain some insight into what Humbaba might be like. Enkidu, meanwhile, walked over to the entrance to the forest. Standing beneath the arch he suddenly groaned and looked back at his friend in disbelief. An invisible wall of pain and fear seemed to bar his way. The wicked enchantment had stopped him from going further and at the same time prevented him from going back.

"Do not come closer," he shouted to Gilgamesh. "It is horrible and it will not release me."

"Fight it, Enkidu, defeat it."

"It is too much to bear, we cannot go through."

"We can and must," Gilgamesh said with determination, stepping up beside Enkidu. He too was gripped by terror and held fast by the force of the magic doorway. "We have not come this far to be thwarted now," Gilgamesh groaned, gritting his teeth and straining against the power pressing against him from all sides. "Not after all the difficulties we've faced, the battles we've fought. Be brave and stand by me."

"We can beat it," Enkidu screamed at last. "We will protect one another."

"And if we fall in combat, we'll leave behind an everlasting name."

"We are not going to die yet,"' Enkidu snarled against the pain and strain. Together they summoned all their willpower and physical strength.

"On the count of three, we break through," Gilgamesh hissed. "Put everything into it, my friend."

Enkidu nodded, barely able even to move his head.

"One, two, three ..."

With a mighty howl the two suddenly hit what held them with a burst of energy and angry resistance that broke its power. Finding themselves racing forward head long, they could not stop and fell, tumbling to the forest floor, rolling in the dust and pine needles. Hooting and shouting for joy and relief, they climbed to their feet, slapped each other's backs and danced about, laughing and congratulating one another.

Looking around they felt a menacing closeness, an eery silence. They had done something all right. But, what, exactly?

Penetrating far into the forest, they were moved by its beauty as well as haunted by it. They walked the trails made by Humbaba and came to its very heart, where, struck dumb with awe, they saw the Cedar Mountain of the gods. The shade of the great trees around it gave out a sense of peace and happiness. At sunset, Gilgamesh dug a well and climbed some way up the mountain, taking water and food with him as offerings. He asked the mountain to send him a dream that would foretell joy.

That night, after the two friends had lain down to sleep, Gilgamesh awakened suddenly with a start.

"What was that? What did you say?"

"Nothing," Enkidu said after a moment, fully awake now, having feared a threat. "I did not speak."

"My friend, who was it who spoke to me if not you?" Gilgamesh took a moment to emerge fully from sleep. "It was a dream. I remember it now."

The two men lay down again, silently staring at the stars through the treetops.

After a few minutes, Gilgamesh spoke. "I dreamt we stood at the foot of the mountain. Then suddenly the mountain fell and we were, you and I, like two fleas. But there was another dream, too, and I saw the mountain again as it was falling. Then a glow shone out. The radiance and brightness of it grew intense and overwhelmed the earth and carried me away from under the mountain, refreshing me and filling my heart with joy."

"Your dream has a good meaning," Enkidu told him. "It signifies good things. The mountain is obviously Humbaba and we will overpower him and kill him."

In yet another dream he had that night, Gilgamesh identified signs of another good omen and in the morning, when they climbed the mountain once more, they were both in good spirits. The time for the confrontation with Humbaba was nearly at hand.

After sharpening his axe on a stone, Gilgamesh looked at the tree varieties in the immediate vicinity. When he had selected a suitable type, he brought his mighty blade down on the trunk, swung back and cut again, chopping at it slowly, rhythmically, with hard blows that echoed around the forest. Its thick trunk would sustain such loud but slow, measured chopping for hours, Gilgamesh reckoned, and its splendid foliage would hide the fact that Enkidu was concealed up there.

The two men had planned a similar deception to the one that had worked so well at the forest entrance. Gilgamesh would attract the attention of Humbaba, summon him with the sound of his chopping, and when he came to investigate, Enkidu would drop onto him and together the two friends would kill him.

Everything worked perfectly until they saw Humbaba. By comparison, the demon they had killed at the entrance to the forest was knee high to him and soft skinned. With hide as hard as granite, fire in his piercing, withering eyes, a mouth like a cavern and ugly as an ancient toad, he came at Gilgamesh, in a thundering, ground-shaking run.

"Who cuts the trees of my forest?" he roared furiously. "Who trespasses on my mountain and disturbs its serenity?"

Gilgamesh stood gaping at Humbaba, and Enkidu found himself being looked down upon by the giant demon, who could see him easily through the thinner branches at the top of the tree. Slowly, Humbaba lumbered toward the two friends, both of whom were frozen with fear. All thought of fighting the monster vanished from their minds as they watched it come at them. They might as well take their axes and swords to the mountain itself. Instinctively and uselessly, Gilgamesh scrambled up the tree and clung to it beside Enkidu, their eyes enormous and glassy, no colour in their faces as each looked at the other, knowing that death was coming for them and that it would be a hideous one. Battle against an army of men each would have been preferable to combating this evil demon.

They made no bold, noble or witty comments now, for unlike past times and past fights, they were not simply facing death. The two heroes were not afraid of death. They were, however, very afraid of Humbaba. He was horrible, invincible, and the cruelty of his burning eyes terrified them into paralysis and screaming insanity.

Fire shot from the demon's eyes and his mouth opened to gush forth a slimy torrent of water that hit them like a raging river. As if caught in a storm the tree fell, torn from the ground, roots and all, and was washed backwards as the demon's foul breath and scorching eyes cooked them in steam that rose from the combination of all the vile creature's weapons.

"Oh, what have we done?" the two friends squealed in bitter anguish over the rashness of their adventure.

"Shamash, Shamash," Gilgamesh wailed. "Help us."

"Yes," Enkidu begged the god. "Save us from this thing."

Praying furiously, holding to the downed tree for all their worth, they shut their eyes from the horror approaching them and pleaded with Shamash to intercede and somehow stop the monstrous Humbaba from annihilating them.

As they lay among the branches, shivering in terror, alternately praying for deliverance and cursing themselves for fools, the god heard their pleas and his heart was moved. To even have tried to face the evil demon of death was enough to win his support. Perhaps the heroes' mad courage and frank repentance amused him, too.

Shamash stirred up the winds until a tremendous gale began to blow, tearing and whipping at the mountainside, felling more trees, yet blowing at Humbaba, who now fought against it to keep his monstrous feet. Rocking in the great wind that faced him, he teetered violently and seemed to topple slowly, falling almost gracefully for a long moment until with an earth-shuddering crash he met the ground, tossing stones and tree trunks into the air with the jarring, thunderous impact.

With no real thought but acting on warrior instinct, the heroes scrambled out from under the branches around them, stumbled over the shattered wood and rubble left by the torrent and the gale, found their discarded weapons and attacked. Even as they climbed onto the rock-hard chest of the felled Humbaba, they were assailed by doubt that they could harm him. Already the shocked and shaken demon was struggling to rise. With his bulk it would be difficult but not impossible. They had to act swiftly or be in the same danger they had faced only moments before.

Noticing a fissure in the granite-like armour, just over the demon's heart, they aimed a sword at it and prepared to drive it in with the flat of an axe blade.

"Wait," bellowed Humbaba. "Do not slay me. Have pity and I will give you this great cedar forest and all its wealth of trees."

"No," said Enkidu.

"I beg you," the demon pleaded. "Do not kill me, I long to live, and I swear to do you no harm and to cease from the evil that is loathsome in the sight of Shamash."

"What do you think?" Gligamesh asked, looking at Enkidu. "Shall we spare him and show compassion?"

"Don't trust him, evil never changes," Enkidu swore. "If we don't kill him now, while we can, he'll surely kill us once he is free and up again, and Shamash who heard us once may not be so kind again."

Gilgamesh reared back and hit the sword pommel with his axe, driving it like a stake into the breast of the demon, then with its point on the pommel of the first, another sword was driven in, pushing the first yet deeper. With a quake-like shudder, the great demon Humbaba died. Using their axes like chisels and working at it for days, they cut off the demon's head for a prize and wearily, though in glorious triumph, the two heroes returned to Uruk.

Gilgamesh bathed, washed his hair, which he let fall to his shoulders and polished his armour. He put on clean clothes with fine embroidery and wrapped a belt around his waist. Finally he donned his crown. The greatest celebration of his life awaited him as the whole city longed to toast the victory he and Enkidu had won. The elders and heroes of the city applauded them and showed awe and respect, the populace worshipped them and the women of Uruk desired them as bed-mates. Everyone, everywhere wanted them, and this was not limited to mere humanity.

From heaven, the glorious Ishtar looked on Gilgamesh and she was smitten. His beauty, courage and irresistible success filled her with passion. Appearing in his bed-chamber, she admired his body as he dressed, and then spoke in a husky, seductive voice.

"Come to me Gilgamesh," she said, devouring him with a smouldering look from her hooded eyes. "Be my chosen bridegroom and give me your seed to enjoy. You shall be my husband and I shall be your wife."

Startled briefly, Gilgamesh returned her smouldering gaze. He knew her to be the most beautiful and desirable female in heaven or on the earth. For a moment he hardly knew what to say. With studied calm he went on dressing.

"I shall prepare a carriage of lapis lazuli and gold for you," she continued, "with golden wheels and spokes of bronze. Demons of lightning will pull it instead of mules."

"A fine vehicle," Gilgamesh said flatly.

"Our home will be filled with the fragrance of cedars," Ishtar told him, moving slowly and seductively towards him, her shapely body seeming to glide and shimmer, though solid, warm and soft. "When you enter our home, the threshold will kiss your feet and kings, rulers and princes will all bow down to you in submission. They will offer you wealth in revenue from the mountains and the plains. Your goats will bear triplets and your ewes will give birth to twin lambs. Your donkeys will carry more than mules ever can and your oxen will be splendid and without rivals. The horses of your chariots will be the winners of every race they run."

"Glorious Ishtar," Gilgamesh asked with no emotion in his voice. "What do I have to give you if I take you for a wife? Do I offer you ointments and clothes for your body? Do I give you bread and food? If so, what food can I give that will be fit for you, a divine goddess?"

"All you must give to me is yourself, Gilgamesh," Ishtar whispered breathily in his ear, for by now she was next to him and pressing herself against him.

"What good would it do me to have you for my wife, Ishtar?" Gilgamesh asked sincerely. Gently he pushed her away and looked her frankly in the eye. "You are only a hearth when the fire dies with the cold. You are a crack in a door, that keeps out neither wind nor storm."

"Gilgamesh!" she gasped in wonder.

"You are a castle within which heroes decay." He was worked up now, the full shock of her proposal having sunk in. Though briefly fun for her, it would have been disastrous for him. Moved to righteous anger, he waxed lyrical. "Yes, you are an elephant which destroys its harness. You are pitch that soils its bearers, a water skin that leaks over its carrier, a marble wall that collapses. You are a sandal that pinches the wearer."

"How dare you!" She slapped his face.

"Which of your lovers have you loved with any consistency?" he demanded.

She sniffed and tossed her lovely head but did not reply.

"Let me remind you of the sad tales of your past loves, shall I?"

"What sad tales can these be?" Ishtar pouted.

"There was Tammus, the lover of your youth, for whom there is yet wailing and weeping every year. Next you fancied the multi-coloured roller bird but then struck him and broke his wing so that he alights in the garden even now and laments crying; 'My wing! My wing!'"

"An accident," she shrugged, carelessly.

"Oh? Then you wanted the lion, so perfect in his strength and grace, but dug seven times seven pits in which to trap and kill him. You desired the horse yet inflicted the whip and the spur and the harness upon him and forced him to race seven leagues without quenching his thirst until he had muddied the waters. Then you made his mother, Silili, weep and lament forever."

"Vicious rumours," Ishtar said lightly, studying her nails.

"You loved the shepherd after that," Gilgamesh continued. "And he brought you bread and slaughtered the kids of his flock and cooked them for you every day, but you struck him and turned him into a wolf. Now he's chased by his own herd-boys and his dog bites his legs."

Ishtar sighed heavily, feigning boredom, but inside she was seething with anger.

"You loved Ishullanu after that, your father's gardener, who daily brought you baskets of dates and heaped your table with delicacies of all kinds. You looked on him and enticed him. 'Come on, handsome Ishullanu and let me enjoy your manhood,' you said to him; 'Reach out your hand and touch the charms of my body.' Then Ishullanu demurred, knowing you would do him no good, and he asked how a hut of straw could keep out the bitter cold of winter and asked why he should eat tainted bread. In a fury, you raised up your wand and hit him, turning him into a frog just to make him suffer."

"So?"

"Soon enough you're bound to treat me the same as you have all the others."

Enraged, Ishtar glared at him a moment and then instantly ascended to heaven where she went in tears to her father and mother, the god Anu and the goddess Antum.

"Gilgamesh has cursed and insulted me," she cried, flinging herself dramatically at her father's feet.

"Oh, has he?" Anu said doubtfully.

"Well, he has listed all my wicked and shameful deeds," Ishtar said, her lower lip protruding.

"You provoked him and got what you deserved," Anu told her with a smile, while Antum nodded in agreement.

"Daddy," Ishtar said pouting and fluttering her eyelashes. "Let me have the Bull of Heaven so that I can send it down to destroy that bad Gilgamesh."

Seeing her parents exchange a look of impatience and disapproval, Ishtar stood up quickly and glared at them.

"Well," she snapped, "if you don't give me the Bull of Heaven, I'll tear down the door to the Underworld and let the dead rise up and eat with the living."

"But Ishtar," her father said in alarm. "If I gave you the Bull of Heaven then Uruk would go through seven lean years. Have you collected enough crops for those years? Have you stored that much fodder for the cattle and other beasts?"

"Oh yes, Daddy, I've stored more than enough for all the people and animals if the lean years spread. Plenty of fodder and grain."

With a sigh, knowing Ishtar was fully capable of carrying out her threat, Anu gave her the chain of the leading rein of the Bull of Heaven. Taking it gleefully, she led the creature away and down to earth where she placed it in the middle of Uruk.

Panic and terror spread throughout the city at once. At the first terrible lowing of the bull a hundred people died, then two and three hundred more. When it lowed again hundreds of others were killed. With its third lowing, it attacked Enkidu, who had come to investigate. But bravely, Enkidu fought back.

Leaping out of the way of its charge, Enkidu grabbed the Bull's horns as it passed him and was pulled onto its back. Whirling furiously and throwing foam from its mouth and dung with its tail, the great Bull desperately tried to dislodge him. With a mighty buck it tossed him into the dust and came at him with its giant horns aimed at his chest. Gilgamesh, who had arrived just then, ran and threw the full weight of his body into the animal's side, checking its momentum and infuriating it. Only Enkidu springing to his feet and distracting the Bull again, prevented it spinning about and goring Gilgamesh, who then scurried out of range.

"We've boasted about all our other exploits, my friend," Enkidu said. "But they were mostly far from Uruk."

"And they will all have been for nothing if we don't kill this thing and save my people," Gilgamesh replied, all the while watching the Bull in case it charged one of them.

Snorting and digging at the ground with its hooves, it looked from one to the other and bided its time. If it lowed again now many people would die.

"We had better attack it together," Enkidu said. "I'll get it by the tail and going backwards a moment, while you get on its back with your sword drawn."

"A thrust between the nape of its neck and its horns should kill it," Gilgamesh agreed. "Are you ready?"

Enkidu nodded with a doubtful gin.

"Now," cried Gilgamesh and instantly they jumped at the bull.

Enkidu succeeded in grabbing its tail and, as hoped, pulled it backwards long enough to stop it spinning. In those split seconds

Gilgamesh sprang upon the terrible animal's back and fought against its violent leaping and shaking to poise his sword point above the agreed place. Both hands tightly grasping the hilt, using every ounce of his strength, he stabbed downwards.

Without so much as a bellow, a shiver or a last rear or buck, the Bull dropped on the spot, stone dead. Gilgamesh sat on its back trying to collect his wits and Enkidu stood, still holding the tail, staring at the sight in front of him. Suddenly, people burst from doors and windows and climbed down from trees and roofs to take the two men up on their shoulders and carry them in triumph around the city walls.

Returning to the Bull's body, the two heroes were never more loved by the people of Uruk than now. They cut out the heart of the Bull and offered it to Shamash, prostrated themselves and prayed. Then the two brothers, feeling utterly drained, sat down and rested. As they lay, leaning against the carcass, Ishtar appeared hovering over the walls of Uruk, shouting curses at them.

"Woe to you, Gilgamesh," she raged. "For defiling and insulting me by killing the Bull of Heaven."

At this unjust fury of a woman justly scorned, Enkidu lost his temper entirely. Deftly leaping up, he sliced off one of the Bull's haunches and he flung it at Ishtar, hitting her square in the face with it.

"If I'd caught you, I'd have done to you what I did to him, and tie his entrails around your limbs."

Disappearing in high dudgeon, Ishtar gathered the priests and vestal virgins and performed lamentations and wailing over the Bull of Heaven's right haunch, while in Uruk, Gilgamesh summoned craftsmen and armourers, finding uses for other parts of the dead creature.

Everyone was amazed at the thickness and size of the horns, for each of them was lapis lazuli, weighing thirty mina. The thickness of the outer layer was the span of two fingers and could hold six gur-measure of oil. This Gilgamesh offered up to his protector god, Lugalbanda. Then he took the horns and hung them in his bedroom.

The two heroes washed their hands in the Euphrates River, embraced and rode again through the streets of Uruk to hear once more the people's praise. Crowds proclaimed them, and sang of their courage.

"Who is the most glorious of men?" Gilgamesh shouted with a grin.

"Gilgamesh is the most glorious of men," the singers cried.

"Who is the most splendid of men?" he asked again.

"Gilgamesh," they sang as one. "Gilgamesh is the most splendid of men."

In his ear, suddenly worried by his own rashness, Enkidu muttered of the consequences of so infuriating Ishtar.

"She at whom we flung the haunch of the Bull of Heaven in our anger," Gilgamesh assured him, "the glorious Ishtar herself, will not find anyone to console her. She was wrong."

Alas, Gilgamesh should not have been so certain.

They held a great celebration in the palace and when it was late, the two heroes went up to their beds. In his sleep, however, Enkidu had a disturbing vision and sat up violently half-awake, asking; "Why did the gods meet for deliberation?"

The next morning Enkidu told Gilgamesh about his dream."

"My friend, it was very strange," he said. "The gods came together to confer and Anu said to Enlil: 'Because they killed the Bull of Heaven and Humbaba, the one who cut the cedar trees on the mountainside must die.' But Enlil said: 'It is Enkidu who must die, but Gilgamesh will not.' Then the divine Shamash said he had ordered us to kill the demon and the bull. He asked them: 'So, why should Enkidu, who is innocent, have to die?' But Enlil grew indignant and said to Shamash: 'You are too close to them, you appear to them daily and are nearly becoming one of them."

Even before his eyes, Enkidu seemed to grow weak and pale and Gilgamesh was frightened for him.

"But my brother," he said desperately. "Why should they absolve me and not you?"

Enkidu made no reply and inside his head Gilgamesh wondered, beset with worry; 'Is it my fate to watch the spirits of the dead and sit at the gateway of death? Is it for me never to see my dear friend again?' He did not speak of his deep concerns but tried to encourage Enkidu and nurse him, as daily he grew weaker and more confused.

At one point in his delirium, Enkidu spoke to the door of his room as if it were a living being. He had chosen its wood from a forest twenty leagues away before he ever saw the lofty cedar trees.

"Your wood, oh door," he told it. "I have never seen the like of before in all the land. You are seventy-two cubits high and forty-two cubits wide. A skilled carpenter made you in Nippur and brought you from there. Yet, if I had known that your beauty would bring disaster upon me, I would have taken up my axe and destroyed you, I would have made a raft of you. But what can be done now, door? I made you and brought you and now maybe some future king will use you, remove my name and have carved on you his own."

It broke Gilgamesh's heart to hear his friend speak this way and he tried to calm his fears and inspire him to get better, but still the illness grew worse. Even while lucid, Enkidu, in his despair, regretted leaving the wilds for the temptations of civilization. Angrily, he cursed the hunter and the whore.

"Oh divine Shamash," Enkidu cried in his agony, "blight the life of the hunter who first saw me. Take all his strength and let all his prey escape him. May nothing he desires ever be attainable. Shamash, Shamash damn the whore who lured me from the wilderness. Let me predict her future, which I pray will be grim. May all my curses have effect at once. Whore, you will never be able to build a house to befit your beauty, may your vanity be great and may your charms fade quickly and be horrid in your sight."

Gilgamesh was saddened to hear this and ashamed to tell his

friend that the whore had been his idea and his gift.

"Let your food be the rubbish of the city," Enkidu went on cursing her. "And the corners of the dark streets your refuge. May you stand in the shadows of the walls where the sober and the drunk will slap your face alike. May your lovers leave you as quickly as they have satisfied their lust for your fatal beauty."

Then the god Shamash or Enkidu's vision of the god produced by his own inner guilt for what he had said, appeared to him from heaven and asked him why he so cursed the harlot.

"She is the one who first taught you to eat bread fit for the gods and made you drink wine fit for royalty and made you wear elegant clothes. It was she who made it possible for you to become the bosom friend and companion of your brother, Gilgamesh."

"Oh harlot," cried Enkidu in his misery and sorrow. "I that cursed you would rather bless you. Let me tell your future again. Kings and princes will love you dearly. No one will ever strike his thigh and ridicule you. For you, the aged man will shake his beard and the young men will undo their belts and offer you lapis lazuli and gold. Punishment will fall on any who scorn you and their houses will be empty. The priest will let you enter the presence of the gods and for you, wives will be deserted, even if she be the mother of seven children."

In the night Enkidu dreamt he was entrapped in a hellish underworld and his vivid description of it so deeply disturbed Gilgamesh that he carried the horror of it for the rest of his life. In the dream, Enkidu recounted, the sky thundered and the earth replied and while he stood between them, a boy with a dark and threatening face appeared before him. The boy's face was like that of an eagle and he stripped Enkidu naked, holding him in his claws and choking him until his breathing stopped. Enkidu, in his dream, was dead. The eagle then changed Enkidu's appearance into that of a bird, giving him feathers that covered his body and wings where his arms had been. He was led to a house of darkness, the house from which none who enter ever returns, the house whose dwellers see no light, where sand is their food and mud is sustenance. Here, Enkidu saw kings and princes, mighty in life who were lowly now, heaped on the ground and wearing no crowns. Only the deputies of the gods Anu and Enlil were given meat, bread and cold water. The queen of the underworld also lived in this place. All prostrated themselves before her, as she read from a tablet in her hand. When she lifted her head and saw Enkidu, she said; 'Who brought this man here? Take him away from me.' Enkidu then experienced the worst of the horrors of the underworld, and when later he woke from the dream he was convinced that it boded ill for him.

Until now, he had often been able to move about, though weakened and saddened. After this dream he was confined to his bed and for many days he stayed there. Gilgamesh, in anguish, went to his mother Ninsun for help and advice, but nothing could be done. Enkidu grew worse still and did not rise again from his sickbed.

"A curse is upon me," Enkidu said, fading quickly now and in great pain, angry at his helplessness. "My friend," he told Gilgamesh. "I am under a curse and I will not die in the fury and action of battle. I feared to die in battle, of course, but now it seems a good way, for I will die a despised and ignoble death. Believe me, those who perish on a battle field are truly blessed."

Sitting up all through the night with his friend as he faded, Gilgamesh attempted once more to revive his spirits and stood beside where Enkidu lay. Patting his shoulder and smiling at him as the dawn came up, he teased him and prayed for a retort.

"Your mother was a gazelle and your father a wild ass. You were raised on the milk of asses …" But it was plain that Enkidu did not hear, though lightly he yet breathed. The knowledge that his friend would never respond, never open his eyes again, overwhelmed Gilgamesh.

"The paths you walked among the cedar trees will grieve for you," he said over his friend. "And he who pointed the way for us and blessed us will weep for you. The echoes of the weeping will echo about the land and the bear and tiger, the lynx, stag and lion will mourn you. Let those who glorified your name weep for you, and those who anointed your back with fragrant oils and gave you beer and wine and fruit to eat. May all grieve for you, all the brothers and sisters of the land."

Still, though, he could not accept that Enkidu would never recover and he railed against it. By now the elders of Uruk had gathered around the sickbed and stood watch with their king over his dying brother.

Turning to the elders as the horror of Enkidu's end drew near, Gilgamesh tried to express his feelings, even as they attempted to draw him away, to distract him or present false hope.

"Listen to me, oh elders, and hear me," he shouted. "It is for my friend and companion that I weep. Mine is the lament of the mother who has lost a child. Do you not see that he is the hatchet that protects me, the sword and dagger at my belt, the shield that defends me? He is my happiness, my joy, my festive attire. An accursed devil has appeared to steal him from me. My friend and little brother, who hunted with the wild ass in the high hills, with the tiger in the deserts. Together we defeated the Humbaba and the Bull of Heaven, so Enkidu, what is this sleep that has overcome you now?"

Approaching the bed, Gilgamesh touched his friend's hand and froze in shock, for it was so cold.

"Does the darkness of night enfold you?" he whispered. Enkidu did not open his eyes and when Gilgamesh laid his hand on Enkidu's chest it was still and no heart beat within it. Solemnly, he covered the body with a veil and turned away. Then he began to roar like a lion that has lost its cubs, to pace up and down the room, tearing at his hair and ripping his clothing. Through the night he sat on the floor beside the bed, his dead friend's hand in his, and at dawn he rose.

Gilgamesh left the bedchamber in a dazed state and ordered that a beautiful statue of his brother be made, with lapis lazuli for his chest and gold for the rest. He ordered also, though it was not needed – for all would have done so out of love and honour – that all the people of Uruk mourn and lament the death of Enkidu.

On an oath to Enkidu's memory, Gilgamesh let his hair and beard grow and wearing only a lion skin, he went into the desert. For a long time he wandered there, weeping and half-mad in the wilderness, grieving for his lost brother. When the horrible inevitability of the death sank in, the certainty that no god could or would change it, knowing that death was the fate of every man, he began to be frightened.

The sudden illness and lingering death, the helplessness of watching his only friend die, had scared him, as had the hellish dream Enkidu had experienced before his passing.

"When I die," Gilgamesh dared to ask himself at last, "will I be like Enkidu?"

In fear and grief he had wandered the desert, overwhelmed by sorrow, anger, doubt and fear. Then, with some of the determination of old, he decided to find out the truth, and see if he could defeat the very nature of death.

Thus was Gilgamesh set on to the path of his further destiny and the great quest with which he made even greater his heroic name. Venturing into the underworld and up to heaven, he found his grandfather, Utnapishtim, the only mortal to achieve immortal status. Gilgamesh ultimately failed in his mission to win immortality for himself, however, and even lost a plant, which rendered eternal youth, that Utnapishtim told him how to find.

There is a legend, however, that, at last, he did become a god, reach heaven and dwell there, but that is another story. Certainly, the lasting name he craved and cajoled Enkidu into helping him achieve, is immortality enough for any hero, for no such name is greater or more enduring than his. Few friendships as that of Gilgamesh and Enkidu's have been as lasting, either. Indeed, it could truly be said they fight the monsters, chase the girls, protect the people and entertain the gods to this day.

Osiris,
Bringer of Civilization

Osiris, or more properly Ousir,
was once worshipped throughout Egypt as the god of
the dead and as a nature deity,
and many references to his life and deeds
are to be found in Egyptian hieroglyphic texts.
A cult of Osiris spread widely
and in the Roman empire
became established in many provinces as a religious sect.
His fate as a physical being is enough to make
any fellow wince.

From the nothing that was before creation, Atum, the 'all-formed', made himself into a human shape. It was moulded of the essence of everything that would be male and female, divine and human. In a great cosmic act of masturbation, he shot forth the seed that became Shu and Tefnut, ancestors of the gods. To them were born Geb and Nut, god of earth and goddess of the sky, parents of Osiris, Isis and Seth. As Ra, Atum also became the sun-god.

At the birth of Osiris, a voice echoed out across infinity, but the gladness engendered by this auspicious birth was leavened by sadness at the future the new-born god faced. Ra himself rejoiced, however, and recognized Osiris as his great-grandson and heir to his throne.

Growing up to be handsome, taller than most men and dark of features, Oisiris became king of Egypt when his father Geb retired and returned to the heavens. He married his sister Isis. Seth married their other sister Nephthys, but she wanted a child by Osiris and remained barren until she lay with him after making him drunk one night. Anibis was born of this union, but this act was not what made Seth hate his elder brother. The evil Seth was jealous only of his brother's power.

The chief order of business for the new king was to abolish cannibalism and then to instruct his semi-wild subjects in the skills of agriculture and how to make tools related to this foreign enterprise. From Osiris they learned to grow grain and grapes, and how to produce bread, wine and beer.

Worship of the gods did not exist as such until he introduced the practice, along with the rules for religious observance. He created two types of flute and composed the songs to accompany religious ceremonies, as well as sculpting the first divine images and having the first temples built. Osiris also constructed towns and instituted just laws. The fourth divine Pharaoh, he became known as the 'Good One' among his people, so great were the benefits of his reign.

Nor did Osiris' zeal to civilize stop with Egypt. He travelled the world spreading knowledge and culture, conquering lands with charm, intelligence and the earnest desire to teach and assist humanity. Accompanied by his grand vizier, Thoth, and his aides Anibis and Upuaut, Osiris did not need to use violence to get his way. His gentleness and music disarmed people wherever he went.

Returning to Egypt after bringing civilization to the whole world, Osiris found his country in good order, having been ably ruled by his excellent wife, Isis. However, all along Seth had been plotting against him and now, the jealous younger brother was more than ever determined to take over. Gathering support among men as ruthless and ambitious as himself, Seth was soon ready to carry out his act of betrayal.

Many celebrations greeted the return of Osiris to Egypt and it was under the guise of such a festival that Seth made his move. Seth was in appearance unpleasant to the Egyptian eye, with his pale skin and red hair. A violent individual and always regarded as dangerous, he is said to have torn himself from his mother's womb. His plan was subtle, though, and in some points almost resembled a practical joke.

Surrounding himself with 72 accomplices for safety's sake, Seth invited Osiris to a lavish dinner party. During the merry-making after the food was eaten and taken away, a beautifully made, very ornate and valuable coffer was brought before the guests. It would be a present, Seth declared, to anyone who could fit perfectly inside it.

Now between the contrivance of his cohorts and having had Osiris measured in his sleep, the coffer did not seem to fit anyone else. It did indeed fit Osiris perfectly though, as in the spirit of the fun he lay down inside it. Suddenly all the conspirators darted forward and shut the lid of the coffer, hammers and nails appeared from their cloaks and the lid was nailed down in an instant by many willing hands. Together, swiftly without pause for second thoughts, they carried the coffer to the banks of the Nile and threw it in.

Osiris died and his body, still encased in the coffer, was carried out to sea and drifted far until it reached Byblos in Phoenicia. It came to rest at the base of a small tree which thereafter grew with strange rapidity, completely surrounding the coffer. The tall, thick, very solid tree eventually found its way into the palace of King Malcandre as a central pillar.

Meanwhile, heartbroken at the loss of her husband, Isis had been searching the world for his body and it had taken all her powers to locate it. Word of the magnificent scent given off by the tamarisk tree at the court of King Malcandre eventually reached her, and, understanding its significance, she set off at once, in disguise. Too much openness about her whereabouts and purpose would have alerted Seth to her mission, and this she wanted to avoid at all costs.

Isis found work at the court looking after Queen Astrate's newborn son. She grew very attached to the child and decided to confer immortality on him. She was in the process of doing this, bathing the infant in purificatory flames, when its mother, Astrate, walked in and, understandably, given the strange scene, screamed the house down, unfortunately preventing the completion of the rite. Isis was forced to reveal her true identity and tell of her suspicions about the tamarisk tree.

Awed, honoured and embarrassed by their divine nanny, the king and queen of Byblos happily gave her the tamarisk tree and, sure enough, she found the coffer containing her husband's body embedded within its truck. This she secretly took back to Egypt and hid in the swamp of Buto.

By chance, while hunting by moonlight, Seth discovered the body and recognized it as his brother's. Enraged and intending to make certain it did not turn up again, he hacked it into fourteen pieces which he scattered far and wide. At last, the usurper felt secure on the throne.

All the gods were in an uproar over Seth's actions, however, even going to the extreme of turning themselves into different sorts of animals to escape the tyranny of his rule. Nephthys was so outraged that she had left him, feeling the same as everyone else, who had taken the side of Osiris.

Isis had not given up hope of somehow saving her husband, however, and searched out and found every part of Osiris with the sad exception of his phallus. This, apparently, had been eaten by a river crab or a crocodile. Isis was determined to reassemble her husband and, using sorcery, bring him back to life.

With the help of her sister, Seth's estranged wife Nephthys, her nephew Anubis as well as Thoth, Osiris' grand vizier, she went to work. Her potent charms and magical spells constituted, for the first time in history, the rites of embalmment. With all this, the women taking turns weeping over him, Osiris was restored to life. He was even, despite his missing member, miraculously able to give Isis a child.

After Horus was born, Isis took him to be brought up in the swamps, safe from Seth until he was old enough to avenge his father. Beset by accidents and misfortunes as a child, bitten by savage beasts, stung by scorpions, and suffering pains in his abdomen, Horus only survived to manhood with the magical help of his mother.

Osiris, meanwhile, might have remained among the living,

regained his throne and ruled Egypt once again, but he preferred not to. Instead he became god of the underworld, that realm where the Sun goes at night, far to the west, the place of the dead, where he judged men's souls by the weight of their sins. Only the good were accepted, the wicked went to hell. Nevertheless, he found time to appear to his son, Horus, to instruct him in the use of arms and help him to grow into a strong and courageous warrior.

In time, Horus was ready and, leading those who held the memory of Osiris dear, he went to war against his uncle Seth and his followers. Long and savage was the combat, Horus fighting skilfully with his favoured weapon, the lance. His men cut up Seth's body in battle and then it was their turn to take refuge in the bodies of wild animals such as crocodiles, antelopes and hippopotami.

At last a council of the gods was convened to bring the war to an end. Seth maintained that Horus was not the true son of Osiris but a bastard. However, with the help of his mother's fame for sorcery and proofs the other gods readily accepted, Horus was recognized as legitimate, as was his cause. He was at last fully restored to his inheritance and ruled Upper and Lower Egypt thereafter.

Good had triumphed over evil, light over darkness and Horus became the most honoured ancestor of the future Pharaohs. With his father and mother, he was worshipped throughout the land of Egypt for all its long existence as a great empire.

Sir Gawain and the Loathly Lady

The earliest reference to King Arthur is found in the Historia Brittonum
of a ninth-century Welsh monk called Nennius.
In this Arthur is referred to rather blandly as a 'leader of troops'.
By the time of Malory's Morte d'Arthur *in 1485,*
he had become a legend and leader of a colourful band of
knights noted for their great chivalry.
Gawain is the most gallant and generous of them all,
and this story should perhaps be more properly titled, 'Virtue Rewarded'.
Gawain is always represented as popular with the ladies
in his many adventures, and his advanced views and respect for
women are central to his character

King Arthur rode along dejectedly, his spirits lower than the mud beneath his horse's hooves. The worst of it was that he knew he had only himself to blame. It had all started because he had so vocally yearned for some adventure to break the monotony of the long and otherwise welcome period of peace his reign had brought about.

Only a week before, on Christmas day, King Arthur had been celebrating with great pomp and ceremony. He had been seated in the grand hall at Camelot, beside him his lovely Queen, Guenever, the cleverest and most beautiful queen a king could ask for. All about them were gathered the Knights of the Round Table. In his heart the king knew that never before or in the future would any leader assemble so noble a band of courageous warriors. Arthur's chest had swelled with pride as he looked upon this throng of feasting heroes.

On his right had been the invincible Sir Lancelot, sharing a jest with brave Sir Bors and Sir Banier. Beyond them sat the ever-loyal Sir Bedivere, next to surly Sir Kay, Arthur's foster-brother, the churlish steward of the king's household. Then there were King Arthur's nephews, the young and valiant Sir Gareth, the gentle and courteous Sir Gawain, and the gloomy Sir Mordred, always full of dark looks and seemingly a dark secret. As he plodded along alone days later, Arthur banished thoughts of Mordred from his mind. It would have depressed him even more to think of the boy.

All the other knights, he remembered, had been engaged in banter, drinking and feasting, as were their lovely ladies, while servants and pages scurried here and there waiting on them, carving meat and filling their golden goblets. In a gallery above minstrels played their harps and sang lays of heroes from long ago.

Arthur belonged in such company and was himself a mighty and noble knight. A melancholy mood had descended upon him at the feast, however, and he began to daydream about having some new adventure. For some time nothing even remotely adventurous had happened to any of them. Indeed, this Christmas was like all the others in recent years, as were so many other high holidays and feasts in general.

The fear had assailed him that in these times of peace and plenty he and his knights were growing soft. If a real threat appeared now they might not be equal to it. Maybe they all needed a shake up. Suddenly he had pounded his fist on the table, and bellowed:

"Are we all sluggards or cowards, that none of us goes forth adventuring? I swear every one of us will soon be better fitted to feasting in this hall than fighting in the field. I ask you, or rather I ask providence, has our fame so withered of late that no one even comes to ask for our help or support against evildoers?"

The assembly had fallen quiet, and everyone had looked a little shamefaced.

"I declare by the food before us and all the saints in heaven that I'll not rise from this table unless an adventure or quest of some sort is embarked upon, if I have to undertake the mission myself."

"But sire," Sir Lancelot had smiled, trying to reassure his agitated monarch. "It is Christmas and even a noble king and his gallant knights must pause for celebration and reflection."

"Dear uncle, we are not cowards," Sir Gawain had said. "There simply aren't many evildoers to deal with under your rule. It isn't your fault nor ours if we seem idle."

"Without risk to the kingdom and its folk, I would that it were not so for myself," the king had muttered.

Even as he had spoken the most distressed damsel imaginable had ridden into the hall, her long, fair but dishevelled hair flying and her elegant dress disordered. The hooves of the woman's excited palfrey clattered on the stone of the floor and its eyes rolled, the whites showing as it tossed its head. Dismounting from her steed with difficulty, even though a page had rushed forward to hold its head, she fell to her knees, sobbing at Arthur's feet.

"A boon," she had wailed, her voice ringing out through the hall so that everyone heard her. "I beg a boon of you, oh brave King Arthur. Please, in Heaven's name, do not deny me."

"What boon is this?" the king had been taken aback yet intrigued. The poor girl's apparent horror had been touching to see and it had moved him greatly. "Dry your tears, my dear, and tell me what we can do to help."

"I crave your pity and plead for vengeance on a wicked knight, who has imprisoned my beloved."

"When did he do this? What were the circumstances and where did it happen?"

"My betrothed is a gallant knight, and I dearly love him. All was bliss until yesterday, but out riding together, planning our marriage, we passed through the moorlands and into wooded country beside a pretty lake."

"What lake?"

"Tarn Wathelan. Beside it stood a great castle with streamers flying and banners waving. It seemed a very solid and pleasant place, but it plainly stood on magic ground. To our woe we discovered that inside the enchanted circle cast by its shadow, an evil spell affects any knight who enters. As we stood staring in amazement at the strange place, my love and I observed a rude and horrible warrior, twice the size of any mortal man, emerge. He rushed at us in full armour, a wicked grimace on his fierce-looking face. Armed with a huge club, he arrogantly ordered my knight to ride away and leave me to his lustful attentions. My betrothed drew his sword and would have defended me, but the evil spell robbed him of every ounce of his strength. His sword fell from his weakened grasp and he could do nothing as the giant beat him to the ground with his club. The wicked knight then took hold of him and dragged him to a dungeon in the great keep. Returning before I could flee he badly used me, though all the while I prayed for mercy in the name of chivalry itself and of the Blessed Virgin, Mary Mother of God. When he allowed me to go free, in fury I told him I would come straight here to you, to your court, where I would beg for a champion to avenge me, perhaps even the king himself. At this the giant laughed aloud."

"He laughed out loud?" King Arthur had cried. Oh, why had he not seen the trap from the start?

"Yes," the damsel had nodded. "The giant said: 'Tell your stupid king where I can be found and say that I do not fear him. Say also that I'll do just as I please with anyone who comes into my power. I have in my prison quite a few knights already, besides your beloved, some of them King Arthur's own men. So, tell him to come and fight with me if he wishes to get them back. If indeed he dares come at all.' Then he laughed again, Sire, jeering loudly at you as he returned to his castle. After that I remember little but riding here as quickly as I could. Please help me, my king."

"By my knighthood," the king had shouted, "by the Holy Rood, I swear I will find this evil, boasting giant and beat him or perish in the attempt."

If only it had been so simple, Arthur reflected now.

Naturally, the knights had all applauded their sovereign's vow, while Queen Guinevere looked with concern at her husband. The damsel stayed in Camelot that night, and after Mass the next morning Arthur had said farewell to Guinevere and the court, riding away alone on his quest.

The journey was a chilly one to Tarn Wathelan at that time of year, but the country was very beautiful, though wild and rugged. In due time Arthur saw the lake gleaming clear and cold below him, and there beside it stood the enchanted castle towering above the water, its banners flapping defiantly in the breeze.

Drawing Excalibur and putting his bugle to his lips the king blew a loud note to summon his enemy. Three times he blew without reply, and then in exasperation he shouted at the castle.

"Arrogant knight, it is I, King Arthur. I am here to punish your crimes or see you repent and seek forgiveness from on high. Come out to fight or to yield."

Suddenly out came the giant, swinging his massive club. He rushed straight at King Arthur and in that moment the enchanted ground struck the king and rendered him defenceless. His arms became leaden and too heavy to hold up even without the burden of the mighty sword Excalibur and his shield. The giant bellowed with laughter as he saw Arthur's arms drop to his sides and the weapons fall on the ground.

"Now you yield or fight, King Arthur. You have no power to resist me."

"Then strike, Sir Braggart. Kill me while your magic makes courage useless."

"I can easily slay you, and my magic makes it possible, I do not deny it. With Excalibur you yourself are invisible, but you must wield her first and you cannot. I do not wish to kill you, though. If you do not yield, however, you will die slowly in my dungeon after many interesting games have been played with you and my other prisoners."

"And if I yield?"

"I will hold you to ransom."

"What ransom?"

"Terms I shall set and you must swear to accept."

"What are these terms?" King Arthur demanded, furious at his helplessness.

"You will have to swear by the Holy Rood, and the Virgin, that you will come back on New Year's Day to bring me the true answer to a question I shall pose."

"That's the ransom?" the king asked disbelievingly. "Alright, what is the question? What is the best torture known to man, I suppose?"

"I already know that. No, your question is this: 'What is it that all women most desire?' A good one, eh?"

"Is that all?" the king smiled, then repeated the question. "What is it that all women most desire?"

"Yes, that is it. If you do not bring me the correct answer your ransom will not be paid, and you will remain my prisoner. These are the only terms I offer, do you accept them?"

With no choice and no chance of fighting back as long as he stood on the enchanted ground, King Arthur swore he would return on New Year's Day with the answer. After his initial amusement at the question, it had quickly dawned on him how difficult it would be. As he rode away, he realized it might be well nigh impossible to find the answer in so short a time, indeed in a whole lifetime.

Too ashamed and humiliated to go back to Camelot, he decided he would not return home until somehow he had triumphed. Riding in every direction, ranging as wide over the land as time allowed, he interviewed every woman and girl he met, asking them the question; "What is it that all women most desire?" Alas they had all given him different replies and none was satisfactory. Riches, pomp, beautiful clothes, mirth, flattery, a handsome lover – these were some of the suggestions he received. In the end, King Arthur felt confused and regretted the whole enterprise. A fine lot of good he had done in his quest except to bring himself to this pretty pass, where his life, his freedom and the future of his kingdom were in jeopardy.

Naturally, he had written down every answer he and been given, hoping against hope that one of them might satisfy the giant knight of the Castle of Tarn Wathelan, though at heart King Arthur knew that none of them was the truth, the whole, frank truth. So now as he rode towards the giant's home on New Year's Day, he thought of how it had all begun and how much more lonely the journey was this time compared to when he had ventured forth on Christmas Day, so full of hope, courage and self-assurance.

Passing sadly through a lonely forest, dreading his coming encounter with the giant, Arthur heard a woman's voice greeting him.

"God bless you, Your Majesty. God bless and keep you."

Turning quickly to see who was addressing him, Arthur could spy no one for a moment, then finally he perceived a woman warmly clothed in a bright red cloak. She was seated between a hollybush and an oak tree, and the berries of the former were hardly more vivid than her dress, while the brown leaves of the latter were pale beside the brown of her wrinkled cheeks. Upon first seeing her, King Arthur thought he had been bewitched. Surely this nightmare of a human face could not be possible otherwise. Her nose was long, hooked and covered in warts, while her chin was also long, curving upwards and hairy. She had one eye and this had a milky cast over it and was almost covered by her wrinkled and overhanging brow. Her mouth was a red, toothless gaping slit, and the whole head was framed by snaky locks of ragged grey hair.

The king's stomach involuntarily turned upon first sight of her. Indeed his shock was so great that he was lost for words and did not reply to her greeting.

"Now, Christ be with us," the loathly lady said, striving for patience, angered by the insult of King Arthur's silence. "Who do you think you are to ignore me? So much for the courtesy of you and your

knights of the Round Table, if you can't even be civil enough to return a lady's greeting."

Arthur worked his mouth up and down but could still not find his tongue.

"Even so, my proud King, it just might be within my power to help you, hideous though I am, though I'll do nothing for anyone who cannot be bothered to display simple good manners towards me."

"Please forgive me, lady," King Arthur said at last, ashamed of his lack of courtesy. He was also gripped by the sudden thought that here might be a woman who could help him. "I am very distracted with troubles and my mind is clouded. I am heartily sorry for my lack of courtesy, and apologize for having missed your greeting."

She nodded her ugly head and seemed to see that he was telling the truth.

"Did I understand you to say that perhaps you could help me?"

"I did."

"Lady, if you would do this ... Perhaps you have heard of my dilemma ... if you can show me how to pay my ransom, I will give you anything you ask for that is in my power to give."

"If you will swear by all you hold dear and sacred that you will grant me whatever boon I ask, then I will tell you the secret you wish to know."

"You can truly tell me? You know what it is I wish to learn."

"By secret means I know the question you seek to have answered. 'What is it that all women most desire?' Is that not it?"

"It is."

"You have consulted many women and they have given you many replies. They have only told you what they felt you wished to hear, or what they thought they wanted to believe was so, or they were too frivolous and not honest with themselves. I alone can give you the right answer. Never fear, it will pay your ransom."

"Please tell me," the king all but pleaded.

"Only when you have sworn to keep faith with me."

"Very well. Indeed, I will take the oath gladly," the king said. "For one who would help me I would happily help also." With that he duly lifted up his hand and swore. The lady nodded with satisfaction and told him the secret directly. Laughing out loud in relief, Arthur knew at once that this was undoubtedly the correct answer.

Convinced of the wisdom of the old crone's words Arthur rode on to the Castle of Tarn Wathelan, and blew his bugle to summon the giant. Because it was New Year's Day, his adversery was ready for him, and hurried out, club in hand, eager to take whatever advantage the enchantment offered, convinced that Arthur could not have found the answer to the question.

"I have collected these answers, Sir Knight," said Arthur. "And having written them down I bring them to you. Here, I offer them to you as my ransom."

The giant took the writings and read each one with a derisory snort and growing excitement.

"As I suspected, you have failed utterly," the giant chuckled. "So you are my prisoner, for though these answers are numerous and not totally unwise, none is the true answer to my question. Therefore, your ransom is not paid. To keep your vow, your life and all you have is forfeit to me."

"Ah, but Sir Knight," said the king. "Wait but a moment and let me try once more before I yield. It is a small favour to ask when a man risks his life and kingdom for good and all."

"Go ahead," said the giant with an indulgent smile, glad to let the king wriggle a while and draw out the moment. "I am listening."

"Might the answer to the question 'What is it that all women most desire?' be 'To do their own will'?"

"Who told you?" gasped the giant, turning pale and then red with fury all in an instant.

"It is the right answer, isn't it?"

"Yes, blast you."

"And my ransom is paid? I am free?"

"Yes, yes, but how did you discover the answer?"

"Just this morning when I thought all was lost, I was riding this way through a wood when an old woman in a red cloak greeted me and told me the correct reply to your question."

"Old you say, in a red cloak and ugly as an aged and diseased boar?"

"That was the lady, yes."

"By thunder," cried the giant. "I vow that if I catch her I will burn her alive, for she has cheated me of being King of Britain. Now, be gone Arthur, your ransom is settled."

"Very well," Arthur said, dismounting to retrieve Excalibur and his shield. "But two things must be said. Having me and all I possess would not have made you king, for no Britons would have followed such as you for a moment. They'd die first. Secondly, unless you can take this enchantment with you wherever you go, which you cannot, you had best leave the loathly lady be. It will be the worse for you if you do not." After remounting, Arthur looked once more at the giant knight and said, "Repent of your ways and find grace," before riding away, back to the forest where the loathly lady sat waiting for him.

"Much thanks to you, lady. I am free now because your answer was the true one. What boon would you have as reward? As I promised, anything you name shall be yours."

"The boon, King Arthur, is this," said the malformed old woman. "I wish for you to bring some young and courteous knight from your court at Camelot to marry me. He must be both brave and handsome, too."

"Oh, but lady ..." Arthur began.

"Nothing else will do. Remember, King Arthur, you have sworn. Would you now break your word?"

"No, no, lady, I'll not break my word." he said reluctantly. He had indeed been about to try to dissuade her from such an unreasonable notion, but he now realized this would be futile.

The old woman watched him ride off back to Camelot with a mixture of emotions. Both pain and excitement stirred in her bosom.

Arthur was almost as sad returning to Camelot as he had been when trudging around trying to find the answer to the giant's question. He arrived home to be greeted happily by his wife and knights, but he could barely raise a slight smile in response and could not hide his distress. Seated in the great hall where it had all begun, he and Guinevere caught up on what had happened while he had been away.

"I suppose the damsel went home after I left." Arthur said first.

"Why yes." the queen affirmed.

"I failed her, but we will find a way to defeat the giant soon." He then told Guinevere about the giant's tricks, the enchantment and the ransom. "I was able to answer his question and buy my freedom only with the help of a loathly lady. But it seems that her help came at a very terrible price and one that I cannot meet myself."

"Why not, uncle?" asked Sir Gawain, who had entered the room and heard all without the couple realizing. The sight of his favourite nephew cheered the king for a moment until he recollected what it might mean for the young man.

"Never mind," the king mumbled.

"But tell us, husband," said the queen.

"Why can you not pay the loathly lady for her secret, uncle?" Gawain asked.

"I promised to grant her any boon she asked, and she has asked a thing impossible."

"What was her boon?" asked Guinevere.

"A promise is a promise," Sir Gawain said.

"Why can you not grant her boon?" the queen asked again.

"Can I help you grant it somehow, sire?" Sir Gawain offered, supposing that money or some quest far from home might be involved.

"I cannot pay the price myself," the king said sadly and a little exasperated, "because I am a married man."

"I ask again, uncle, is it possible that I can be of service in this matter?" Gawain smiled. He would gladly have died for Arthur and they both knew it, so anything else was also the king's for the asking. It must be said, however, that the young knight was thinking along the lines of a kiss or even perhaps some more intimate contact with the old woman as her price for helping his uncle.

"Oh, you could help me indeed, dear Gawain." said King Arthur. "But I can not ask you to do so. It is too horrible a thing."

"I am ready to do it, uncle," Gawain laughed, highly amused at the king's supposed embarrassment before his wife in speaking of such things. "Why, I'd do whatever it takes to pay this debt for you, even marry the loathly lady herself."

"Gawain," Arthur said seriously. "That is exactly what she asks, that a handsome young knight should marry her."

"Well," Gawain said after a long pause while he turned a little pale and swallowed hard. At last he saw that the king was truly upset and not merely uncomfortable. "I said I would do it and I will."

"But the poor woman is old, hideous and deformed. No man can make her his wife."

"Uncle, if that is all that is worrying you," Sir Gawain told him, "then everything is settled. Let nothing trouble you. I'll marry this ill-favoured dame, and settle your debt to her."

"You have no idea what you are agreeing to," said the king. "I have never seen so deformed a being. While she speaks well enough and nicely, her face is terrible, with a warty crooked nose and pointy chin. Why, the unfortunate creature has only one eye and that with a cast in it."

"Ill-favoured as the lady may be, it does not matter," said Sir Gawain gallantly. "Not if I can save you a moment's care. I am in earnest."

"God be praised for you kindness, dear Gawain," cried Arthur, moved to tears. "And a thousand times thank you. Now through your devotion I can keep my word."

For a moment he simply held his beloved nephew in his arms in a great bear hug and then stepped back and smiled apologetically.

"To-morrow," the king said shyly. "We must bring your bride from her lonely lodging in the greenwood, but I think to save everyone's feelings we will find some excuse for the trip and not excite the curiosity of the people. We'll make it a hunting party, with horses, hounds and riders. No one will know we are off to fetch home so ugly a bride."

"Lord have mercy, uncle," Sir Gawain shrugged. "Until to-morrow then, I am still a bachelor and a free man."

The following morning King Arthur called all his knights together to go hunting in the greenwood close to Tarn Wathelan. He did not take them near the castle with its giant and the enchanted circle about it. Things were likely to become awkward if they went there and yet all the while he was applying his mind to ways of defeating the giant and freeing his prisoners. But for now there was little reason to disturb him or put him on his guard.

The hunt soon roused a noble stag which the party pursued far into the forest until they lost its trail among the dense thickets of holly and yew interspersed with copses of hazel and oak. The chase had been thrilling, despite the loss of their quarry, and the train of knights laughed and talked gaily as they rode back through the forest. Seemingly the happiest of all was Sir Gawain, who rode wildly down the forest drives. Drawing level with the churlish Sir Kay, who always rode alone by preference and because he did not make good company, he fell silent, lost in his own thoughts.

Sir Lancelot, Sir Stephen, Sir Banier and Sir Bors eyed him curiously, wondering at his reckless mood, while his brother, Gareth, began to feel concern, for he knew Gawain must be troubled by something. Sir Tristram, absorbed in his love for Isolde, far off in

Cornwall, noticed nothing and rode heedlessly, wrapped in sad musings.

With a jolt, Sir Kay reined in his horse and sat staring at the large flash of scarlet he had caught sight of under the trees. As he studied the apparition, he realized he was looking at a woman, wearing a dress of finest scarlet, sitting between a holly bush and an oak tree.

"Good morning, Sir Kay," said the lady.

The churlish knight could only stare in morbid fascination, sure that he had never imagined that such a face could exist. As he gaped, he ignored her salutation.

Seeing his attention so absorbed the rest of the knights joined him, curious to discover what it was that so held his gaze. When they found out, they too stared in astonishment at the woman's hideous features. Sir Kay was the only one among them willing to put his thoughts into words. He was almost proud of his strange discovery and, basking in the presence of an audience, showed his rude and thoughtless nature. The king was still some distance off when Sir Kay began to jest loudly and to point at the woman in the red cloak.

"So which of you gallant swains will woo this fair lady?" he asked. "Tempting, ain't it? Though I fear it will take a braver man than I. But who will try to win a kiss? Careful though that you do not miss her mouth. Ah, I hear you say, that might be best wished but look at the alternatives and wonder if t'were so. Yet come, who will pay her court, perchance to win a charming bride?"

King Arthur rode up and at sight of him Sir Kay fell silent though by now the loathly lady had hidden her face in her hands, deeply hurt and mortified by Kay's cruel scorn, and she wept piteously.

Touched with compassion for this uncomely woman, Sir Gawain felt a lump of shame in his throat. Here she was alone, helpless and ill-favoured, among these strong, well mounted, confident and very handsome knights.

"Be still, churlish Kay, we do not choose our faces and it is not a matter of poor taste in fashion. What right have you to jeer at anybody?

Such behaviour does not become a knight of Arthur's Round Table. Besides, it is fated that one of us here will marry this unfortunate lady."

"Marry her?" cried Kay. "You must be insane, Gawain."

"My liege, is this not true?" asked Sir Gawain, turning to the king.

"Yes, I have promised, for the lady gave me help when I was in great distress. The boon she craved was for a young and noble knight to be her husband. Sir knights, I have given my royal word and I must keep it. That is why I've brought you all here to meet her."

"What?' Sir Kay burst out with derisive laughter. "You'd actually ask me to marry this foul female? You can't be serious. Whoever I wed, be she the devil's sister, she'll be more comely than this hideous hag."

"Silence, Sir Kay," snapped the king. "I'll not have you abuse this poor lady as well as refuse her. Watch your tougue or you'll be no knight of mine any longer."

Turning to the others, he said: "Will someone not wed this lady and help me to keep my pledge? Would you all refuse over a little ugliness and deformity, for my promise is given and surely you would not let your king and kinsman break his plighted word of honour."

He observed them all intently to see who was sufficiently devoted to him, and as he did so the knights began to excuse themselves and move away. They called their hounds to them, and made ready to search for the track of the lost stag, some of the knights becoming absorbed in tightening a girth while others dismounted to feel the leg of a perfectly sound horse.

Then Gawain spoke up. "Before you all disappear or become fascinated by nothing, my friends, stop worrying. I will wed this lady myself. Lady, will you have me for your husband?" He asked, slipping from the saddle to kneel at her feet.

Lost for words at first, the poor lady then struggled to express her gratitude to the young knight.

"But truly, Sir Gawain," she said after recovering her wits a touch more, "you are only joking, are you not? How could you marry someone as ugly and deformed as me? What kind of wife would I be for so handsome and gallant a knight as you, the king's own nephew? Imagine what Queen Guinevere and the ladies of the Court will say when you return to Camelot with a bride like me. You would be shamed by me, and through me."

She now wept bitterly, and her tears and swollen cheeks made her more hideous than ever.

"Lady," said Arthur, "rest assured there will be no knight or dame at my court who dares mock my nephew's bride. They'll not be there long if they do." The king glared meaningfully at Sir Kay.

Raising her head the lady looked into Sir Gawain's eyes as he took her hand.

"Lady, if you will have me, I will be a true and loyal husband to you. Trust too, that I will know how to guard my wife from insult. Come to Camelot, lady, and my uncle will announce the betrothal."

"Sir Gawain, may God bless you," the lady. "And believe me when I say you shall never regret this wedding, and the great courtesy you have shown."

A horse with a side-saddle was brought for Sir Gawain's bride, but when the lady moved towards it to mount, everyone saw that she was lame. She not only halted in her walk but there was a slight hunch to her back, neither of which showed when she was seated. As she moved, the other knights looked at one another, and then quickly away, pitying Sir Gawain even more for being bound to a deformed wife.

The bride rode between King Arthur and her betrothed, while the rest of the train rode behind, some of the knights whispering and sneering.

There was great excitement in Camelot when people at the gate and in the street saw the ugly dame. In the hall of the castle there was even greater confusion and embarrassment when it was learned that this loathly lady was to be Sir Gawain's bride.

Queen Guinevere was the only one who understood, and she

showed much courtesy to the deformed lady. At the wedding that evening she acted as her maid-of-honour while King Arthur was best man to his nephew. After the long banquet a time came when the bride and bridegroom need no longer sit beside one another. The tables were cleared away and the hall was made ready for dancing. All the men supposed that Sir Gawain would free himself and come away to chat with his friends, but he did not.

" 'Tis tradition that bride and groom should take the first dance together. Would you like to?" he asked.

As she only smiled in surprise, he held out his hand and asked again.

"Shall we?"

"My sweet husband, thank you," she said and, taking his hand, she moved forwards with him to open the dance.

His dignity was so perfect, the courtesy and grace with which he danced so natural, that even the meanest heart among them never dreamt of smiling with derision as the deformed lady moved clumsily through the long and intricate movements.

When the evening was finally over, the last dance had been danced and the last toast drunk, the bride was escorted to her chamber by a group of ladies. All the guests went to their rooms, the lights were extinguished and Gawain was left a moment to reflect on what he had done, and to dwell on how he had wrecked any hope of happiness he might have had. He also thought of his uncle's distress, of the poor lady's gratitude and the blessing she had invoked upon him. He determined always to treat her gently, though he knew he would never be able to love her properly as his wife. With all the will in the world, he did not believe it possible.

As he entered the bride-chamber he tried not to appear like a man condemned. He felt he must endure and be kind, and with a whistle and as light an air as he could manage, he sat on a chair beside her at the fire. He looked into the glowing embers and searched for something to say.

"Why, husband, have you no word for me?" asked the lady. "Can you not even spare me a glance?"

"Of course, my dear," said Sir Gawain, attempting a smile and turning his eyes to her.

Suddenly, he leapt up and stepped back, his eyes wide in amazement. There sat no loathly lady, no ugly and deformed old woman, but a lovely girl of two and twenty, with long black curls, a beautiful face and a tall and graceful figure.

"Who are you, miss? And where, pray tell, is my wife?" asked Sir Gawain.

"I am the very wife you found between the holly and the oak, whom you married this night and danced so gallantly with."

"But how can such a thing be?" He asked, marvelling at her beauty.

"I am in bondage to an enchantment," said she. "Our marrying has partly set me free from it. Now, for a time, I may appear to you as I really am."

Stepping forward with shyness he admired her lovely face and clear bright blue eyes.

"Is my handsome knight pleased with his loving bride?" she asked with a little smile as she rose and stood before him.

"Pleased?" he said, taking her gently in his arms. "How could I not be pleased with the fairest dame in Arthur's court? If the beauty I somehow felt was within you even before is not only in the flesh now, I am the most fortunate knight in Christendom. I thought to save my uncle and help a hapless lady, and it seems I have won my own happiness thereby."

"There is one more thing you must know, husband. A weighty choice awaits you. You see, I am still under the spell of an evil witch. Even now I am only allowed my own face and form for half the day. I must have the hideous appearance in which you first saw me for the other half. You must choose whether to have me fair by day and ugly by night, or hideous by day and beauteous by night. What do you say?"

Sir Gawain was fully awake now, though moments before he had been feeling quite sleepy. The choice he was presented with was too difficult. If the lady was hideous in the daytime he would have to endure the taunts of his fellows and probably be in endless fights, causing the whole kingdom trouble. If she was ugly at night, he would be unhappy himself. Then again if the lady was so beautiful all day, other men would attempt to woo her, also causing trouble. Yet if she became beautiful to him after dark, his love would make them both look ridiculous at court and embarrass the king.

"Oh, be beautiful just for me, that I might love you by night," he said, unable to think properly and prompted by his immediate desire.

"So, that is your choice? I must be ugly when all around us are so beautiful? The other ladies are fair and shown respect. Must I seem foul to all men?" Turning away from him, she wept.

Gawain was filled with pity and remorse as he heard her lament. He cursed himself for putting his own pleasure before his lady's feelings.

"Please, I did not think," he said, his natural courtesy and kindness winning the upper hand. "My dear, if you would rather that you be beautiful while in the world of daylight, I will choose that. To me, of course, you'll be always as you are right now, so be lovely in front of others and deformed to me alone. Anyway, at least the others need never know that the enchantment is not wholly removed."

Looking pleased for a moment, the lady suddenly turned grave, and said:

"But have you considered the dangers a young and lovely lady is exposed to at court? Surely there are bad knights who would try and seduce an innocent dame who has led such an odd life and may be susceptible to flattery and attention even though her husband is the king's favourite nephew? Heaven forbid, but one of them might please me more than you. Many are bound to be sorry they refused to marry me when they see me in the morning. It may be a great risk to leave my beauty under the guard only of my own virtue and wisdom. If you want me young and fair, that is the consequence. Do you dare it?" She was grinning merrily now at him and he finally smiled and shook his head.

"No, no, my dear love," he said, his hands raised in surrender. "I'll leave the matter to you. It is only just that it should be left to your own judgement. I will be happy with whatsoever you decide."

With a gasp, the lady threw her dainty hand over her tender mouth and looked wide-eyed at her husband.

"Oh, Gawain," she cooed, tears of joy welling up in her lovely eyes. "Bless you, my own dear lord. With these words you have entirely released me from the spell. Now I will always be as fair and young as I am now, that is until old age changes me as it does every other mortal."

Relieved, happy and rather proud of himself, Gawain swept her into his arms and twirled her around the room, showering kisses on her lips and face, then falling on to the bed with his bride.

"How did all this happen?" he asked, catching his breath.

"My widowed father, a great duke of high renown had one son and one daughter, both of goodly appearance, whom he dearly loved. However, about the time when I came of an age to be married, my father decided to take a new wife. Alas, he wedded a witch and she used her powers to be rid of his two children. She cast a spell upon us both, and that is how I was transformed into the woman you wed, while my gallant and gentle young brother was turned into the churlish giant who occupies the enchanted castle at Tarn Wathelan."

"The very one who ransomed the king?"

"Yes; in his guise as a cruel giant he certainly meant me no good. Our step-mother condemned me to keep that awful shape until I married a young and courtly knight who would grant me all my will. That seemed an impossible dream until just the day before yesterday. But Gawain, you have done all those things for me, and I shall always love you and be your good and faithful wife."

"And what about your brother?"

"That is part of the wonderful thing you have done. He too is now released from the spell. He will become once again one of the truest and most gentle knights alive."

The great hall was full the next morning when the knight and his bride appeared. Every single knight and lady had turned up at court to see them. The men were all thinking scornfully of the hideous hag Gawain had married and wondering how the wedding night had gone for the poor self-sacrificing fool. The ladies thought it a terrible pity that so good looking and well placed a young knight should be tied to an ugly old crone. All their scorn and pity disappeared when they saw the bride on Gawain's arm as they slowly came down the long staircase into the hall.

"S'wounds, who is this delightful dame?" Sir Kay whispered loudly. "So Gawain," he called, "for all your sweet courtesy yesterday, you got rid of your ancient bride quickly enough."

"Where is you wife?" asked the king, alarmed.

Everyone awaited the answer with bated breath.

"Why, uncle, do you not recognize her? This is the lady to whom I was married but yestere'n," Sir Gawain replied with a grin.

"I was under an evil enchantment," the young lady explained, blushing prettily as everybody gaped at her.

Sir Kay stared with much the same expression he had worn when he had first seen her in her hideous form, except that now it was his pinched-looking mouth that was turned slightly up at the corners instead of his nose.

"The spell has vanished now that I have a fine husband," the lady went on. "What is more, my lord King Arthur," the lady smiled winningly at her husband's uncle, "the giant knight of Tarn Wathelan is my brother, who was also under a spell. It too is now lifted, and he surely will soon come to ask your pardon and assure you all that the ground on which his fortress stands will have no more power to sap the strength of other knights." His prisoners, of course, were all set free.

"By God's good grace, dear liege and uncle," Gawain said as he came before the king and queen. "When I married the loathly lady yesterday, truly I thought only of your happiness. Perhaps for that reason He has blessed me beyond measure. I am now the happiest of men."

The miraculous good fortune of his nephew gave King Arthur much joy. His guilt for allowing Gawain to pay his debt was lifted and it was glorious to see such sincere virtue so profoundly rewarded. For her part, Queen Guinevere welcomed the fair maiden as graciously as she had the loathly lady. The wedding feast began anew with greater merriment and with all tongues wagging over more uplifting subjects or more gentle fun, as befitted the end to the Christmas festivities.

Thor, Loki the Trickster, and the Twilight of the Gods

The Germanic tribes and pagan Norway put Thor (or Donar)
at the head of their pantheon of gods.
He is often ifentified with Jupiter (Zeus to the Greeks)
and honoured in the German language by having a day named after him
– Donnerstag (Thursday). Thor crops up in many legends and
took a hand in the careers of many other gods,
including Loki, who was a creation of Scandinavian myth-makers.

When Thor woke up and stretched, his hand landed naturally on the spot where the hammer, Mjolnir, should have been, but his touch only met with empty space. Fully awake instantly, he looked around for the famous weapon, which could shrink to such a small size as to fit into a pocket when he wished it to. He searched among his blankets, under his bed, through all of his clothing. Alas, 'the Destroyer' was nowhere to be found.

His first thought was of his fellow god, Loki. From mischief to downright skulduggery, Loki could always be counted on to keep the lives of gods, giants, demons, and even ordinary people, interesting. He was decidedly light-fingered and knew more than anyone ought to about theft and trickery in general. One way or another he would be able to enlighten Thor.

Of course, it had been through some of Loki's shenanigans that Thor came to have the hammer in the first place. Gungnir, the famous spear of Odin, was acquired by similar means, as well as several other remarkable possessions of the gods. Thor found himself recalling the matter as he made his way to Loki's home.

He ground his teeth a moment as he recollected how Loki had cut off the hair of his wife, Sif, while she slept, and how he, Thor, had nearly broken the miscreant in two upon finding her shorn like a sheep. Loki had escaped with promises of getting the dwarfs to fashion for Sif hair of pure gold that would grow and feel like real hair.

So skilful were these renowned workers of metal, and so flattered by the divine commission, that they made Odin two fine gifts in addition. There was Gungnir, the spear that would never stop in flight, and a wonderful ship that could be shrunk so small as to fit in a pocket and yet sail straight to its destination when full sized, all of its on accord.

Loki had been so impressed that he thought he was on safe ground when he bet other dwarfs that they could not make anything as special. Now these dwarfs diligently worked to rise to the challenge and were on the verge of succeeding when Loki, in fear for his head, for that had been the wager, turned himself into a gadfly and vexed them so much they could hardly work. Despite his attentions, they finally completed the task and produced several wonderful things. There was the ring Draupnir, which had the virtue of constantly enriching its owner, the golden boar which later became the property of the god Frey, and Thor's now stolen hammer, which never missed its mark when thrown and always returned to him.

Of course, the gods, who were also known as the Aesir, were asked to be the judges in the matter. They found that these works were indeed as fine as the earlier gifts. Loki fled. When Thor brought him back to face the music, the mischievous god's quick wits and slippery tongue saved him. Loki pointed out that the wager had only been for his head, therefore no part of his neck could be taken. In the end the cheated dwarf was satisfied with having the tricky god's lips sewn up as punishment. Loki, of course, promptly untied the stitches.

Thor now reasoned that, even if Loki was not responsible for the theft, he might be a source of good advice about who might have taken the hammer. Aware of his own shortcomings, Thor knew he could be too naive and unworldly at times. A mind like Loki's would be invaluable in a matter such as this.

"Don't look at me," were Loki's first words. And his second remark, with perfect understanding, was: "Some giant has obviously stolen your hammer. Who else would dare and who else would most wish to remove the greatest weapon in the defence of we gods of Asgard?"

"All right," Thor nodded, accepting this logic.

"Do you want me to help you get it back?" the trickster asked with a yawn.

"Just help me find out where it is and I'll get it back," Thor said, cracking his knuckles. He would not have been so confident and not so keen to set out if he had known what it would involve.

"I'll need Freyja's feathered cloak," Loki said, trying to hide his smile. He had long wanted to use the thing and fly with it as himself and not in the guise of some bird or insect.

"I'll ask," Thor shrugged. It would be a big favour but, on the other hand, all the Aesir would be anxious to see him get his hammer back. After all, it was their champion's favourite weapon.

Shortly afterwards Loki set off wearing the magic robe of feathers, flying to the domain of the giants. He went with the blessing of the gods. Their hereditary enemies must not be allowed to get away with this sort of thing or life would become unbearable. As it was, almost constant fighting persisted, though not open warfare.

In the beginning the gods and the giants had sprung from the same parents, though the giants came first. When the seed of the universe was made from the icy region of Nifleim in the north meeting the fiery realm of Muspell in the south, the first giant, Ymir, was formed. As he lay frozen in sleep he broke into a sweat. From his armpit a new male giant and a female appeared, then another male from his legs. But it was the cow Audhumla, also born of this frost, wet nurse to the giants, who licked the salt from the ice and uncovered first the hair then the head and body of yet another being, Buri.

The son of Buri, Bor, married a female frost giant and their offspring were the first gods, Odin and his brothers Vili and Ve. They eventually killed Ymir and created the world from his body. They made the first humans and a region for them to live in, as well as one for giants, elves and dwarfs. Their own realm was Asgard, home of the Aesir, the sky gods and some of the Vanir, their one-time rivals, gods who also had a home beneath the earth. All of these lands and beings had their place on, around, or under the great tree of life, Yggdrasil.

The enmity of the giants had been a given ever since, of course, and keeping them at bay was a major part of the lives of the Aesir, who were mortal, despite being gods. Like the giants themselves, they could be killed and defence of their primacy in the world, their homeland of Asgard and their lives was vital. As in the beginning, sex, love and marriage between them was possible, despite size differences, due to magic, but affairs and jealousies only added to the trouble between the two races.

As Loki flew over Jotunheim, the giant's homeland, he had no difficulty discovering the identity of the thief. A certain giant named Thrym had been boasting of having purloined Thor's hammer to everyone he met. When Loki found him, he again proudly admitted it.

"The hammer," Thrym told Loki, "is hidden eight fathoms underground, but I will return it under one condition."

"And that is," Loki wondered, studying the giant with hooded eyes, relishing the coming revelation.

"I wish to wed the goddess Freyja. If the Aesir will give her to me as my wife, I will return the hammer to Thor."

Loki laughed out loud at such audacity and could not help but express his admiration. When he took this news back to Asgard, he had to hide his glee at the consternation it caused. Freyja flatly refused to marry the giant. Her outrage was so great that the veins in her neck swelled up and burst her golden necklace.

Embarrassment and consternation reigned, until Loki himself suggested a possible solution.

"We could give him a false Freyja."

"What?" everyone cried. "How?"

"I think if we dressed Thor up as Freyja ..."

"Are you mad? He would never pass ..."

"I am not going in drag to some horny giant's lair ..." Thor thundered.

"Hear me out," Loki shouted. "First of all, with a little bit of illusion, Thor can pass."

"I am still not ..."

"And secondly, Thrym is not horny; he's love struck. Remember, it is matrimony he's after, not simply to lay with Freyja. He will be respectful and easily fooled. Freyja's reputation for beauty will aid us as well as Thrym's over confidence and vanity. Besides, does anyone have a better idea?"

No one did and so, feeling like an idiot, Thor put on women's clothes, a bridal veil and Freyja's famous necklace, freshly repaired. Some of the fun of the plan backfired on Loki when Thor insisted that his fellow-god should accompany him disguised as a servant girl. It was thus that the blushing and uncomfortable pair made their way to Thrym's territory.

On the journey Thor saw Loki glancing occasionally at the necklace and knew he was recalling the trouble it had caused him in the past.

There were four dwarfs who lived in a grotto not far from Freyja's palace and as a great collector of jewellery she often went there to see what they were working on. One day she found a fine and cunningly wrought gold necklace, which they were just finishing off, and she knew she absolutely must have it.

She offered much gold and silver but the dwarfs only laughed. As lords of the underground world, they had access to all the gold and silver they could ever want. It was as clay to the potter for them. What they demanded as payment was a far more tender currency. Freyja was to go to bed with each of them. She agreed in a trice and thought nothing of it, until Loki told on her to Odin, who was enraged and ordered Loki to steal the necklace.

Loki succeeded in the theft, by turning himself into a fly and entering her locked bedroom through a hole in the roof. When the ingenious god was then unable to get at the catch of the necklace, he turned into a flea and bit the sleeping Freyja's cheek. As she stirred and rolled over, Loki was able to turn back into himself, undo the clasp and walk out of the room. Intending to keep the trinket, he hid it under a reef. Later, when Odin made a bargain with Freyja and said she could have the trinket back, he did not wish to co-operate. The god Heimdall, guardian of the gates of Asgard, and to Loki a mere drudge, turned himself into a seal and fought Loki, who had also assumed the form of a seal. Heimdall won the battle, took the necklace from beneath the reef and returned it to Freyja.

"All your own fault," Thor said, sensing that Loki was brooding on this old sore.

"It was not ... I don't know what you mean." The trickster corrected himself quickly, reluctant to admit anyone could tell what he was thinking. "I am just puzzling over how we should proceed when we get to Thrym's place. You could always help the illusion along a little by swaying your hips and treading a deal more lightly."

"If this turns out like half the other things you've pulled, Loki, my last act will be to tear your head off your shoulders." Thor threatened.

"Charming sentiment, when all I'm doing is trying to help."

"You could walk a bit lighter too, you know," Thor accused bitterly. "And mind how you go with any females we meet. None of your usual lechery or you'll give the game away."

"I won't forget myself. I'm a born actor. It's you we have to worry about."

"Well, just remember you're supposed to be my maidservant."

"Yes, mistress," Loki curtsied primly, buoyed up by the thought that no matter how ridiculous he felt, the excruciating embarrassment of Thor was multiplied ten-fold. "If we don't get the hammer back until after the ceremony," he wondered aloud, "would that mean you'd actually be married to Thrym?"

Loki had to step lively to avoid a kick in the backside, but soon they had to stop bickering and teasing one another for they crossed into Jotunheim. Here they had to take seriously their roles as women, keep up the illusion and maintain their respective social status. Thor got his revenge by ordering Loki about mercilessly, though when they got to Thrym's palace he wanted the other god very near him indeed.

The giant was overjoyed at their arrival and they were lavishly received. Thrym gave orders for the wedding banquet to be prepared at once. By this time Loki had been promoted from maid to handmaiden and finally lady-in-waiting and his presence at table was not unusual. Thor, however, soon forgot himself once the food was placed before them, and ate and drank ravenously.

Every morsel meant for the women of the palace, which constituted one whole roast ox, eight large salmon and dozens of side dishes disappeared down the supposed Freyja's throat along with three barrels of mead. Everyone was amazed, especially Thrym.

"You see," Loki whispered into his ear by way of explanation, "my lady was so excited about coming to the land of the giants and her impending nuptials that she has not eaten in many days."

The giant was more enraptured than ever. "I like a woman with a good appetite." Of course, the dear thing was excited. "And it is right that she should now make herself at home."

Emboldened by this news of Freyja's eagerness to be his bride, he lifted her veil to steal a kiss only to draw back as if bitten. The fire in Thor's eyes had been impossible to disguise and perhaps some impression of his ruddy face had also got through to the lecherous giant.

"Alas," Loki said swiftly, "my lady has not slept these eight nights, so anxious has she been to come here to Jotunheim and be with you. It was her weariness and bloodshot eyes combined with the heat of her passion which you saw."

"By eternity, I'll be bound it was," Thrym exclaimed, now keener than ever to have the beautiful creature, and wouldn't she rest so much better afterwards?

Rubbing his hands together he ordered that everything be made ready for them to be married at once.

"And what of your promise?" Thor said as softly and shyly as he could. "A girl doesn't want to be taken for granted."

"Of course, your bride price, I'll fetch it at once."

Thrym was gone some time, going down so many fathoms into the earth. When he came back, all had been made ready for the consecration of his union with 'Freyja'. By now he was so hot and bothered he practically breathed steam. His eye roved over his fiancée's body and he was sure he discerned a beautiful figure under the flowing gown. As was the custom he placed the dowry – which was, of course, Thor's hammer, Mjolnir – on the bride's knees. As he put it there Thrym could not resist a little feel of the goods, imagining that his shapely bride was a very firm and fit young woman. Thor, flexed his well-developed pectoral muscles, hefted the hammer and smiled. Right, he thought, let's see how he likes it now.

Throwing off the veil and roaring in fury, Thor rose up brandishing Mjolnir, all illusion dispelled. The look on Thrym's face was enough to give him pause for a fit of laughter, and then he laid into the giant with a will.

"You're not just a thief but a damned masher," cried Thor, swinging the hammer down on the gaping giant's skull.

Next he flew at the rest of Thrym's band and slew or frightened off the lot of them. Loki, meanwhile, only had to stand aside and give him elbow room. When at last Thor's fury was exhausted and all the giants were dispatched or had fled, the two gods made their way home to Asgard.

The whole affair did nothing to improve relations between the Aesir and the giants, however, and Loki soon found himself embroiled in another intrigue between the feuding sides. Again it involved his enjoyment of the use of Freyja's feathered robe and subsequent flight in his own form. While on this jaunt he fell into the hands of a giant who thought he was a rare bird and put him in a cage. Geirrod, the giant who captured him, was not a very attentive collector, and failed to feed his latest prize. After three whole months with nothing to eat and no chance of escape, the tricky god had had enough. He got Geirrod's attention, removed the robe and announced his true identity.

After the giant had regained his composer, for his laughter had been long, deep and straight from the belly, he refused to release the god unless he agreed to a particular bargain.

"I would rather have one of the Aesir among my menagerie than any bird," he chuckled, "so it makes little odds to me whether you accept or not."

"I'll agree to whatever you want," Loki said without hesitation. "Just let me out and give me some food, will you?"

"You will have to swear such an oath that even you would never dare to go back on the bargain I have in mind." Geirrod grinned, wagging an enormous finger in Loki's face. "You have a reputation."

"I'll swear to anything you like or on anything you like."

"Because what I want will be both difficult and involve selling out one of your own. What do you say to that?"

"How difficult? Would it involve a lot of work?"

"Is that all that troubles you?" Geirrod laughed again. "Probably it will be very easy for you of all people, now I think about it."

"Pass over a goose leg or a bit of cheese and tell me all about it."

So it was that then and there Loki agreed to betray Thor. The slippery god had so little compunction about doing this that Geirrod was still shaking his head and laughing as Loki flew back to Asgard.

The jolly giant had been quite correct. It was simplicity itself for Loki to trick Thor, even though the deal involved delivering him without his iron gloves, the hammer, Mjolnir, or the girdle that gave him supernatural strength. Abandoning these would make him virtually helpless and easy meat for Geirrod, who could then kill or keep him prisoner at will.

"Where have you been, Loki? Visiting Hell? You look like death warmed up and not very warmed up at that." Thor said on their first meeting after Loki's return.

Until this moment Loki had not been sure what tack to take but suddenly he began to improvise.

"I tell you, Thor, I am worn to a frazzle, but what a time I've had. The drink, the women, the music. That Geirrod can certainly throw a party. And it never stops. I had to come home for a rest before I was carried off entirely by sheer pleasure."

"Who is Geirrod?" asked an intrigued Thor.

"Oh, you wouldn't like him, not your sort at all. And anyway he is a giant. But so are his entertainments. Mercy!"

"I don't hate all giants."

"No, but you want to fight and kill them."

"Not every single giant in creation, I don't."

"Well, Geirrod is certainly no fighter. Doesn't even own or approve of weapons of any sort. He just wants peace between gods, giants and men. He doesn't have any prejudices against anyone, even dwarfs, elves and demons, would you believe? No, he is not your sort. I probably couldn't get you an invitation. But it has to be said, you're really missing out."

"I'd like to think I can get along with anyone, given half a chance," said Thor, a little taken aback. "I have friends among the giants and dwarfs, and you know it. How is the food and drink at Geirrod's?"

"Unbelievable, but I was too busy to eat much, as you see. Look at all the weight I've lost. But the girls are fantastic and they come from every realm, drawn by Geirrod's open-minded views. And don't they have open-minded views themselves!"

"Be a sport, Loki," Thor grinned. "Get me an invitation."

"No, you are a militant and it just wouldn't work. He wouldn't take to you."

"I am not a militant," Thor assured him. "I like peace. True, just peace as much as the next god, man or giant."

"Well, you'd have to prove it. I mean you'd have to go unarmed. I doubt you'd even be welcome wearing your iron gloves and that girdle. They are weapons too, after all. To a passive sort like Geirrod they surely would seem to be ..."

"I'll go unarmed then," Thor assured Loki. "No problem."

"Well, I'll see what I can do," Loki said doubtfully. "Look me up in a few days."

Eventually Loki told Thor he had managed to get him an invite to the 'great unending festivities' at Geirrod's palace. If the mighty Thor were willing to come unarmed, he said, he could be assured that the celebrating and feasting would be more extraordinary than ever. The girls would be especially impressed by Thor's gesture of peace and trust.

Thor could hardly wait to get there and thought nothing of it when Loki insisted that he was not yet rested enough to return to the rigours of such lavish and extravagant partying. Alone Thor set off in eager anticipation of having the time of his life. Only chance, not any scruple from Loki, saved him.

On the way, and indeed very near Geirrod's home, Thor ran into an old flame, and luckily, one who still carried a torch for him. This was the giantess Grid, who was also the mother of his child, born of an affair they had enjoyed years before. For some time now they had been 'just friends', but she was very glad to see him and they spent a pleasant half hour exchanging news.

"Where are you off to now?" Grid asked.

"I've got an invitation to one of the big parties that Geirrod gives. Or rather the one always in progress at his palace."

"Parties? At Geirrod's place?"

"I hear they are really something, the food, the drink, the music, the wom ... the food," Thor checked himself.

"Are you kidding? Geirrod is too cheap even to feed his pets, and he hates the Aesir. The only thing he would invite a god to is a fight, or rather an ambush. He isn't the bravest of souls."

Turning bright red with rage, Thor said only one word in explanation before storming off to Asgard, bent on revenge.

"Loki."

Grid understood perfectly and looked forward to seeing Thor some time when he was not so occupied. Loki himself looked forward to not seeing him at all and went into hiding for quite a long while, which everyone appreciated.

It was not in Loki's nature to learn his lesson or to be loyal to his fellow gods, however. There came a time when, after being forgiven by Thor, Loki yet again betrayed not just one of the Aesir, but all of them. The initial trouble was not his fault but all that happened later certainly was.

Odin, Hoenir, Loki and three other gods were on an expedition wandering the earth, when hunger got the better of them and they stopped to roast an ox. For some reason the meat simply would not cook, in spite of the blazing fire they had placed it over. Above them, an eagle was perched in the branches of a tree and suddenly it spoke to them.

"I have cast a spell on your food," the eagle said. "And will not lift it unless you agree to share your meal with me."

Reluctantly, the gods agreed but when the creature sat down with them and proceeded to take all the best cuts for himself, they lost their temper. Loki was especially perturbed and grabbing a rod he beat the interloper with it. The eagle, finding the rod stuck into him, flew off so suddenly that he carried Loki with him and flew so high that it would be suicide for the god to let go. Periodically the great bird would dip down to drag Loki through trees and to scrape him along ledges.

Crying out in agony and despair as he was torn, cut and battered, Loki begged for mercy. Now, the eagle was really a disguised giant named Thjazi and though he was in pain himself, he pretended he could fly forever or until Loki let go of the rod and fell to the ground.

"If I land softly and release you, Loki, you will have to do something for me. You will have to swear a binding oath to do just as I ask."

Naturally by now everyone knew what Loki was capable of and how his betrayal had nearly spelled the end of Thor.

"Just name it," Loki shouted over the rush of the wind, seeing a tall fir tree coming up.

"I want nothing less than Idun and her apples."

"I have to say you think big," Loki called. He could do this. The pretty goddess had a weakness for him and he knew how to get to her, how to manipulate her. "It's a deal, Thjazi. Now let me down easy."

"You swear by your own precious skin?"

"Yes, I swear! I swear!"

"Good, and don't take your time about it. I'll drop you off ..."

"What?"

"Sorry. Set you down in Asgard. If anyone asks, I was just some crazy bird."

"Thjazi," Loki said laconically, "don't tell your grandmother how to suck eggs." Already he was planning this fresh crime against his fellow Aesir and not minding a bit.

It was a crime, too, and an even more serious one than simply aiding in the abduction of a goddess. The apples Idun regularly gave to her fellow gods were very special and only she knew how to grow and gather them. It was the magic in them that kept the gods young and vital, and to let a giant kidnap her and take them away would condemn the Aesir to a terrible decline. Without the apples they would grow old, weak and vulnerable.

Telling Idun that he had discovered in the forest apples even more beautiful than her own, Loki lured her to a spot where Thjazi was waiting. The giant grabbed poor Idun and with her apples carried her off to his hideaway.

It was not long before Idun was missed, and so were her apples. The gods began to age, to grow a little shaky on their feet, and begin to go grey.

Despite their enmity, the lives of the gods and giants were too interconnected for anything of such magnitude to remain a secret for long. Soon all the Aesir turned on Loki with such fury and dire threats that he was forced to admit what he had done, and to promise to rectify matters. He would find Idun and bring her back, with the precious apples.

Changing himself into a hawk, Loki flew to the kingdom of the giants and searched for Idun. Upon finding her he turned her into a nut and flew away with her. When Thjazi realized what had happened he shape-changed into his eagle guise, and went after them.

Dodging through clouds, in and out of valleys, between trees, and along steep-sided gorges the eagle that was Thjazi chased Loki the hawk carrying Idun as a nut. The speed at which they flew was tremendous but as they drew near Asgard, the eagle was perceptibly gaining on the hawk with a gleam in its eye and its talons flexed menacingly.

What happened next has been attributed to some quick thinking god in Agard and his accurate reading of the situation, but that is only because no one wanted to give Loki credit for anything after all he had done and would yet do. This particular twist was too obviously planned, and too well timed to have been spontaneous, and while all the gods were adept at serving the giants a dirty turn, this one smacked of the work of Loki himself.

Streaking for the walled city as fast as his wings could propel him, with Thjazi only a few feet behind him now, Loki darted for a particular place on the high wall. An instant after he had passed this point flames shot into the air from an enormous bonfire, lighted, stoked and controlled by the waiting gods. A metal sheet was snatched away and grand bellows were pumped right on cue. The leaping flames caught the eagle in their midst and burning like a fire arrow, fanned by his own speed, he flew on, screaming, trailing smoke until he fell to earth a mere cinder.

That was the end of Thjazi. Idun resumed her natural form and her generous distribution of the magic apples to the gods and goddess. But it was not the end of Loki's bitter relationship with the other Aesir. Indeed, things went from bad to worse, and from worse to horrible and then to horribly final. Consequences never much mattered to Loki, though.

Just before his penultimate crime, Loki had a field day of abuse, insulting nearly every Aesir in existence at a banquet given by a diplomatic giant named Aegir, lord of the seas. Only Thor, who was travelling in the east, was not there to witness it.

Everyone was enjoying Aegir's fine hospitality when suddenly Loki forced open the door to the hall. Needless to say he had not been invited. By unspoken agreement, the entire assembly ignored him and did their best to carry on as if he was not there.

Undeterred by this cold reception, Loki addressed the diners in a loud but respectful, even humble, voice.

"I am only a thirsty traveller, surely you will not refuse me the cup given unasked to all passers-by, even strangers?"

Nobody answered him as still they tried to pretend he was not there.

"At least offer me a chair," he went on mildly and as if hurt, "according to the basic laws of hospitality. Otherwise just say in so many words that I am not welcome."

The gods held a whispered conversation. Aegir himself stayed well out of it, though he was the host. Rightly he felt this was a matter best settled by the Aesir, and that anything he might do would offend somebody. It was a family squabble of sorts, after all.

Everyone was reluctant to give Loki a seat, including Bragi, the god of poetry, whose usual duty it was to welcome new arrivals at gatherings.

"No," Bragi said emphatically. "I must insist. He was uninvited and does not deserve a place here."

"Odin," Loki turned to the chief of gods, spreading his arms appealingly, a slight quiver in his voice. "Have you forgotten that we once swore an oath to be forever blood brothers?"

Touched by the memory, Odin slowly nodded.

"Vider," Odin said gently to the god next to him. "Be a good fellow and give Loki your seat for a while. A cup, please, for Loki," he added to a serving girl then apologetically to the others. "As is the custom."

Loki made himself comfortable, accepted his cup and proposed a toast to the health of everyone present.

"Except Bragi, of course, who would have kept me out."

Feeling a little ashamed for what he felt was rather shabby behaviour in front of their giant host, Bragi stood with his hands up and smiled at Loki.

"I am sorry. It was very discourteous and I do apologise. Let me make it up to you. I'll tell you what, you can have that new horse of mine, and this ring." He plucked a nice one from one of his fingers. "And a sword I shall have made just for you."

The approval and charm of such open-handedness buzzing around the hall was cut short by a curt gesture of Loki's dismissive hand.

"Keep them," he said arrogantly. "I do not accept gifts from cowards who hang back in battle and let others do their fighting for them."

It was such an obvious and terrible lie that Bragi's wife, Idun, easily prevented him from attacking Loki or even losing his temper.

"This needs no reply," she said looking at Loki with such utter contempt that it gave even him gooseflesh. "How can anything so ridiculous possibly offend." Her look made it clear that she meant him, not just his words.

Stung by this beyond what he would have expected of himself, all pretence of good manners where the others were concerned left Loki. It was not just Bragi that he insulted now. In a pitiless stream of invective and minute detail he tore in to each of the gods and goddesses with every scandal and humiliating episode for all their lives. Who had betrayed their husband or wife. Who had cheated at a game or long owed whom money. Who had said what about someone else behind his back.

"There is not a goddess here who has not betrayed her husband. Very few that I haven't enjoyed the favours of myself" he boasted. "Which means just about all of them who aren't too damned ugly to stomach." On his feet again, swaggering, a bit unsteadily, around the hall, he was getting into the faces of people, breathing on them. Until now he had hidden the fact that he was already drunk when he arrived.

"You were good," he singled out one goddess after another. "You were very good, but you were an utter bore. A yawn. Glad she's not my wife," he turned to her astonished husband. "Ha! Not bloody likely." Between Loki's good looks and tricky ways, no one doubted the truth of any of this.

Everyone tried to defend themselves however, make excuses to others, talk Loki down, or return insult for insult. Certainly he had done far more shameful things than anybody else. The trouble was he was shameless. Nothing touched him. Gleefully Loki himself recounted every crime he had committed against all of them, both known ones and many unknown.

Even the poetical and wordy Bragi was struck dumb by the onslaught and yet more surprisingly, Odin. Renowned for his presence of mind and his eloquent speaking, he failed to silence Loki. Completely flabbergasted, Odin too fell victim to Loki's mockery and abuse.

Sif approached him with a cup of mead, trying to placate him, get him to sit down and desist. He only laughed at her, grabbed her by the waist and danced her around, spilling the mead on those nearby.

"And here is another beauty I have bedded," Loki squeezed her rump. "The wife of good old Thor. Yes, you've been in my arms before, haven't you, willing, nay desperate, for my particular attentions."

As if by evoking his name the thunder god had been summoned. Thor was heard as a rumble in the mountains, then in moments, outside the hall as his chariot drew up. Bursting in full of life and merriment, an apology to his host for being late on his lips, Thor instantly sensed the strained atmosphere and looked around confusedly. His eyes alighted on Loki and, slowly, understanding dawned.

"Ah the very fellow," cried Loki. "That look on your face just now reminded me of the time the enchanter giant Utgardaloki hoodwinked you so badly. Friends, I saw through him quickly enough but played along. He had Thor going for ages, though, convinced him his hammer blows on his head hardly left an impression, felt like leaves landing, cheated him in eating and drinking contests and then foot racing ... Why poor naive Thor was well and truly flummoxed. What a picture his face was when he found out. Of course, Sif," Loki turned to Thor's struggling wife, whom he had not yet let go, "we can hardly complain about him being naive, can we?"

Without a word Thor raised his mighty hammer and deliberately started for him with fire in his eyes. At this point Loki realized he had gone too far, challenged the wrong person and bitten off far more than he could chew.

"Only joking. No harm done, everybody. Just a bit of fun. Doesn't time fly. Must dash. Good night all." Smiling broadly, patting backs that shrank from his touch, he made for the exit, away from Thor around the other side of the great table.

At the door he turned to them once more and leered at the assembly.

"Enjoy this feast, my friends. It may be your last. I prophesy that soon this hall and all in it, outside it, and everywhere else, will be but ashes."

Whether this parting shot was truly a prophesy or he was already plotting with the enemies of the Aesir to bring about their downfall and the end of the world, is uncertain. The truth of what he said is indisputable, however. Soon, the end would come in a great all-consuming battle.

The final straw in his relations with the Aesir was what Loki did to Balder, a handsome god like Loki, but unlike him, well loved and popular with everyone for his wisdom, kindness and gentleness. In a warlike race an individual with such attributes must have a great deal of goodness, charm, integrity and fortitude to be so well thought of, and Balder had all this and more.

Like Heimdall, whom among all the gods, Loki also particularly despised, Balder was a god of light. But while Heimdall's duty was to stand watch over the gates to Asgard and guard them from surprise attack, Balder seemed to perform the function of a mediator, and represent gentility and civilization within a divine but nevertheless tough and brutal society. In Heimdall, Loki hated and mocked the selfless sense of duty, standing sentinel in all weathers, uncomplaining while others had fun or slept warm in bed. In Balder he deprecated that seeming softness, sweetness of nature and lack of malice which his fellow-gods found so oddly admirable.

So beloved and valued by the Aesir was Balder that when he reported having strange and disquieting dreams and presentiments of evil, everyone was deeply concerned. His usually harmonious and blissful life was suddenly darkened by these feelings of impending danger and the gods resolved to do something, so worried were they by the idea that something bad should happen to Balder.

Though the son of Odin and the goddess Frigg, Balder would have been everyone's favourite whatever his parentage, but as it was, concern ran even higher and his mother took steps, with the approval of all, to forestall any harm to him. She begged every being and thing on earth never to hurt him. She beseeched elements like fire, metal, water and stone, minerals, plants, trees, illnesses, animals, snakes, fish and all else. Every single one of them swore an oath never to harm Balder, and the gods were satisfied.

Eventually they made a sport of attacking him with weapons, to which he was now invulnerable. He would stand in a ring at their feasts and gods would throw spears, and hammers, shoot arrows and sling stones at him and laugh as he smiled and let them strike, causing him no pain or damage. It was a great trick to pull on guests of other races, too, and everyone delighted in it but Loki.

Going to Frigg during one of these sessions disguised as an admiring old lady, Loki praised and questioned her carefully about how she had protected her son so well.

"Incredible! And you left nothing out? In all the world?"

"Nothing," Frigg said with pride. "Well, there was one thing, I suppose. A little plant called Misteltein, or mistletoe. It seemed too young to be made to swear an oath. Just a baby, as plants go."

"Of course," laughed the old woman, as did Loki inside the image, for what he had learned might be useful. "But where does such a rare little plant grow?" the old lady wondered gushingly.

"Oh, to the west of Valhalla," the unsuspecting Frigg replied. Loki left, changed back into his own image at once and set off to find the mistletoe.

As time went by the plant grew enough for him to cut a hefty wand from it. The next time the gods played the game of flinging things at Balder, Loki was ready. He had had to be patient, as the novelty had worn off by now and the game was rarer.

Seating himself beside Hod, who was blind, Loki asked him why he was not joining in the game.

"Why do you think?" Hod turned vacantly to him.

"I'll help you, direct your arm."

"I don't have a weapon …"

"Try this stick. Come on, let's get closer," Loki said taking Hod's elbow.

The other gods saw Loki lead Hod nearer to Balder and guide his arm, though the stick missed. Each time Loki retrieved it and helped Hod again and everyone thought it nice but out of character for Loki to help the blind god to enjoy the game.

"A bit higher, Hod," Loki would whisper. "Head height, you know. More fun."

Then suddenly the stick struck Balder in the temple. Between the unaccustomed noise of real impact and seeing the gentle god go down as if pole-axed, everyone gasped and stared a moment in disbelief. As they saw the look on Loki's face, understanding dawned. After first rushing to Balder and finding him dead, as one they closed in on Loki.

The only thing that saved him was the fact that they stood on sacred ground. It was the law that in this place dedicated to peace, no blood could be spilled, even in righteous revenge. As grief and lamentation assailed the assembly, Loki slipped away and stayed hidden for a long time.

"Who will volunteer to go to Hel, goddess of the kingdom of the dead, and try to rescue Balder for us?" Frigg cried. "I will give myself to any man who will attempt it, in advance, no matter who he is."

Hermod, one of Odin's sons, by another mother needless to say, volunteered with alacrity. After enjoying his reward he mounted his father's famous charger, Sleipnir, and set off at the gallop. He had liked Balder as much as the next man and now a life-long desire had been fulfilled. Full of vim and vigour, he felt he could face Hel and even win a hostage back from her.

In the meantime, the gods carried Balder's body to the sea and built a funeral pyre on a boat, which had belonged to him in life. Here they placed the body and as Thor gravely raised his hammer, consecrating the ritual, the pyre was set alight. Balder's fully equipped horse was led to it so that the flames consumed the animal at the same time as its master. Nearly all the gods, and even many giants, were in attendance, so greatly loved was Balder. No one made a secret of his or her sorrow.

As the body of the dead god was being wept over, Hermod was making his way down to the realm of the dead. Riding through dark valleys and deep crevasses, he did not leave the saddle for nine full days. At last he came to the river Gjoll, which bordered the underworld. This could only be crossed by a bridge of gold. In conversation with the guard, he learned that Balder and five hundred others had passed over only the night before.

Hurrying onward Hermod came to the gates of the Kingdom of Hel. Here he dismounted a moment, tightened his saddle's girth, threw a leg over Sleipnir once more, collected himself and his magnificent steed and rushed at the wall. Leaping majestically, the fantastic horse cleared the top without even brushing its hooves on the stone.

Once inside, however, Hermod was somewhat intimidated and bewildered by all he saw. Going as near as he dared to the throne, he sought after his half-brother and spotted him seated in a place of honour beside Hel herself. It was late in the day by now and Hermod felt all his weariness settle upon him. He resolved to wait until the morning to speak to Hel. He knew he would need all his wits about him and full command of his nerves.

Early the next day, but not too early, Hermod presented himself respectfully to Hel and explained his mission. He did not see Balder anywhere nearby and that made it easier. He would not have wish to get his hopes up if they were only to be dashed and, equally, he did not want to risk the embarrassment of asking if Balder had no desire to return to the land of the living.

He need not have worried, nor about his interview with Hel in general. She took pity on him and on the sadness of the gods and everyone else at Balder's death, and she explained that Balder had not been with her long enough to truly wish to stay or even be utterly required to.

"If, as you say," she told Hermod. "the mourning for him is universal among all things in being, and if all agree – and I mean all – that they desire his return to life, then I will set him free. But remember, if just a single creature, object, element or what-so-ever in the universe refuses to weep for him, then he must stay."

"Oh, none will, I assure you." Hermod bowed low, kissed Hel's hand and hastened back to Asgard with the happy news.

The Aesir sent out messengers all over creation to canvass the opinion of all things in it and to beg them to shed a tear for Balder and thus display their grief so that Hel might see that the sorrow was truly universal. At the god's behest everything – men, animals, wood, stone, plants, fire, water and the rest – began to cry honest tears for Balder.

Just when the messengers were about to return to Asgard to proclaim the success of their efforts, it was discovered that there was yet one who would not grieve for the so beloved god. A certain giantess called Thokk, living in a cave deep inside a high mountain, had refused all their pleading.

"I'll not shed so much as one tiny tear for him," she swore. "Not while he lived, nor now he's dead. Let Hel have him. What did he ever do for me?"

No one knew at the time that this supposed cruel giantess was Loki in yet another disguise, but he surely enough prevented Balder's return to life among the Aesir. When the truth came out, it was as if Loki had murdered Balder twice. The gods moved heaven and earth to find and arrest him. In the end, they chained him and threw him in to a deep dungeon to rot.

Almost inevitably the crafty Loki escaped and fled to Jotunheim, where he allied himself with the Aesir's greatest enemies, whose forces were already gathering. A final showdown was threatening, for the giants and other races felt that a reckoning was overdue. The haughty Aesir had had the upper hand too long.

For some time now they had been rather too cavalier in their treatment of others. If Loki was the trickster and villain of Asgard, the Aesir were the Lokis of the world at large. Indeed, they'd often enough used that wily god's talents for their own ends against giants and other races when it suited them.

In the early days of creation the gods in their palaces in Asgard had led peaceful and industrious lives. They had taken pleasure in building temples, erecting alters, working in gold and forging tools with hammer and anvil or playing draughts together. This blissful existence might have gone on forever had they been able to control their passions. As it was, they brought down on themselves the grave destiny that was about to overtake them.

There had been the day in Valhalla when in order to extract her gold, they had tortured the Vanir goddess Gullveig, who had come to them as an envoy. This crime had precipitated the first wars. Later they broke their word to a giant who had constructed their celestial dwelling. As the price of his labour he had been promised the hand of the goddess Freyja, along with the sun and the moon, if he could complete the project in a specified time.

When it seemed he would fulfil his end of the bargain, they set Loki on him. The trickster shape-changed into a fine mare in season and so distracted the stallion helping to carry the building materials that the work was not done on time and the gods reneged on the arrangement. From then on the word of the Aesir was deemed worthless. If that was how the gods behaved, it was natural that all treaties concluded in the world quickly lost their force and validity.

An era began characterized by perjury, violence and war. Hatred and anger equally swayed men, giants and gods. Evil dreams began to trouble the sleep of the Aesir. Odin uneasily watched the sinister portents accumulate. He realized that the supreme struggle was about to unfold. Calmly and resolutely he made ready to face it.

The murder of Balder, Loki's escape and defection and events in a distant forest where a giantess gave birth to a brood of wolves fathered by Fenrir, himself a giant wolf, were all dark omens for the immediate future. When one of these monstrous young wolves chased the sun, it found the pursuit long and difficult but eventually it caught up, coming near enough to take a bite from it. As with each season the wolf grew in strength it began to eat more and more of the sun. Its rays were extinguished one by one as it turned blood-red and finally disappeared. For many years the world was plunged into darkness, and yet still war raged as brother killed brother, snow covered the earth, all sense of family vanished and everything descended rapidly towards the abyss of nothingness.

From everywhere, hostile forces of all kinds gathered. On the edge of the sky, Heimdall, watchman of the gods, looked out for their attackers. No one in the world had an eye more piercing or an ear more acute than he, yet Loki managed to steal his sword and to delay his sounding his horn to warn the gods until the giants' army was already on the march.

The great wolf Fenrir, whom the god Tyr had sacrificed his right hand to chain up, pulled himself free and escaped. As he shook off his chains he made the whole world tremble and the tree of life, the ancient ash Yggdrasil, was shaken from its roots to its topmost branches. Mountains crumbled or split from top to bottom, and the dwarfs who made their subterranean homes therein scrambled vainly to find exits once so familiar but destroyed now as the earth shook and fell in on itself.

From the west, in a ship manned by a crew of phantoms, the giant Hrym came, ready and eager for battle, standing erect, his shield in his left hand and the tiller in his right. The ship was propelled by great waves created by the writhing of the sea serpent Midgard, an old enemy of Thor with a score to settle.

Another ship appeared from the north, its sails bellying in the wind, carrying the inhabitants of the underworld. Loki was at the helm of this craft and beside him his fellow escapee, the dreaded wolf Fenrir, fire spurting from his eyes and nostrils, his great jaws dripping blood.

From the south Surt, lord of enormous land holdings in the giant kingdom, raised his flaming sword and led his innumerable fire giants toward the scene of the coming battle. Lightning flashed from this blade and all around him flames sprang from the cracking earth. As he passed nearby, rocks crumbled and people fell dead.

The vault of heaven shook at the tumult of this hoard on the march. Scorched, then frozen, then baked by the fiery furnace below, it finally cracked in two. When the fire giants, last of the enemy host, rode their wild horses across the rainbow bridge linking earth with Asgard, it was set alight, and burned and collapsed behind them as they rushed joyfully to bloody combat and slaughter.

Drawing up for battle at an agreed place, as was the ancient custom, they met at the field of Vigrid, which stretched before Valhalla, a square measuring a thousand leagues by a thousand leagues. Here gods and giants and all other races existent at the time, countless in number, met and clashed in pitiless and relentless, seemingly inexhaustible butchery.

Odin, wearing a golden helmet plumed with eagle's wings, and gripping the good spear Gungnir, would lead the Asir attack. Swarming endlessly out of the gates of Valhalla came the gods, the Valkyries closest behind Odin on flying chargers.

Seeing Fenrir, Odin went for him personally, but the giant wolf's fangs were so large and powerful that the chief of the Aesir was torn asunder and gobbled up. Thus the father of the gods was the first casualty in the apocalyptic struggle, though his son, Vidar, avenged him. Pinning the enormous wolf's lower jaw to the ground with his foot, shod in leather that was indestructible and could not be penetrated by Fenrir's sharp teeth, he held the upper jaw aloft in his strong left hand.

Driving deep with his sword he found the beast's heart with his thrusts, finally killing it.

Thor met with his old adversary the sea monster Midgard, who crawled toward the thunder god spitting venom and poisoning the air around him. Thor crushed its skull with the hammer Mjolnir and destroyed it. He then staggered away from the encounter with failing strength and after taking nine steps fell dead.

On the other side Loki had no qualms about fighting against his own kind. In the chaos and mist of battle, he too sought out a personal enemy. Heimdall, who had taken Freyja's necklace back from him, Heimdall whom he had always denigrated as a bore, a dutiful watchdog, a drudge. There was no god he hated more.

When at last they came across one another, both quickly dispatched his present adversary and made straight for the other.

"Is that a new sword I see?" Loki called. "Recognize this one? It would be fair to say it has your name on it." Holding aloft the weapon he had stolen form Heimdall, Loki waded in with mighty blows, going for a quick kill. Old fury mixed with the bloodlust of this great satisfying war. He was thrilled and invigorated by this fight against his kith and kin and longed to slaughter this adversary and go on to another and another.

As in their underwater encounter in the guise of seals, Heimdall was a match for Loki, however. Every thrust was parried, and counter thrusts or slashes followed from each man with neither finding a way through the other's guard.

At last, true to his nature, Loki employed a trick. Looking relieved and focusing his eyes at a specific point behind Heimdall, Loki let his guard down, dropping as if exhausted to his knee.

"Oh, kill him then, Surt," he cried resignedly.

Turning to face the chief of the fire giants, Heimdall saw no one behind him poised for attack, only the throng of struggling warriors intent on one another.

From his kneeling position Loki swung his sword at his enemy's legs, striking at them just above the ankle. Heimdall was already turning back, however, and his movement became a falling strike at Loki's side, embedding his sword half way though the renegade god's body, even as Loki held his own sword point upwards, aiming just right. Heimdall fell, impaling himself and dying as the blade pierced his lungs and heart. Mortally wounded, Loki crawled away, dying in agony some time later.

Everywhere gods and giants died bloody and miserable deaths; few were cut down by some swift blow. One by one they fell, and with them order in the universe. Finally, the chief fire giant, now in his own death throes, set the world aflame. The human race was driven out, ultimately to be consumed along with all other forms of life by the inferno.

As fire and steam shot from the ground, the earth began to lose its shape and became an empty, cracked, burning ruin. Then the rivers, lakes and oceans rose and the earth, engulfed by the waters, sank deep beneath them.

When things quietened down it seemed that two of Odin's sons, two of his nephews and two sons of Thor had escaped to live in the sky. Odin's old faithful companion Hoenir also survived. By studying and reading runes engraved on magic wands, he penetrated the secrets of the future and was able to tell the new race what happiness awaited them.

Men reappeared also, a few humans having escaped by shielding themselves in the wood of the old ash tree, Yggdrasil. Impervious to the conflagration, the tree had kept them alive, and provided their nourishment in the form of dew as they awaited the renewal.

The Death of Tutunui

*A tale told throughout the Pacific islands
with slight variations, this is much in the international tradition
of duels between magicians and sages.
The tactics employed here
are in some ways unique, however.*

The Maori chieftain Tinirau looked far out across the blue waters surrounding his island home, his face showing excitement and anticipation. Over his shoulder he shouted last-minute instructions to his children and people for the feast they were preparing. His guest of honour, Kei, was a famous magician and a powerful chieftain. Tinirau was relishing the prospect of impressing Kei, and making a friend of him.

From high in a palm tree a sharp-eyed boy called out that he could see a canoe. Tinirau squinted into the distance, trying to make it out. He thought of the surprise he had in store for Kei and looked forward to springing it. A modest man and, like Kei, a fine magician, although he did not consider himself as such, Tinirau hoped it would be appreciated by his honoured guest.

Slowly the canoe came into view. Tinirau could just make out the figure in the middle of the craft, staring straight ahead as the strong young men around him rowed, rhythmically and with ease. When it entered shallower water Tinirau waded into the surf to help his guests disembark and to greet Kei warmly.

Though their islands were not far apart, a history of suspicion had long separated the two chieftains, and this was their first meeting. A strange feeling of disquiet came over Tinirau as they went through the traditional greeting, but when this quickly passed he thought no more of it. After each chieftain had given a formal speech of greeting and

153

friendship, everyone sat down to the feast.

Kei was a small, energetic fellow with an appetite that was on a scale with the largest of men, and while he took his pick of the bountiful array of fruits he was looking forward with relish to the arrival of the meat course. There was no sign of anything being roasted, nor the smell of so much as a bird or fish cooking. As the remains of the first course were cleared away, it was all he could do not to comment on this, though the distraction of the beauties waiting on him, particularly his host's eldest daughter, helped.

"Next," Tinirau smiled, having noted the greedy look, "whale meat."

Rising, Tinirau beckoned to his guest to follow him and they walked onto the sands of the beach.

"That is a rare treat," Kei allowed, aware of how hard it was for the young men to catch anything as big as a whale. Still he was wondering why he had smelled nothing of the cooking of such a delicacy. Beside him Tinirau, spreading his arms and looking out to sea, took a deep breath.

"Tutunui," he bellowed. "Tutunui!"

Out among the gently lapping waves a water spout suddenly shot into the air, then a moment later, leaping clear of the surface, a whale sailed across many feet of sea before spectacularly splashing down, disappearing underwater.

With satisfaction Tinirau saw the wide-eyed look on Kei's face as again the whale appeared, gliding along in the surf heading straight for where they stood. Again shooting water into the air almost as a salute, it came to a halt in the shallows. Tinirau waded out to it as a small boy ran up to hand him a large knife. Intrigued, Kei followed, although at first wary of approaching the whale too closely.

Running his hands along the whale's side, Tinirau whispered happily to the beast and it seemed to respond to him. As Kei stared in amazement, Tinirau brought the knife up as if to show it to the mammal then slipping along its flank proceeded to cut a big slice out of its flesh. The whale appeared to accept this without alarm or protest.

Handing the generous portion of meat to the boy, who ran back to the beach to give it to the women to barbecue, Tinirau stroked the whale, still somehow conversing with it, and then turned to Kei.

"Come, let us eat some more," he smiled, as the whale wriggled its way into deeper water and swam back out to sea. The other magician's astonishment was most gratifying, though once more Tinirau momentarily felt uneasy at something in Kei's expression. But again the moment passed and soon they were drinking together without a care in the world. When the meat was served, Kei's praise was lavish and his enjoyment obviously immense. For the rest of the day he charmed everyone by performing small magic tricks, which he deprecated as illusions, and entertained his hosts enormously. Tinirau was very glad that he had extended the invitation to Kei and looked forward to seeing him again soon.

As the sun began to set, Kei regretted that he had to return to his own island and reproached himself for staying too long.

"I have lost track of time in such company, enjoying such hospitality," he sighed. "But there is a sick child that I must look in on and already it is late. My rowers will still be weary, however, and the trip will take a long while. I wonder if you might do me a very large favour, Tinirau."

"Anything."

"Would it be possible to have your pet whale carry me home on its back? I am sure it would shorten the journey."

"Well," Tinirau demurred. "Tutunui has never performed such a task ..." For some reason he felt very reluctant to do as his guest proposed. The rowers would surely be rested by now, though perhaps a little tipsy and full from feasting. It did seem surly of him to refuse, though. "All right," he said finally. "I will have him do this."

He waded into the surf and called the whale, which had been

cavorting offshore. It came immediately and once more Tinirau met it in the shallows and ran his hands over its head. After a few minutes he turned and nodded to Kei, who came up beside him to be hoisted onto the whale's back.

Many others now waded out to wave him off, followed at a leisurely pace by his canoe and young rowers. With mixed feelings Tinirau watched his guest disappear into the distance as around him his people sang and laughed and began drifting back to their homes. The day had been a complete success. Kei had been gracious, appreciative and amusing and everyone had enjoyed themselves. Yet still, the sense that something was wrong would not leave Tinirau.

Out on the waves Kei was thrilled by his ride on Tutunui's back. It had not escaped him either that it seemed the great wound in the animal's side had already healed. Using all his cunning and artfulness he began to speak to the whale, to charm it, attempting to seduce it away from Tinirau. Try as he might, however, he could not establish communication with the whale. It swam on, not reacting in any way, and finally Kei gave up and began to think along other lines.

Whether out of jealousy, greed, laziness or cruelty he made up his mind to act. As they neared his island Kei refused to respond when Tutunui gave the mighty shiver which was his signal for the magician to dismount. Again, Kei tried sweet talking the whale, begging the animal to swim just a little closer inshore, so that he could get off without danger of the water being too deep, for he was but a small man. His real purpose, though, was to attract the attention of the many villagers sitting on the shore.

As if he understood, Tutunui did as he was asked and headed further inshore. The waters in this part of the bay were deceptively shallow, however, and the waves rushed in more quickly than one might have thought due to the shape of the coral either side. Picking his moment, Kei attacked, stuffing the whale's blow hole with his clothing, and jumping onto Tutunui's head to hold it under the surface of the water. As he struggled with the fast-weakening creature, Kei shouted to his people to hurry out to him with knives.

Seeing their chief single-handedly assailing the whale, they rushed out and joined in, hacking the beast to death. This sort of 'kill' was very rare and the meat would feed them for a long time to come. Only the clever Kei, the islanders said, could have actually caused such a thing to happen right on their doorstep.

The feasting and celebrations went on late into the night and the smell of the cooking whale meat drifted far over the waters, even reaching the nostrils of Tinirau, who was growing increasingly concerned because Tutunui had not returned. Soon confirmation of the whale's unhappy demise came from a girl who had married a man of Kei's island. Tinirau was overtaken first by grief and then anger with himself. Eventually these feelings wore off and were replaced by an overwhelming sense of outrage at Kei's ingratitude and treachery.

Calling all the men of fighting age together, he stood before them, but as he was about to incite them to wage war on Kei, Tinirau stopped, his heart sinking. This was the first such assembly in years and, looking round it, he was appalled by how few warriors he had. A generation seemed to have come where most people had delayed having children and there were too few young men of fighting age. It would be years before a force of sufficient strength could sally forth with any hope of success against so large and ruthless a bunch as Kei's people.

"Let us women go and capture Kei," Tinirau's daughter whispered.

"You are not trained in war," Tinirau began dismissively. "not strong enough in body ..." He stopped abruptly, turned to her and smiled, seeing the look in her eye.

Forty women and girls were chosen and with an abundance of flowers, strong drink and musical instruments they set off in canoes for Kei's island. Arriving in an apparently festive mood, denigrating their own men with a wink, and expressing a wish to join the on-going celebrations, they were welcomed by Kei. Singing and dancing and entertaining their hosts, passing around drink and promises never quite fulfilled, they kept the celebrations going until late into the night.

Shortly before dawn, all around Kei's large house people lay sleeping but still the chief himself seemed to be awake, though he had not moved in ages. At last, Tinirau's daughter, who had been watching carefully, crept up to him and looked deep into his seemingly wide-open and unblinking eyes. Suppressing a gasp and a giggle, she saw that the wily magician had put mother-of-pearl discs over his eyes so that in the dying firelight he would appear to be awake and still vigilant.

Tinirau's daughter and the other thirty-nine women, who were only pretending to be sleeping, quietly rose and gently lifted the small body of the slumbering Kei. Forming a line in the moonlight, running from the house to the beach, they passed him easily from one to the other. For all his eating and drinking he was still light. Even as he was bundled into a canoe and the women crowded in around him and began paddling, he barely stirred.

When they got home, again they silently formed a chain and passed the snoozing magician from hand to hand until he was safely and comfortably installed in Tinirau's house. Everyone then settled down to waiting, the whole village walking on tiptoes, with even the smallest children making no noise and no work being done.

At about midday Kei gave a yawn and stretched his limbs, the shells falling from his eyes as he opened them. The first thing he saw was the face of Tinirau.

"What are you doing here?" he asked with a start.

"I should be asking you that question."

"The magician smiled and relaxed again, yawning. "Ah, of course, you have come for your women. I take this as a sign that you recognize that we are the stronger and accept ..."

"I think you are the one who needs to understand. What are you doing here?"

"But this is my house," Kei snapped, rubbing his eyes. Hung-over and suffering an upset stomach, he was in no mood for foolishness.

"Is this your house? Is it really?" Tinirau chuckled softly.

Looking around, and with growing desperation, Kei saw that he was not at home, that there was a crowd of silent people behind Tinirau and not his people. He saw the grinning faces of Tinirau's daughter and several other women, and then he knew. He knew where he was, that he was in Tinirau's power and that the other man's vengeance was at hand. With a sickening sense of poetic justice as well, he knew what his fate would be even before Tinirau spelt it out for him.

"As you can imagine, Kei, we are very happy for you to be here," Tinirau smiled. "And we will be most pleased to have you for dinner."

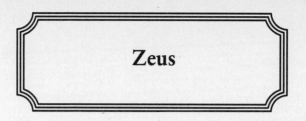

Zeus

*Number One in the pantheon of Greek gods,
Zeus was originally god of the sky and of the elements,
of the winds, clouds, rain and thunder.
Later mythmakers gave to him the attributes of divinity
and with this power he ordered the world's affairs
according to the law of fate and his own will.
He did not always get his way, and because of this he is
perhaps one of the most likeable – certainly the most human –
of all deities from any tradition included in this book.
He certainly gets up to much that one thinks a lusty god
should get up to, troublesome for himself
or others though it might be.*

First there was Chaos, or empty space, then came Gaea, the earth mother, and Eros. This was not the Eros of later times but a symbol of the attraction of forces, of magnetism itself. Eros presided over the formation of things and beings, while from Chaos came the night and the day. Gaea, meanwhile, gave birth to Uranus, that is the sky and the stars, giving him equality with her, that he might cover her entirely. Then she brought forth the lifeless sea, Pontus, with its rhythmic waves.

From the mating of Gaea and Uranus came the first race. These, the Titans, were twelve in number, six males and six females. The Cyclops also sprang from the union of Gaea and Uranus, as did the many-headed and many-handed monsters called Hecatoncheires or Centimanes.

Alas, poor Uranus was terrified by such progeny, and shut them up in the earth, even the rather comely Titans, not to mention the three with one eye in the centre of their foreheads and the three who seemed mere conglomerations of limbs and craniums. This situation, however, was not to last.

Gaea was grief stricken at first, but then the desire for restitution and an awful revenge swelled within her bosom. So it was that from this same bosom she drew a sliver of steel, which she had created there, forming it into a sharp sickle. She went to her children and told them of her grisly plans. All save the youngest of the Titans, Cronus, baulked at assisting her.

When Uranus came to Gaea again, as usual in the evening, and with the Night lay down beside her to sleep, the scheme to punish him was in place. Cronus, waiting nearby, armed with the sickle, crept out of hiding and cut off his father's testicles. These he threw into the sea but the blood dripping from them and the horrible wound was soaked up by the earth and brought forth new life in the form of giants, monsters and nymphs. The severed parts floating on the waves became a white foam which turned into a young goddess, Aphrodite.

The impotent Uranus fades from our story, leaving Cronus to free his Titan brethren but not Uranus' other prisoners. Together this new coalition continued creating the world, from the dawn to the rainbow, along with gods and demi-gods to watch over them. Furies, Harpies and humans also appeared around this time, as did the offspring of the Titans, who bred with each other or with nymphs. Cronus, too, fathered six children, mating with his sister Rhea.

These births were not regarded as happy events by Cronus. It is not clear whether he was aware of a prophecy which declared he would be deposed by his own progeny, or whether he had simply inherited his father's dislike of children. Either way, as his daughters Hesetia, Demeter and Hera, and his sons Hades and Poseidon entered the world, he swallowed them whole.

Rhea was overwhelmed with sorrow each time this happened, and by the time she was carrying her sixth child, Zeus, she had had enough and went to her parents, Gaea and Uranus, for help. Taking their advice, she journeyed to Crete, where, deep in a cavern in the thick forests around Mount Aegeum, she gave birth. Gaea took the baby away to bring up, and Rhea wrapped a large stone in swaddling cloths and gave it to Cronus, who swallowed it without hesitation, noticing nothing unusual.

Zeus was placed with the nymphs Adrasteia and Ida, who were the daughters of Melisseus, King of Crete. They lavished care and attention on the little god, and gave him a golden cradle. Adrasteia made him a present of a ball made from hoops of gold.

So, hidden from the evil eye of his father, Zeus spent his childhood in the forests around Mount Ida. Some believe his wet nurse was a nanny goat named Amaltheia, a magical animal whose appearance frightened even the gods. Zeus is said to have rewarded her later by giving her a place among the constellations. Her hide, which could not be penetrated by arrows, became his invaluable aegis. He gave his nymph foster-mothers one of her horns, the cornucopia, or horn of plenty, which could never be emptied of food or drink.

Zeus grew up happily enough in this situation. Besides the goat, he was also wet nursed by the wife of the King of Crete, while the nymphs gave him ambrosia and nectar. It may well be that the ministrations of these charming creatures affected his erotic inclinations, for goddesses would not be the only objects of his considerable passion later in life.

As he came to adulthood Zeus knew that there must be a reckoning with his father, and that Cronus must be punished for his wickedness. With the help of another immortal, he managed to get Cronus to consume a drink that made him violently ill. Retching copiously, Cronus vomited up not only the stone he had gulped down, thinking it his last born, but all the other gods he had swallowed as well.

Deposed and under the power of Zeus now, it is unclear what became of Cronus. He may have been thrown into the belly of the universe and confined there in darkness, sentenced to an enchantment of perpetual sleep in faraway Thule, or merely superannuated to live happily enough on the other side of creation.

To commemorate his triumph, Zeus laid the stone thrown up from the gut of Cronus in Pythos, at the foot of Parnassus. This later found its way to the tomb of Neoptolemus at Delphi, where it could be seen for many years.

The Titans came to resent the usurpation of the new gods, who made Olympus their home, and they rebelled. Only Oceanus, whose daughter Metis had helped him against Cronus, sided with Zeus. From their stronghold on Mount Othrys, the Titans mounted savage assaults on the Olympians.

For a decade the battle see-sawed back and forth with neither side quite strong enough to overcome the other. Then, in an act of wisdom, courage and belated justice, Zeus went into the bowels of the earth, to where the Cyclops and the Hecatoncheires had been imprisoned long before by Uranus. Unlike the Titans, they had not been liberated when Cronus defeated his father and it is easy to understand their feelings towards their brothers and sisters who had abandoned them. As allies against the Titans, they were invaluable to Zeus.

Again, battle was joined, a battle not royal but divine. Earth and sea echoed with the horrible roar, heaven itself shook and moaned, Great Olympus was made to tremble at its foundations by the combat of the immortals. They used their deadly weapons and clashed repeatedly, shouting at each other so loudly and vehemently that the noise reached up to the stars themselves. At last Zeus gained the advantage and grew ever greater in strength. His might showed forth, as straight from Heaven and Olympus he rushed at his enemies, hurling lightning bolts together with flashing thunder. The earth and all upon it burned, the sea boiled and the heat blasted the divine ether. It was as if heaven and earth had crashed together at blinding speed.

Even the Titans could no longer withstand the onslaught, as the Hecatoncheires, Cottus, Briareus and Gyes, the so-called Hundred-Armed giants, lusting for battle and foremost among Zeus's host, each hurled one hundred stones in rapid succession. This cloud of missiles overwhelmed the Titans, and drove them back down into the bowels of the earth. Here they were bound in chains and guarded by the brothers they had abandoned. All that is, save Atlas, who was forced to hold the world upon his shoulders.

No sooner had Zeus seen off the threat of the Titans than other enemies arose to challenge his power. The giants and other creatures given birth by the dripping blood of Uranus' testicles making contact with the earth now forced a new struggle on Zeus and his fellow Olympians.

Some of these formidable creatures were mainly of human shape but with feet like the tails of snakes. They had sprung from Gaea and commanded the islands, rivers and the plains around Olympus. Wearing gleaming armour and bearing enormous spears, they could lift whole mountains and fling them as weapons, or take the snows from icy regions and crush an enemy under them.

Using the surrounding hills, they built a ramp for an assault on Olympus. Zeus and the other gods stood firm and together they killed many giants but, as the oracle foretold, gods alone could not defeat the sons of Gaea. It was Hercules, son of Zeus and his last mortal concubine, Alcmena, who turned the tide in this battle.

A useful piece of intelligence won the day for him in his desperate struggle with the champion giant Alcyoneus, who had killed all the adversaries sent against him. Before the battle Athene had told Hercules that the earth of his home territory and the connection to his mother was the source of the giant's invincibility. In the ensuing battle Hercules discovered for himself the wisdom of Athene's words. He threw the giant to the ground, only to find that he was stronger when he regained his feet. Hercules changed his tactics and, hoisting him aloft, carried him away from his homeland to slay him beyond its protection.

Another powerful champion of the giants, Porphyrion, succumbed to a clever ruse. Inspired by Zeus to become enamoured of Hera, Zeus' wife, the creature pursued her, giving the god a clean shot at him with a divine arrow. Athene also entered the battle, overcoming the giants Enceladus and Pallas, making an aegis from the skin of one and burying the other under the island of Sicily.

Angry at Zeus' emphatic victory over her children, Gaea brought forth a monster called Typhoeus, which was born out of her coupling with Tartarus. This terrible creature had hands and feet that constantly moved, a hundred snake heads coming from its neck, black flame spewing from its eyes, vipers hanging from its thighs, and sprouting bristly hair all over its truly horrible body.

From each head of Typhoeus came a different voice, from yelping puppies to the sounds of the speech of gods and men, roaring lions, terrible winds, the cries of birds or of infants. Everything about the god-beast so frightened the Olympians that all fled before it except Zeus.

In the mighty struggle that ensued, Zeus was bested by Typhoeus, who cut the tendons of his hands and feet, and imprisoned him in his den. Hermes rescued his father, by stealing back the sinews. Zeus escaped, flew back to Olympus to replenish his supply of thunderbolts, which the monster had taken from him, and then resumed his attack. Typhoeus was chased to Sicily by the irate Zeus, who, picking up Mount Etna, finally imprisoned the monster beneath it and left him to rule this domain with his fiery breath.

Now the time of upheavals was over. The world settled down, volcanoes subsided, the elements were calmed, the ground no longer shook violently and mountains remained upright, rivers stayed on their established course and the sea ceased to rise up and engulf the land. The great moderator of the universe had tamed all. Evil had been defeated and harmony reigned. The authority of Zeus would never be questioned again. He was master both of the gods and of man.

This is not to say there were not annoyances. Prometheus was a considerable irritant to Zeus, though he was a friend to humanity. Vexing Zeus was part of his motivation for this, of course, though some say he even had a hand in the creation of man.

Son of one of the Titans, but judiciously neutral in the war, Prometheus was allowed into Olympus and was one of the circle of

Immortals. Perhaps he harboured a resentment of the gods who had supplanted his race, or just liked doing mischief to Zeus.

With the dominance of the Olympians, things changed greatly in the relations between humanity and Immortals. Whereas they might easily sit down and break bread together while Cronus reigned, Zeus stood on ceremony. His supremacy had to be recognized in all things. The days of mutual understanding were over. Part of the fault lay with Prometheus and it may be that he felt he had something to make up to humans. In cheating Zeus out of the better portions at one of the last feasts where gods and men sat down together, giving the best bits to the mortals, he angered the chief god so much that Zeus withheld fire from humanity. Prometheus, either from the forges of Hephaestus or the heat of the sun itself, lighted a brand of the sacred element and later brought it down to the mortals.

Furious at such temerity, Zeus cursed man further. He caused a clay and water body to be made, gave it the spark of life and with the form of a lovely virgin he sent it forth, endowed by each of the gods with some attribute, looking like the goddess of beauty herself. She was called Pandora. The contribution given her by Hermes was deceit.

Zeus sent Pandora to the brother of Prometheus, who warned him against her, but such was her seeming charm that Epimetheus ignored the warning and succumbed to her. Epimetheus became besotted with Pandora, making her welcome among humanity and little realizing what lay in her baggage. From her 'box' or, more precisely, a clay jar she carried, sprang all the terrible things suffered by man ever since.

Not stopping at this, so fed up with man was Zeus, that he brought down upon them a flood that covered the earth and drowned nearly the whole race. However, Prometheus was alert to the situation and helped his nephew and his wife, Deucalion and Pyrrha, to escape. For nine days and nights they floated in an ark until they ran aground on the peak of Mount Parnassus. There as the waters subsided, they offered prayers and displayed such profound and sincere piety that Zeus was moved to spare them and grant them a wish.

Deucalion and Pyrrha wished only for the rebirth of humanity. His anger now dispelled, the god granted this wish, though he did not forgive Prometheus, whom he had taken away and chained to a mountainside. Here an eagle would daily attack and tear at his flesh, eating part of his immortal liver, which grew back again at night, to be eaten again the next day. Despite this suffering, Prometheus did not complain, beg for mercy or do anything but continue to defy Zeus and show a rebellious spirit. He also insisted smugly that he was party to a secret that concerned Zeus, a secret involving a grave danger that might befall him.

For thirty years this torture and resistance went on until Zeus allowed Hercules to rescue the malefactor. The secret, which Prometheus now revealed, was to do with yet another of the god's amorous pursuits. If the philandering Zeus continued to court the comely Thetis, daughter of Nereus, there was every chance a son would be born who would grow to be his enemy, supplanting him.

Zeus took this sound advice and gave up his attempted seduction, letting Thetis become the bride of a mortal. However, nothing could prevent him from falling into other lusty entanglements with mortal women, nymphs, Titanesses, goddesses and just about anything else that moved. One of his favourite tactics was to appear to them as a beguiling and gentle animal of some sort, such as a beautiful white bull or a swan. Largely, the objects of his attention were flattered and overwhelmed by the interest of the greatest of the Olympian gods.

It was such an episode that resulted in the birth of Hercules himself, of course, much perturbing Hera, the chief goddess and wife of Zeus. Poor Hercules was to suffer from her wrath ever after, and lose a kingdom to a man who would be his sworn enemy and sometime master. But that is another story.

Big Trouble
with Little Gods

*Much of the mythology of Eastern Europe was
lost when Christianity extended its 'civilizing' influence into this
part of the world. Nothing much is known of their great divinities
and all that is left is the host of minor rustic gods which the Slav
peasants would hope to placate in order to make their harsh
lives a little easier. Even once the Slavs were Christianized
they continued to observe the traditional niceties where
these small spirits were concerned. It obviously must have
entailed an awful lot of effort.*

Ivan shouted and reeled about the house in anger, knocking into things and searching for his wife so that he could beat her. He considered himself the very model of a hard-working Russian peasant and more than entitled to get drunk upon occasion whether she liked it or not. It was only natural, after all.

All the way back from the village he had brooded over the inevitable nagging he would receive on his arrival home. He had decided to take none of it, and to attack rather than defend. He would point out Natasha's negligent housework and thrash her before she could argue about his drinking.

As he wandered out into the farmyard and called for her, he began to suspect that she had been tipped off by the Domovoi, one of the small household gods which invariably took a wife's side in domestic quarrels. He well knew they would have pulled her hair as a warning that he wished to beat her and that she, Natasha, would have heeded the signal and gone into hiding. In his fury and inebriation Ivan dared to shout a curse at the Domovoi before stumbling back into the house, where he fell asleep on the floor.

The Domovoi were diminutive divinities, relations of the creator, but they had rebelled against him and been thrown out of heaven. After falling to earth they had landed on people's houses and in their yards. The Domovoi liked to live under the threshold of a front door, or near the stove, while their wives, Domovikha, preferred the cellar. In time they had become attached to the humans who lived there and were sometimes helpful. Certainly, they were never as mischievous and downright dangerous as their fellow exiled spirits who had landed in the fields and forests. They would often notify the inhabitants of the house of some impending trouble. The humans would hear weeping if there was to be something like a death in the family, for example.

That night, as Ivan dropped into a drunken sleep, he imagined he heard such weeping. When he woke the next morning he looked about him and knew that the mess that greeted him was of his own making. He had been unjust in intending to accuse his wife of bad housekeeping. There was another female spirit who lived in people's houses beside the Domovoi and Domovikha and she was called the Kikimora. This little goddess would help a human wife in her domestic chores if the wife were conscientious. If slack in her duties, the Kikimora would tickle the children to keep them awake at night and do other things to make life more difficult.

Ivan had to admit that Natasha had never been particularly hampered in this way or forced to make a fern tea with which to scrub out the kitchen pots and appease the deity. Obviously, she always pleased the Kikimora and received her aid. Hung-over and ashamed now, Ivan went into the kitchen to find Natasha preparing breakfast, stony faced but saying nothing about his latest binge.

They ate in silence and then Ivan went out and about his work, but all along he was uncomfortable about the weeping he had heard the night before. Everyone in the family was well, though that did not mean someone might not become ill or have an accident. Some instinct told Ivan this was not the problem.

He was worried about the harvest and the white horse he had craftily bought very cheaply the week before. He decided to take certain precautions, some of which should have been seen to as soon as he got the horse. It had already kicked out several boards in its stall, which would have to be replaced, trodden on his toe twice and bitten him once. These things were not the horse's fault but that of the Dvorovoi, the spirit of the yard, who hated animals with white coats.

Ivan put sheep's wool in the horse's stall, hung about it some glittering pieces of tin and glass and left a slice of bread to appease the Dvorovoi.

"Tsar Dvorovoi," Ivan said ceremoniously. "Master, friendly neighbour, I offer thee this gift in a sign of gratitude. Forgive this beast its colour, be kind to the cattle, look after and feed them well."

If these measures did not work Ivan would take more drastic action against the Dvorovoi. He would stab the fence around the yard with a pitchfork and carry a whip with a thread from a winding sheet with which to beat the Dvorovoi. Worse still, he might hang up the dead body of a magpie, a thing the wicked little deity dreaded.

Next, Ivan went out into his fields, having gathered eggs and a small cockerel, thinking as he did so that at least white chickens were safe from the Dvorovoi, because they were protected by the god of chickens, represented by a round stone with a hole in it and kept in the yard.

Then Ivan wondered if the barn spirit, the Ovinnik, would become jealous of his offering to the Dvororvoi. This type of god habitually lived in the corners of barns and looked not unlike a rather scruffy black cat. The Ovinnik could bark like dogs or laugh their little heads off, but they could also be very mean spirited and were known to burn a man's barn to the ground. Ivan's unease increased.

Out in the fields, he looked carefully around to make sure he was not being observed by anyone. Not that he would have been thought superstitious, but the exercise itself would be useless if it was seen by anyone else and the Polevik would not be placated. With two eyes of different colours, and grass instead of hair on his head, the Polevik ruled the field.

Ivan took the two eggs and the old rooster who could not crow anymore, as stipulated in tradition, and placed them in a ditch. No one saw him make the sacrifice and he felt a little better as he walked home. The spirit of the field would not damage his crops and hopefully not throttle him, if on some summer night he fell asleep in the field a bit drunk.

So it was that as days went by Ivan began to feel better about everything and after his next drinking bout, receiving a mild rebuff from his wife, he only beat her mildly. The trouble was he had been sick on himself, and had spent a further night on the floor.

Again he felt bad for beating Natasha and was also troubled by rumours he had heard the night before, of plague afflicting people several villages away. It might mean bad times were ahead for them, too.

When he stumbled out to the bathhouse, Natasha had already washed his shirt and was hanging it up outside. She did not look at him as he shuffled by. Was it possible that she resented the mild beating he had administered, or did she simply sense that he regretted it himself and did not respect him for that? Her father, after all, had been tireless and uncompromising in beating her mother, an excellent woman, who had obviously benefited greatly from it.

Hung-over and depressed, Ivan would be especially careful to leave a little water in the bath for the Bannik, the god of the washhouse. This deity would allow three bathers or three groups of bathers into the bath without receiving an offering, but he expected the fourth to do so and leave him some water. Ivan intended to do this. To anger the Bannik was never wise. The god was known to invite devils and forest spirits to visit him and could be nasty if crossed. Anyone disturbing him during his own bath would have boiling water thrown on them, and some might even be strangled.

The Bannik was not all bad and dangerous, however. He could

agree to tell fortunes. Ivan decided to test his luck, to see if the Bannik would tell him something of what the future held, whether it was to be good or bad.

After taking his bath, Ivan, in the prescribed manner, opened the bathhouse door slightly and presented his naked back to the open air. Patiently he waited for the Bannik to communicate. A scratch with its claw meant bad luck, a soft stroke with its palm showed the future would be bright. Just as Ivan was thinking the deity would not oblige, he yelped painfully, slammed the door behind him and leapt back into the bath. Something sharp had just been dragged down his naked back.

Shivering, he sat in the hot water, which Natasha had heated for him. In spite of it being late on a summer morning, goose pimples crept over his skin. What was going to happen to them? What darkness awaited them? Ivan was distracted in his work all that day and went again to the village that night to drink away his fears.

Natasha accompanied him this time, saying she wanted to visit her mother and younger sister, with whom she would stay the night. Ivan was glad of the chance to come home alone, to find no disapproving presence awaiting him and no temptation to lash out at.

It was late when he started to weave his way home, just as full of anxiety as before he had begun drinking. Everyone in the village had seemed in a similar worried state, the men depressed and the women full of whispering and shifty looks, though extra gentle with the children and more tolerant of their menfolk.

There was no moon and though he should have found his way back to the farm in his sleep, Ivan became disoriented. He stumbled down the wrong path and before he knew it he was in the forest. When he realized this, a new fear assailed him. The Leshy would surely be about on such a night as this. This bearded forest spirit could change his size from as tall as an oak in the deep woods to so tiny it could hide beneath a leaf. The Leshy delighted in leading travellers astray, or worse.

These spirits threw no shadow, had green hair and eyes that often popped out of their heads, wore a red sash and, most peculiarly of all, they had their left shoe on their right foot. Ivan knew that he could be forced to blunder all around the forest trying to find his way out only to come back to the same spot, and all the while hearing whistling, human voices, the sounds of birds or animals, sobbing or the laughter of an over-excited woman. The last thing Ivan wished to encounter in his feeble condition was the Leshy. Then suddenly, sure enough, as if to confirm his fears, he could hear a woman-like voice somewhere in the distance.

Without hesitation, Ivan took the only measures he knew would save him. Plopping down beneath a tree, swiftly he began to undress. It was a clumsy business, but at last he managed it. Then as quickly and with even more difficulty, he began to dress himself again, but with everything on backwards.

At last he was finished and started to make his way through the trees, hoping it was the way he had come. Then he remembered something and with a shudder he dropped to the ground once more and pulled off his shoes. He had nearly forgotten to put his left shoe on his right foot and the right on the left. This done, he gave a relieved sigh, struggled to his feet again and carried on.

After a while he seemed to come out of the forest. He could feel a cool breeze and see starlight above him, not just the darkness of branches, and he could hear running water. At this point he lost his balance and with a great splash fell into the millpond.

He scrambled to his feet and, slipping and sliding, desperately tried to drag himself out of the water. This was no place to be. He was certain that a Vodyanoi was about to grab him, to pull him down to a palace made from crystal and parts of sunken boats. These water spirits hated humans and loved to drown and then enslave them. Inhabiting lakes, pools, streams and rivers, the Vodyanoi particularly liked to congregate around a milldam. Often they appeared to have a human face, ridiculously big toes, paws instead of hands, long horns, a tail and eyes like burning coals. They could change colour with the phases of the moon and would even take the shape of a pretty girl sitting in the water combing her wet hair – anything to make it easier for them to drag an unwary late bather or passer-by to his death.

Finally hauling himself out of the millpond, Ivan followed the stream back towards the village. At least now he knew where he was and in the circumstance deemed it best to face the scowls of his wife and female in-laws, rather than try to make it home. The trouble was, he realized that being so near the water he was still endangered. Not only might some Vodyanoi be lurking there, but the Rusalki, as well. He did not know which frightened him more.

Rusalki were the spirits of the drowned women and infants who had died in this stream. There had been quite a number over the years. Like the Vodyanoi, they would try to drown him too, though at this time of year they might just as well be up in the trees in the forest or frolicking about within it. Shrivelled and corpse-like, the Rusalki would be naked and have eyes that shone like green fire. They would drown him slowly, tortuously. How he wished he was carrying a leaf of absinthe with which to ward them off.

There was far more forest ahead of him, towards home, than in the direction he had come. He sprinted through the woods and joined the road he had meant to take in the first place. For an instant, while catching his breath, he thought better of going to the village and to his mother-in-law's house. Then he heard more strange noises coming from somewhere to his right. That decided him. The village was not far.

Now, what Ivan did not know, what none of the men of the village knew, was that the women were abroad that night performing a secret ceremony to ward off the plague. At midnight, the old women had crept out of their homes and prowled around the village summoning the other women to slip out to join them. Nine virgins and three widows from their number were chosen and led out of the village. The chosen women would strip off down to their shifts, the virgins loosing their hair from the braids they customarily wore and the widows covering their heads with shawls. One of the widows was harnessed to a plough, which would be driven by another, while the virgins armed themselves with scythes. The rest of the women carried macabre objects, such as the skulls of dead animals. As was the custom, the procession set off marching, howling and shrieking, ploughing a furrow around the village from which the powerful spirits of the earth would emerge to destroy the germs of evil that caused the plague.

Stumbling along the road, wet and still drunk, Ivan froze in his tracks when the terrifying noise made by the women assaulted his ears and he caught sight of the weird parade looming up out of the darkness. He took them for a band of vicious Rusalki bent on taking him back to the stream to drown him, but so horror-struck was he that he could not move a muscle.

The women did not hesitate to do what was traditional when a man chanced to encounter such a procession. They quickly surrounded him and beat him silly, knocking him out cold.

In the morning, Ivan awoke in a ditch, amazed that he was still alive. Why had the Rusalki not drowned him? Battered and bruised, yet not as hung-over as might be expected, he ran home as fast as his condition would allow.

Natasha was shocked, utterly dumfounded at his appearance. His nose was definitely broken and his right ear would always resemble a garden vegetable now. She did not say a word, did not nag him, question him or so much as shake her head. He had to admit to himself that even if she had nagged and complained, he did not have the strength or heart to beat her. Indeed, he silently vowed never to beat her again.

Both now as she set about cleaning and bandaging her husband's cuts, lumps and scrapes, and forever afterwards whenever she smiled over his bent nose and cauliflower ear, Natasha forgave him his former ways. Ivan did not abandon drink altogether, of course, but he made a point of coming home a good deal earlier and less drunk than before.

The plague did not come to the village and the little gods tended to give less worry. Ivan, though, took very good care for the rest of his life to please the benevolent ones and avoid the rest. The Rusalki were always his chief concern and once or twice they visited him in his dreams, as if to ensure that he would continue to fear and respect them in equal measure.

Sedna, Mother of Sea Beasts

The goddess Sedna appears in her most attractive
form in this story. In her one-eyed guise, though,
she was such a horrible sight that only a shaman or medicine man –
called an 'angakoq' in the Inuit language –
could bear to look at her.

They were gawky youths, milling around outside the igloo and being pests, so shy that they had come courting in a group. All hung back, teasing each other, pushing first one forwards then the next, no one daring to speak to the object of their dumb admiration. From what she could see, none of them was the least bit handsome, strong or prosperous and, as for wit, that didn't figure in their scheme.

In those early days of creation, Sedna was regarded as the loveliest girl alive among the Inuit people. The attentions of all sorts of young men, both local and from far away lands, were nothing new to her and not particularly welcome. She could choose and so she felt it was within her rights to be choosy. It was only sensible.

"Go away," she told them. "I would more gladly marry a dog than any of you."

That was her favourite way of dismissing suitors, and she said it often to many disappointed young men.

"Oh, Sedna," complained Angusta, her father, when she came back inside. "When will you meet someone good enough? I need help with the hunting. Ever since your mother died, it has only been the two of us. Would not a husband for you and a son-in-law for me be a fine thing?"

"What if I married one of the men from far away and went off with him? How would you like that?"

"I would be lonely but if you such took a foreigner, at least I would only have to hunt for myself."

"I'm not marrying just anybody," she said firmly.

Time went by and still not a week or month passed without some fellow arriving to ask for Sedna's hand, to awkwardly try to show off his prowess as a hunter or to moon around ineffectually. All were turned away with a flea in their ear. One or two of these suitors wished he were a dog so as to have stood a better chance, because she was so beautiful and spirited. Others were glad they were not dogs, and need not have a wife so sharp tongued and pitiless. Eventually the stream of suitors became a trickle.

"At least stop saying that about dogs," her father advised. "We have a dog." He patted their pet's eager head and went on. "There is ugly talk that you have married it and that such a thing is bad luck and will bring bad luck on everyone."

"Nonsense," Sedna sniffed.

One day a handsome, mysterious young man came to their seaside dwelling. Dressed in furs and armed with an ivory spear, he was a striking figure. For some time however, he sat in his canoe, saying nothing, just riding the gentle waves, watching Sedna going about her chores. Finally, she faced him, hands on hips, ready to dismiss him. Then he spoke.

"You work hard for a beauty," he said in rather a nice voice. "That is very good to see."

"But no good to you," she replied. She did not turn away though, add a cutting remark or speak of a preference for dogs.

"Come away with me. Come to the land of the birds. Come with me to where you will never be hungry or cold. Where you will rest in my fine home on lush bear skins, your lamp will be ever filled with oil and the cooking pot always full of meat." He seemed to sing to her rather than merely to speak.

"No thank you," Sedna sneered before giving her habitual

response. "I would rather marry ..."

"A dog, I know. Everyone says so. But why not something else for a change?"

"What?" she exclaimed.

"Never mind, but I think you would like my country, if you would only come there. What fine ivory necklaces I would give you and ..." He continued in melodical vein, painting such a wonderful picture of his home that in spite of herself Sedna became fascinated both by it and by the handsome stranger.

Gradually, as he talked she moved closer to the edge of the water and he paddled nearer too.

"So," he concluded. "Will you come?"

"Why not?" Sedna shrugged. As she glanced in the direction of her home, her father appeared and looked curiously at her and the strange young man. "I'll marry this one, then," she shouted to him with a brief wave to him and the dog at his heels.

The stranger helped her into his canoe and they rowed away, leaving her father and the dog inconsolable. They would never again see her on the shores where their home stood and, despite everything, they had been fairly happy.

When, after a long time on the water, Sedna and her new husband came to the place he had so boasted of, she was shocked, though she had been subtly warned on the journey. Up close, once she was over her rather foolishly abrupt parting from her father, and the tears in her eyes had cleared, she could see that her husband was not the man she had thought he was. There was something not quite right about him and his possessions, even the canoe.

His home was a rocky island where nothing seemed to grow, where no animals could survive but the many squawking birds surrounding the place. The fine abode he had described was just a shabby hut of twigs and stones where no human could live. The furs were nothing but a few scraps of uncured animal hides.

She turned to him in anger and horror at his temerity, but her words froze in her throat. The handsome young man appeared even less human now. His shape was changing before her eyes, the human figure fading and the rather vague and ghostly image of a bird taking its place.

"You are a bird spirit," she cried in anguish. "A Kokksaut." That is what the Inuit call such creatures.

"Yes," her husband squawked. "But I can look human, I will be a handsome man again for you in a moment. I will bring you good food, and just look at the home I have made for you."

"You have tricked me," she said, sitting down on a rock and bursting into tears.

"I saw you first while I was flying and that is when I fell in love with your beauty."

"With my beauty," she muttered between sobs.

Of course the bird spirit did not know how people lived and Sedna was physically miserable on the desolate island. The scraps of carrion meat he brought were disgusting to her and the shelter was quite inadequate. Most of all she could not get used to her husband. Neither as himself nor in his guise as a vague and unreal man could she overcome her repugnance or her anger at the cruel trick he had played on her.

Now, Angusta had never got over the sudden departure of his daughter and missed her very much. One day he and the dog set off in a canoe to find her. People had seen where the young man had come from, more or less, far though it was and difficult to find. Eventually Angusta arrived to find Sedna utterly forlorn, lamenting her fate and delighted to see him.

The bird spirit was away and, taking Sedna in his arms, Angusta carried her to his boat as the dog barked its greeting. Covering her with furs, he set off, paddling as fast as he could.

When the bird spirit returned and found Sedna gone and the marks where the canoe had been drawn up on the rocky beach, he took to the air again in search of her. Guessing what had happened, he knew which direction to go in and soon came within sight of Angusta's canoe. Changing into his man-shape again some distance behind, the bird spirit paddled hard to catch up. As he neared the fugitives, he shouted for them to stop.

"Where is Sedna?" he cried. "Please let me see her."

Angusta ignored him and rowed on as the bird spirit followed, calling out to Sedna. Finally he gave up and turned back into a bird, swooping on them, still crying out like a loon. Then he disappeared, flying up into the growing darkness where he caused the sea to become very rough and dangerous, throwing the boat about and frightening Angusta almost as terribly as the bird spirit himself had begun to do. The more he thought about what had happened the more he realized his offence. As the storm worsened, he knew he had made an enemy of the powers of nature.

In despair of his life, certain that it would bring bad luck on his people if he did nothing, and suspecting it was the fate of his beautiful daughter all along, he picked her up and threw her over the side of the boat.

"It must be," he called to her in sorrow.

When Sedna, pale and in shock, came to the surface she reached up and clung to the side of the boat. The waves pulled at her, claiming her as she struggled to climb back into the craft.

Franticly her father beat at her hands, pried at her fingers and in the end chopped at them with a paddle. Sedna's fingertips were cut off and for a moment she disappeared beneath the waves but then she kicked and swam up once more, clutching at the side of the boat.

Again Angusta struck with the paddle and now Sedna's fingers were cut off at the second joint and she fell away under the sea. But then a third time she surfaced and held onto the boat with her bleeding hands. Flailing at them in near delirium while the dog shivered in the prow of the small boat, Angusta chopped off Sedna's fingers at the knuckle.

Slipping for the last time beneath the waves, Sedna sank. But the severed bit of her fingers turned into new sea creatures even as she died a human woman. Her fingertips had become seals, the second joints 'ojuk' or deep-sea seals. The next joints caused walruses and whales to come into being.

With the sacrifice complete, the sea calmed and soon the boat reached the shore. Angusta tied Sedna's dog to a tent pole and went inside. Horrified at what he had done, exhausted by his labours and by grief, he threw himself upon his bed and fell into not so much a deep sleep as unconsciousness.

Overnight there was an unusually high tide which came far up the shore and swallowed up the tent and everything in it. Thus Angusta and the dog were reunited with Sedna in the depths of the sea, where they still rule over the Adlivun, 'those beneath us'. Here souls go after death to expiate the sins committed during life, for a period of time or for eternity, according to their deserts.

As the Spirit of the Sea and Mother of Sea Creatures, Sedna must be placated. This is not always easy as she has little regard for humans. An Angakoq, or shaman, must spiritually journey to her domain, confess the sins of men, beg forgiveness and comb the goddess's hair, for with no fingers she cannot do this herself. This simple act of homage makes her feel better, and in return she will allow people to take some of her charges for food.

Hercules and His Labours

Hercules (or Heracles) is the undisputed hero of Greek mythology, as befits his parentage, being the illegitimate offspring of the god Zeus and a mortal woman. Although he is thought of as the mythological personification of superhuman strength, in pagan Greece his name was principally invoked when men were in need of protection and facing great danger. Medical powers were also attributed to him. Spiritual descendant of Gilgamesh and ancestor of Superman, Hercules is the most enduring Western-world hero. He is also one of the few anywhere who has a foot firmly planted in both myth and legend.

The fair Alcmena gazed lovingly on the face of her husband, a nobleman of Thebes. He had just returned from the war upon the people who had killed her brothers and, at last, she would give herself to him. Of course, they had been married for some time but she had refused him until her family was avenged. And here he was – more handsome than ever, full of news of the successful conclusion of the fighting; strong, tender and very, very eager.

Amphitryon took her in his arms and kissed her with an electrifying passion that thrilled and surprised her. There was something magical in that kiss and something enchanted about the night that followed. In a truly wonderful sense, it seemed to last for ages, or at least more like three glorious nights instead of only one.

In the morning, while he went to wash, and her attendants came into the chamber to help her, Alcmena dwelt with pleasure on her memory of their embrace, the ecstasy and the tenderness. She lived again the happy, satisfied look in her husband's eyes moments ago, as he left her.

Then, suddenly, Amphitryon was back, shouting impatiently for the attendants to leave the chamber. He was very different now. His clothes were dusty, he smelled of the sweat of horses and his hair was not clean. He pulled her to him roughly, kissed her hard and began excitedly to repeat the news of the night before, finally proclaiming that, having killed her brothers' killers, he desired nothing more than to consummate their marriage without delay.

With that, he threw the confused Alcmena upon the bed and with unshaven cheeks and reeking armpits took her vigorously before falling fast asleep. Slipping out from under him and shakily getting out of bed, Alcmena left the room in search of her maids. From them she learned that Amphitryon and his men had only just returned from the wars. Only she, it appeared, had seen him the night before.

The prophet Tiresias, a mouthpiece of Zeus who lived nearby, soon clarified matters: Zeus, the king of the gods, had again succeeded in seducing a mortal woman. It was some consolation that the god had not taken the form of an animal this time, and she would not, as others surely must, go around feeling a flutter in her heart whenever she saw a white bull or a swan. In whatever form he chose to assume for his exploits, Zeus was a hard act to follow and after him the real Amphitryon had been more than a little disappointing. How many wives of mortal men have not experienced that?

The joy of finding that she was carrying twins soon expanded her thinking. She looked upon her seduction as just one of those things that happen, a compliment of sorts and perhaps a blessing. Amphitryon shared his wife's attitude, and, cleaned up, rested and less anxious, he soon proved to be as good a man as a woman could hope for.

On Olympus, as Alcmena's time drew near, Zeus became excited by the coming birth of this new son. He went so far as to boast of it and swore a great oath about the future of the child.

"Today shall be born a man of the race of my blood, who shall rule all who live around him." Zeus cried proudly, envisaging his son as a hero who would become a protector of both immortals and mortals.

This greatly displeased Hera, his wife and the principal Olympian goddess, who was very jealous of his dalliance with Alcmena and that she, his consort, was not intended to play any part in the creation of this super-hero. The goddess decided to use the imprecision of Zeus's declaration to her advantage. She knew that elsewhere another mortal woman, whose husband was a son of Perseus, himself a product of one of Zeus' innumerable affairs, was to give birth about the same time as Alcmena. With the help of Ilythia, goddess of childbearing, Hera caused this mother to be brought to term prematurely, while hastening unseen to the bedchamber of Alcmena, she left her lingering in labour for another day. Thus, the first child, called Eurystheus, fulfilled Zeus' oath, and, chief god though he was, he could not go back on it. Eurystheus would be king of Greece, andAlcmena's child by Zeus, Hercules, would spend his life fulfilling a series of arduous tasks set by his king.

Hera wasn't through with Hercules, however. Not long after the birth of Hercules and his twin brother, Iphicles, she sent two snakes to kill them. Iphicles was wholly Amphitryon's son, although neither parent was as yet clear on this point, and the snakes were not minded to differentiate either. The two innocents were asleep in the big bronze shield used for their cradle when the attack was made.

The snakes slithered into the cradle and were not discovered until a nurse came to check on the children. She saw the tails extending from the cradle, writhing and wriggling horribly, and with a scream of terror ran bravely towards the bronze shield. The woman's cry brought Alcmena quickly onto the scene, followed by other attendants and, moments later, Amphitryon and some men of the palace guard.

In one part of the cradle lay little Iphicles, helpless and howling with fear. The infant Hercules, though, was engaged in an almighty struggle against the deadly intruders. By the time help arrived he had throttled the life out of them with his tiny fists, which were wrapped around the snakes, an inch below their heads.

The bitter anxiety with which Amphitryon had been gripping his sword evaporated and his expression turned to joy. He could see the beasts were dead, although all round him the women were still screaming, pulling at the serpents' tails, and Alcmena, pale and determined, was both weeping and furious. Amphitryon knew beyond doubt which of the two children was his son. The spirit and power of Hercules were the gifts of Zeus.

When everyone had recovered from their shock and the celebrations for the infants' escape from danger were beginning, Tiresias arrived. He began to make prophesies about the life of Hercules. He told of how many monsters more he would kill on land and sea, how he would bring low men of wickedness and insolence. He foresaw the hero's future battles with giants on the plain of Phlegra in the war to come, saw him beneath an onrush of missiles. But in the end, Hercules would achieve personal peace for eternity as a prize for his labours and would be awarded a place among the gods.

Naturally the proud parents of such a wonder-child could not lavish enough attention and education on him as he grew up. The best tutors were found in all suitable subjects. He learned chariot driving from his mortal father Amhitryon, wrestling from Autolycus, archery form Eurytus and music from Linus, a son of Apollo.

While the youthful Hercules was not a bad student of music, it was perhaps the least of his accomplishments. In any case, he found it frustrating, and, during a particularly tiresome lesson when still only an adolescent, he hit Linus with a lyre and killed him. As happened so often with this hot-headed man-god, he hardly knew his own strength.

As punishment for this deed, Hercules was sent away to the far Theban pastures on Mount Cithaeron to mind cattle. It was in this remote place that his adventures began, initially with minor activities such as chasing off thieves and frightening wolves away from the herd. When he was about eighteen, however, things changed.

One day Hercules found himself looking at the mauled carcass of yet another calf, his emotions a mixture of anger and an unwarranted sense of failure. The fact that something was killing his charges the young man took personally. Unlike on previous occasions, this time there was a clear track to follow. The paw prints were those of a lion, and even this knowledge did not alter his determination to hunt the beast down.

Leaving the care of the herd to some servants, Hercules armed himself with a spear and set off alone. He hoped to track the beast to its lair and kill it while it slept off its meal, but the track continued for mile upon mile and as the hours went by it seemed the lion was headed for some far off point, with a purpose. After many hours on the move the young hero wished he had brought along some food of his own and perhaps men and dogs. Cornering the animal by himself would be difficult.

As the day drew to a close and he still seemed to be no closer to the lion, though the tracks remained easy enough to follow, Hercules began to wonder where he might find shelter. The lion kept on, however, not going farther into the hills but down now into a valley below. Darkness came before they reached it and though he was loath to stop, Hercules was forced to find somewhere to huddle out of the wind and light rain and try to sleep. In the night he heard the lion roaring not far off as if to signal that it too had stopped to rest.

At dawn Hercules cast around for the tracks again. The misery of the wet night was made up for by the fresh, clear tracks he soon found. The big cat was again on the move, making steadily for the lush valley in plain view as the sun came up higher into the sky. Pausing only to nibble a few berries, Hercules trailed it relentlessly all that morning.

This was strange country to the Theban lad and he did not know the people who lived there, but he was not going to stop to find out until he had killed the lion or it had killed him. Around noon he heard the sound of lowing cattle. He came upon a herd and shortly afterwards discovered the remains of a half-eaten bullock. The tracks of the lion were much fresher now and Hercules reckoned the beast could not be far ahead.

Just as he sensed he was on the very heels of his quarry, the tracks disappeared, the earth hardened and Hercules surmised the lion must have made for higher ground among the rocks above. As he was contemplating his next move some herdsmen asked him what business he had in their country. When he told them, they conducted him to the nearby town of Thespiae, where he was welcomed and given food and shelter in the king's palace.

Thespius, the king, was overjoyed to see Hercules, especially on learning of his mission. Expert trackers would be put at his disposal the next morning, if he wished them, the king said.

"Indeed," Thespius said as they dined that evening. "We know where the lion has its den, if it has not moved again. We can find the new one if it has, but ..."

"Why then, Sire," Hercules asked, "do you not kill it?"

The king shrugged. "As you see, I am growing old."

"But your younger men?"

"Have you not noticed how few of them there are in Thespiae? We have recently had a war. Though we won it, we lost many, many men. The lion has killed two of our heroes already and lest we lose more, I have banned all our men from hunting it. We can only track it and hope to frighten it away from our cattle and sheep. If a few are taken it is a small price to pay."

"After tomorrow," the young man swore, "you will pay it no more."

However, unbeknown to Hercules, Thespius had conceived other plans, so impressed was he with the fine figure this young man of Thebes cut. A hero, obviously, through and through, and not to be lightly wasted on any lion. Of course, there was little hope that Hercules could be persuaded to stay on in Thespiae; he took his responsibilities to his homeland too seriously for that. Surely, though, some other, longer-term benefit could be realized from his stay among them.

That night one of Thespius' many daughters showed Hercules to his room, turned down his bed for him and did not leave until morning.

Enchanted, the young man hardly noticed the next day when, try as they might, the Thespiaen trackers could not find the lion. Excitedly he ate his dinner that night with the king and went to bed early, only to discover another of the king's daughters escorting him thence. His disappointment was short lived. She too stayed the night and the hero enjoyed her embraces immensely.

Again the next day the trail was cold, though the trackers insisted the lion had not gone back to the high Theban pastures to hunt, or anywhere else. Hercules was not inclined to argue with them. That night yet another daughter of the king shared his bed. Only now did he learn with interest that Thespius had fifty daughters, all of them pretty. Some were widows, others virgins and all had begun to despair of having children to continue the king's line and secure their future.

With such sport at night and the odd return engagement with favourites in the day time, between futile lion hunts, Hercules was in the sort of heaven a man of not yet twenty dreams of. With his heroic stamina, he was able to take full advantage of the opportunity. His divine daddy would have been justly proud of him.

As the days ran into one another and nearly all the daughters had been his bed partners, even such a beguiling situation began to pale. There was never enough time with the ones he really liked. Equal attention among them all was sought after the first carefully regulated night. Some were not as attractive or interesting as others, one or two dropped out of the game early, complaining of fainting fits and upset stomachs in the mornings.

The jealous, whimsical, disparaging looks of some of the old veterans around the court also took their toll. Hercules had yet to prove himself properly in a man's world. Yet out of some strange sense of duty and service, and determined to finish a task he had begun, the young man carried on regardless, until the night the last of the daughters of Thespius had been bedded. Luckily, the final few, rather shy, daughters who were his own age or a bit younger had been far less diverting, and he was left with no great desire to dally with them again. His thoughts now turned once more to the lion.

His mind was set on killing the thing and going home. Both the king and his trackers could sense this. They led him, with an audience of men and women, straight to the creature's lair, where it had just dragged in a new victim. The lamb, not quite dead, could still be heard bleating from inside the cavern, though this was cut short as the royal party approached.

"Wait until the animal has fed and is full and slow, or even sleeping," the guide whispered to Hercules.

"No," Hercules shook his head. "I will take it now. Its anger and agility make no difference to me."

As he strode towards the cave, out of which growling and ripping sounds could be heard clearly, the eldest daughter of Thespius remarked: 'And he was such a nice boy.' Others in the group insisted he had something special about him and that he 'just might stand a chance'. They were actually taking bets by the time he entered the mouth of the cave.

The ceiling was low and got progressively lower the farther in he went, eventually forcing him to crawl on his hands and knees. All the while he could hear the lion, who smelled and heard him too, its growling growing more fierce by the second. The light was bad and getting worse as Hercules reached the back of the cave, where he could just about make out the shape of the lion crouching beside the torn body of the dead lamb. It was a large male with teeth like daggers, blood dripping from its jaws as it roared at him and inched nearer, ready to spring.

Wisdom said let the lion charge and use the animal's strength and forward movement to drive the spear home. But Hercules was not wise; he was young and angry and a storm of ferocious aggression rose in him at the sight of his long-sought prey. Emitting a terrible growl of his own, he charged, as best he could in so small a space. The lion fell back in shock, turned and attempted to leap round him but Hercules was too nimble and drove his spear through the creature's body just behind its heart. This manoeuvre brought Hercules face-to-face with his prey, which, despite its wound, was still very much alive, snapping and clawing at him as it writhed on the spear shaft.

Hercules grasped the shaft and with all his might lifted the lion and slammed it against the wall of the cave, then swung it around and drove its head into the other wall before lifting it again and this time batting it against the ceiling. The lion though was immensely strong and throughout this onslaught dug into Hercules' flesh with the lethally sharp claws of its hind legs, tearing at his arm, left leg and side. Hercules redoubled his efforts and bludgeoned the lion even more ferociously until the beast's grip began to weaken and finally went limp. The ferocious struggle now over, Hercules dragged the dead beast to the mouth of the cave, where he hefted it onto his shoulder before emerging into daylight.

The loud gasp which greeted his appearance was followed by a silence as the group outside the cave stared at him in wonder and horror. His clothes were in tatters, and he was covered in blood – both his own and that of the vanquished beast. With his numerous injuries, Hercules looked almost as bad as the lion. Then the spell broke and everyone ran up to congratulate him and to tend his wounds. The women were solicitous and the men deeply impressed. The young hero instantly recognized the utter sincerity of the gratitude and respect these people showed him. This victory was a turning point for Hercules, who took from it the knowledge that this kind of action was what he was born for. He had discovered his true destiny.

One of the scratches was high up on his thigh and only great consideration would have made it possible for the hero to continue his pleasuring of any of the king's daughters. The ones who might have been careful enough were too shy to try it and the others were certain to become too rambunctious if allowed, so in the end he limited the amount of nursing he received at their hands. In any case, by this time he was more than anxious to go home.

Word was sent to the herdsman in the high pastures of his father when Hercules set off from Thespiae for Thebes. With fine new clothes, a chariot and horses – all gifts from Thespius – Hercules neared his home. Word of his exploit had gone ahead of him and he was lookeing forward to his triumphant return with mounting excitement.

He had only a few miles left to journey when he stopped to rest his horses in a little glade. There was good grazing and a brook beside it where he could water his animals and freshen up. As he sat in the shade of a tree, another chariot, headed out of Thebes, arrived and behind it a loaded cart. The man in the chariot jumped down and harshly ordered his servants about their tasks.

"Good day, friend," the man said to Hercules. "Are you bound for Thebes?"

"Yes," the young hero replied.

"I see you are a Thespiaen by your dress," the other man laughed. "My advice is when in Thebes, kick the men hard and watch your purse around the women. They are a cowardly and dishonest race."

"And who might you be to say so?" Hercules asked, more astonished than angered by the stranger's outburst. "It was not so when I was last there."

"You are young, a mere puppy who would not notice. I am the representative of King Erginus of Orchomenus and I have been collecting tribute from Thebes. We get very rich pickings from the dogs, I can tell you, boy. Rich pickings."

"How so?"

"Why, we threaten war and the cowards pay. Creon, the Theban king, is a helpless fool. Thebes lacks men, too, like Thespiae. Unlike you Thespiaens, though, they have not fought in ages and have become soft."

"Even Amphitryon?"

"As timid as the rest, I imagine," the herald said with a laugh. "I do not know him personally."

Hercules seized the man by his neck and a mere look from his fiery eyes was enough to warn off the servants, who backed away openly smiling.

"I am the son of Amphitryon," Hercules hissed in the herald's face, "who is not a coward and whose country pays no tribute."

Drawing a dagger, Hercules whipped off the man's nose and ears and with a kick to his insolent backside, sent him on his way, without his men or the cartload of booty.

In Thebes everyone's joy at his return and the story of his success in Thespiae turned to trepidation when they saw the cart and heard the story of what he had done to the herald of Orchomenus. War would be the certain result.

"Good," said Hercules. "Good."

The Thebans waited until the enemy came to them. This gave them more time to prepare, to stir their men's hearts in defence of their homes and to encourage the troops of Orchomenus to think them afraid. In the meantime the spirit of Hercules was gradually infused into the Theban army. The men under his command admired his enthusiasm and his confidence, though many an untried youth has those, but most of all they were in awe of his great strength. If this was matched by the courage indicated by his slaying of the lion in Thespiae, then Thebes would have a tremendous advantage.

So it was that when the fighting men of Orchomenus neared the city of Thebes they were confronted by an army arrayed for war and on ground of their own choosing. The confidence shown by the Thebans and the personal taunts shouted across the field displayed their eagerness for battle. When the Theban king, Creon, called for the surrender, on good terms, of the forces of King Erginus, the laughter from the latter's ranks rang a little hollow. What, the men wondered, had got into the Thebans? First the mutilation of the king's herald and tribute collector, now this display of confidence. The men of Orchomenus had set off for battle outraged at the Thebans' effrontery, determined to teach them a short, sharp lesson. Facing the massed ranks of the enemy, standing firm, they stirred uneasily and with not a little trepidation. Something had happened to embolden the Thebens. Wise heads among the Orchomenians knew that it was going to be a straightforward, stand-up infantry fight dictated by the ground, which didn't suit their chariots. Normally they could call on finesse, archery and driving skills, but these were found wanting in the conditions and when faced with the Thebans' methods, which consisted of brute strength coupled with a passionate desire for retribution. The bullied were calling the bully's bluff, with interest.

With no delay, no posturing, no reconsideration or parley, the Thebans launched their first attack. Hercules, with his father Amphitryon and twin-brother to the fore, headed right for the royal party in the centre of the enemy line. They hit with ferocious energy, tearing a hole in the enemy line through which the Theban foot soldiers poured. In a short vicious fight Hercules slew King Erginus. The Thebans swept along behind the bewildered men of Orchomenus, driving them like cattle, slaughtering hundreds. Everywhere the soldiers of the invading army dropped their weapons and took to their heels, or fell to their knees to beg for mercy.

The Thebens did not let up but kept going, killing, capturing and pursuing their enemies all the way to their own city, which fell easily. Creon was crowned the king of Orchomenus that same day. Hercules was the hero of the hour, feted for his valour by both king and country. The one sadness on this otherwise perfect day for him was the death of Amphitryon, his father in every respect but one, who had been killed while fighting bravely in that first bitter and crucial contact with the enemy. His body was taken back to Thebes where it was buried with honour.

As reward for his exemplary courage and leadership, Creon gave Hercules his own daughter, Megara, in marriage. They were young, alas, not in love and deep inside both were unhappy with the arrangement. As a king's favourite daughter, Megara was not an easy woman to get along with at the best of times and while she knew Hercules was a good catch and a good man, he was not her choice. Nor was parenthood something either of them was prepared for, and the three children they had together did not bring them any closer. None of this was any secret at Creon's court, and it was not a particular worry to anyone, including the couple themselves, who simply led separate lives. Hercules would go his own way, taking off on his adventures whenever it suited. The state of their relationship did not make either of them particularly miserable. Most of their contemporaries would have been more than pleased to trade places with them.

The goddess Hera, though, did not look upon the situation at all favourably. Still harbouring a grudge against Hercules, she decided that, as he was now married and thus legitimately within her area of responsibility – or interference, depending upon your point of view –, something must be done to render his life intolerable. The inspiration for her punishment she took from his unsatisfactory marriage and the common knowledge among gods and men that Eurystheus of Tiryns had been given his birthright.

At first Hera plagued Hercules with images of Eurystheus living in splendour, enjoying the adoration of lovely women, never wanting for anything, ruling Greece as he pleased. These were never out of the hero's mind for long and when they were, some other thing vexed him. He could find no rest, no comfort. He began to drink wine in great quantities, which only made matters with Megara worse. And then, he went mad. Hera sent the visions. The delusion and the rage in him did the rest.

One day Hercules fell into the first deep sleep he had had in months. As he slept he dreamed that he killed Eurystheus and his offspring. The peacefulness he felt on waking was in marked contrast to the violence of the dream, which Hercules remembered vividly and he hoped it had some deeper significance, and would resolve the terrible conflicts he had been struggling with. He looked around him. Even as he tried to focus his eyes he noted the unusual silence in the house. Slowly he took in the room and wondered at the destruction he saw. Nothing was whole. Not a stick of furniture and no decoration, no container, no oil lamp was intact. In the corner lay a heap of dirty, stained clothing, so rank the flies already buzzed around it. How could the servants let things come to such a pass?

That is when he saw a little hand poking out of the pile, then the foot of a woman. Stumbling over to the grizzly ruin he saw that it was Megara, not a bundle of cloths. She lay on top of the children and none of them moved. Quickly, fighting confusion and panic he pulled her off the children, but she was limp and cold. So were the children and all of them bled from their eyes, noses, ears and mouths. Cuts and bruises abounded on each body; legs and arms were contorted in odd directions.

A scream of anguish and fury welled up in his throat, stifled by the sudden certain knowledge that he, not another, had beaten his family to death. He ran around the room pounding on the walls, banging his head against them, recalling the dream in which he had gleefully destroyed his enemy and his heirs. Cursing himself and all creation he ran from the house, left Thebes and wandered the countryside in abject despair.

For a time he was hidden and cared for by his fellow hero Theseus, then he went to Thespiae where the king purified him, and his own happy progeny abounded. Here he recovered his sanity but knew that he must seek advice from the Oracle at Delphi if he was ever to live with himself again.

Journeying to Delphi, Hercules climbed the slopes of Mount Parnassus and took the traditional offering of an expensive cake to the Priestess of Apollo. He also had the customary goat to sacrifice. He was met by an attendant who was there to take down what the Oracle said, translating from the often odd sounds and words or mystical references.

His coming to Delphi had been foreseen and so he did not have to wait for an audience. After making the sacrifice of the goat, he was conducted into the presence of the Oracle. She sat near the edge of the mountainside on a tripod above a subterranean fissure out of which emitted noxious fumes. Having taken her seat just before the arrival of Hercules, she was only just beginning to feel the effects of what she inhaled. For the moment her body writhed and strained as she tore at her garments, crying out and involuntarily resisting the trance state that would allow the god to speak through her.

Then at last she calmed down and her body went limp, her facial features relaxed and took on a mild and almost amused expression. Instead of the usually cryptic answers to questions put by the visitor, the Oracle spoke directly, as if the god wanted no misunderstanding.

"Listen well if you would be redeemed from the actions of your madness, which you know was part of you. The violence you showed to those you loved was not all from outside yourself. Pride and anger are your failings, constant service your destiny and only hope. If you succeed in the task that you will be given, you may receive immortality and dwell among the gods you partly sprang from, but know that it will be more difficult than anything you have yet done. It will be a long and nearly impossible process."

"Tell me what I am to do," Hercules asked humbly in a hushed voice.

"A series of labours."

"Only name them," he cried with a swelling heart, "and they shall be done, unless I die in the attempt."

"You will not be directed by me or my priestess," said the Oracle. "But by thine enemy, Eurystheus. You shall be his slave and do his bidding. Only he shall select the labours, only he shall judge them to be completed or not."

The priestess then slumped in her seat and seemed to go into a faint. Hercules was gently led away by attendants who had been taking careful notes, as was the custom. All were impressed with the unambiguous nature of the message.

Hercules was shaking with fear and the horror of what was to come. The utter humiliation of subjecting himself to Eurytheus was beyond anything he could have imagined. Weak at the knees for the first time in his life, he took a seat on a nearby rock.

"Think of it," said the note-taker, handing him a copy of his reading. "Immortality. A seat among the gods."

"But Eurystheus," muttered Hercules in misery and despair. "Eurystheus."

Slowly Hercules made his reluctant way to Tiryns to serve his most implacable mortal enemy.

Over the years, Eurystheus had made no secret of his contempt for Hercules. Wishing to win favour with Hera, and being of a cruel disposition, he revelled in his circumstances and his mortal superiority to the dispossessed son of Zeus. Also Hercules was a hero, a breed Eurystheus could not abide. Being timid and indolent by nature, he saw himself as a far more refined and intellectual sort of man. In fact he liked to have salacious tales read to him by others, indulged in rare foods and wines and dallied with women and boys in the odder sort of ways. The idea of travelling or risking his life for anything was anathema to him.

Word of what the Oracle had told Hercules moved a good deal faster than the hero did himself, and by the time he arrived in Tiryns, Eurystheus was already rubbing his hands together with excitement. For weeks he had been walking around with a secretary carrying a tablet at his elbow, adding or scratching out items on an ever-revised list of impossible tasks he would gleefully put Hercules to.

Their first meeting was suitably short and brusque, with neither man wishing to prolong it. Hercules was dispatched at once to kill a particularly dangerous lion, and at Eurystheus' insistence, told to bring back its skin as proof that the deed had been done.

Now, the Nemean Lion was no ordinary animal; not only was it killing untold numbers of cattle, sheep and people but its hide was so thick as to render the beast impervious to the sharpest arrowhead. Hercules dismissed this notion. He tethered a lamb beneath a tree and sat down to wait for his quarry. When the lion came, Hercules took careful aim and loosed a series of arrows. Each one bounced harmlessly off and the creature escaped with the lamb, which it took away as though it were an offering.

Gritting his teeth in determination, Hercules then cut an enormous branch from a tree and fashioned it into the largest, deadliest club imaginable. Again he put out a lamb as bait, and waited. A few days later the Nemean Lion came.

This time Hercules waited until the huge beast had pounced on its prey before leaping down on it from the tree. For a split second they stood face to face, then the lion leaped towards him, its claws reaching out for his eyes. Hercules swung the club ferociously at the lion's head. The noise could be heard miles off as the hard yet supple wood made contact with the lion's furry head.

Stopped in mid-air, the lion crumpled in front of Hercules, where it remained momentarily, eyes rolling. It shook its great mained head before coming at him once more, growling furiously. Again Hercules clubbed it and again it paused. A third time it shook off the shock of the blow and resumed its attack. Mightily Hercules struck it once again. This time it stopped, grunted, and then started to trot away a little dizzily.

Hercules knew that if the lion was allowed to get away it would recover and start killing again. He ran after it, leaped onto its back and got an arm around its neck. Galvanized into action by this new threat the dazed lion fought tremendously to turn its claws and teeth on to the man. It seemed hours to Hercules before the cat's strength began to wane and finally the struggle ceased. He made certain the animal was dead before he addressed the problem of how to skin it. No blade would penetrate its hide. Inspired, he used the claws of the animal itself and only these proved sharp enough.

Back in Tiryns, Eurystheus seemed almost disappointed to see Hercules return alive and with the lion's skin, which he disdainfully told Hercules he could keep. Of course, if Hercules died it would shorten the fun, but on the other hand he would be safely out of the way. At any rate, Eurystheus reckoned, the odds were overwhelmingly stacked in his own favour, so why shouldn't he enjoy himself into the bargain?

"Apparently there is a rather tiresome serpent of some sort in the swamp of Lerna, near Argos," Eurystheus said, affecting a yawn. "It's known locally as the Hydra, of all things. Go and kill it like a good fellow." He ordered, languidly waving a hand by way of dismissal.

The Lernaean Hydra was a serpent like no other. It had nine heads, eight of which were mortal, the other, immortal. As he neared where the Hydra dwelt, Hercules heard more about it. Some people living near the swamp told him that a giant crab had lately appeared to keep company with the monster.

On the road Hercules had noticed a youth several times in all the places he stopped. The lad kept near him but never spoke and shied away when he approached. There was something familiar about the boy. At last Hercules cornered him by doubling back on his trail and coming up on the youth from behind.

"Hello, friend," Hercules said, suddenly appearing behind the boy, who jumped into the air. "We seem to be going always in the same direction."

"Yes," the lad said, looking at the ground.

"Why are you following me?"

"I'm not, I ..." the boy began but then he stopped himself. "My father sent me."

"And who is your father? Is he an enemy of mine? Have I been accused of seducing his wife or killing his brother?"

"You killed his sister-in-law," said the boy boldly.

After an awful pause Hercules looked hard at the youth.

"By Zeus, it's Iolaus, Iphicles' eldest."

"Yes, uncle."

"Am I thought badly of in Thebes?"

"By some. They say the madness was only drink and resentment."

"And you?"

Iolaus shrugged.

"But what did my brother send you here for?"

"To say that he believes in you, and to help you. If I can."

"And is this your will?"

"It might be interesting," the boy shrugged again.

Hercules did not have to ask why he had not spoken up before. Iolaus had been understandably afraid of his mad and violent uncle. His first instinct was to send the lad away for his own good but some weakness, as he supposed, caused him to let Iolaus stay. It was so good to have a member of his family around. Together they started along the road to Argos once more. Soon Hercules would be very glad of his nephew's help, not just his company.

Before long they were wading through the swamp, Iolaus dressed in the Nemean Lion skin Hercules himself had taken to wearing for protection. Alas, such things would be no use against the poison of the Hydra. The crab was another matter, although this too was another of Hera's creations to imperil Hercules. They encountered it first when it sidled out of the swamp grass, clamped the lad in its huge claw and held him there, squeezing the life out of him.

Like lightning, Hercules rushed around to the side of the crab that was holding the boy, to evade the attack that the crustacean was about to mount on himself. He climbed onto its back. and with his mighty club smashed at its head and beady eyes. Beneath its protective armour the creature's muscles were turning to pulp, and slowly the claw fell open, releasing Iolaus. Apart from sore ribs the boy had no other injuries, thanks to the lion skin.

After taking a brief rest beside the dying crab, they started deeper into the swamp in search of the Hydra. They did not have to go far to find it. Roused by the commotion, the beast was coming to meet them, furious at this invasion of its territory. The thing was so hideous that even Hercules instinctively recoiled and with Iolaus fled from the swamp, pursued by the monster. They reached dry land before stopping for breath and discussing their next move. Both agreed that taking on the serpent in its own environment would be very rash and it would be more effective to try and drive the monster from his patch.

They bombarded the serpent with fire arrows and so irked the beast that it came out of the marsh after them. Hercules stood his ground as the berserk monster lumbered towards them. Ordering his nephew to stay back out of immediate danger, he struck at one of the heads with his club, but to little effect, the head merely bobbling on the long neck while the other heads came at him. Hercules wished he had a great sword, instead of his famous club. Redoubling his strength, giving it all his might, he managed to smash off one head but this grew back almost at once. Again Hercules and Iolaus were forced to retreat, this time with the enraged snake monster hard on their heels.

"Make a fire," Hercules shouted over his shoulder as he desperately warded off the many strikes of the vicious heads, trying not to let any get near enough to scorch him with their deadly breath. "Bring a brand."

Lighting a fire was no easy matter but eventually, as the stamina of Hercules was being tested as seldom before, Iolaus got one going and made a long, blazing fire brand which he took to his uncle.

"Burn the stumps," Hercules gasped, still fighting desperately and with an enormous effort bludgeoning one of the heads so hard that it came clean off, leaving the neck swaying empty of its be-fanged and fork-tongued burden. But before Iolaus could act, another head appeared in its place. The two men groaned. The goal was clear. As soon as Hercules batted off a head, Iolaus would have to be ready with the

fire brand to burn the stump, cauterizing the wound so the head could not grow back. This they did, head by head. It was slow, laborious work, requiring enormous effort and stamina from Hercules.

At last, only the immortal head remained and this Hercules, with one supreme final swing of his club, knocked senseless. He then jumped upon the prostrate neck and, drawing a dagger, cut off the head. This he buried beneath an enormous rock. With Iolaus' help he set about making a large stock of good true arrows whose points he dipped in the poisonous blood of the Hydra.

Hercules returned too soon for Eurystheus' liking. While he was away the king had been pleasantly distracted and had not had the inclination to think up any really good labours. One did spring into his mind, however, after a bit of pondering. Knowing it would take ages, even if it could be accomplished, he sent the hero off to capture the Cerynitian Hind.

Eurystheus was quite right. It took Hercules a whole year to finally catch this beautiful Hind with golden antlers and hooves of bronze. The animal was sacred to the goddess Artemis and perfectly harmless, though highly elusive. In netting the creature finally, on the banks of the river Ladon, Hercules hurt it slightly. For this he incurred the wrath of Artemis. Outraged, she accosted him on his way back to Tiryns, with the poor helpless Hind over his shoulder. When he rightly put the blame entirely on Eurystheus, she forgave him.

The lengthy absence of Hercules had given Eurystheus time to examine all possibilities at his leisure, and gather knowledge of every monster in the known world. He had come up with what he considered his best labour yet. Given how long the Hind business had taken, relative to the other labours, it was obvious that Hercules was rather better at killing things than catching them. What if the two kinds of task were combined? What if he sent the damn heroic fool after something really dangerous, but to bring it back alive?

Eurystheus congratulated himself roundly as he packed Hercules off on the day of his return, as was his habit now. The object of the chase this time was the Erymanthian Boar. It was winter and up on Mount Erymanthus, where the Boar lived, Hercules would soon be freezing his great biceps off, Eurystheus chuckled to himself.

The joke turned out to be on Eurystheus. Hercules pursued the Boar into deep snow where it could not easily run away and netted it without too much difficulty. A sharp tap on its ugly head and that was that. Other than a nasty incident while sharing some special wine with a centaur acquaintance on the return journey, it was all straightforward enough.

By the time he got back to Tiryns, Hercules had tamed the boar and trained it a little. On entering Eurystheus' palace he pretended to be still struggling mightily with it as he presented it to the king. At one point Hercules pretended the boar had escaped him and so frightened Eurystheus that he hid inside a large urn while the animal snorted around it with Hercules desperately trying not to laugh out loud.

Later, when Eurystheus had recovered his dignity and the boar was safely out of the way, he chose to toy with the hero a while. Grinding in the fellow's servitude as much as he dared, he at last announced his new errand and dispatched an indignant Hercules to clean the Augean Stables.

Augeas, King of Elis, was a man after Eurystheus' own heart but he was grateful enough to see Hercules arrive. Magnanimously he swore to give the hero ten percent of his herd of cattle if he could clean the vast stables. The goddess Athene was often as much a help to Hercules as Hera was a hindrance and she now obligingly diverted two rivers to flow through the stables and wash out all the years of accumulated manure. An unpleasant chore had been executed in less than half a day.

Augeas went back on his word and refused to pay Hercules, however, saying the hero was only following the orders of his master, Eurystheus. Phyleus, his only son, sided with Hercules in the dispute, and Augeas expelled them both. Later, though, when the labours were done, Hercules would return at the head of an army and depose Augeas, kill him and put Phyleus on the throne in his stead.

During a rare moment of relaxation after this episode, Hercules instituted the Olympic Games in honour of Zeus. His rest was short lived and soon Eurystheus had him on his way again. Now he must deal with the Stymphalian Birds. These man-eaters had iron beaks, claws and wings and inhabited a marsh in Arcadia. So numerous were they that when they took to the air they blotted out the sun.

Again with the help of Athene, who had a soft spot for heroes, he used the enormous cymbals she had given him to frighten the birds, and keep them on the wing until they dropped, exhausted. While they flapped about on the ground, he finished them off with arrows.

Then came the Cretan Bull, which Minos had been given by Poseidon. Minos had refused to sacrifice it in the end and it wandered destructively about the land until Hercules caught it and brought it back to Eurystheus. After this exploit there were the Mares of Diomedes to contend with.

Diomedes was a Thracian king who owned a herd of female horses that he had trained to eat human flesh. With a small army of volunteers, Hercules entered the country, killed the animals' guardians, rounded up the horses and did battle with the king and his forces. After defeating Diomedes, Hercules fed him to the mares, then tamed the magnificent creatures and brought them back to Eurystheus, who dedicated them to Hera.

While journeying to Thrace and gathering his forces for the expedition, Hercules had stayed with Admentus, king of Pherae. Admentus was recently bereaved and although he tried his best to be a good host he could not conceal his sadness at the loss of his beloved wife, Alcestis, to whom he had been devoted.

Hercules summoned the spirit of death itself, Thanatos, and after winning a strange wrestling match, forced him to return Alcestis to her husband alive. Soon, resisting death and the land of the dead would be a regular pastime for Hercules. Unbeknown to anyone, Eurystheus most of all, Zeus was about to take a hand in shaping the nature of the labours. On the surface, they were just going to get harder.

First, there was one more contest of a more terrestrial nature, but a formative one. With utter frivolity, almost growing tired of the game by now, Eurystheus ordered Hercules to fetch him the Girdle of Hippolyta, queen of the Amazons, which was said to be set with valuable jewels and have magical powers.

Once more the nature of the contest required the help of volunteers. This was no attack on an individual monster but a foray into hostile territory at the far northern end of the known world. There would be terrible hardships along the way, and a world-renowned army to face when they got there.

Accompanied by other famous heroes such as Theseus, Telamon and Peleus, he set off, it must be said reluctantly. While the others looked forward to a fantastic adventure, Hercules could not help thinking that for once there was no good service in this labour, no noble deed. It would be mere conquest or out and out theft. Of course, Hercules was not above such things ordinarily but more and more he began to see his labours in a new light, not simply as ways of placating the gods, suffering humbly in service to a lesser mortal as lesson and punishment, but as holy missions. They were, after all, supposed to lead to his virtual deification.

The first port of call of the warriors was Paros, where they ended up fighting the sons of Minos before moving on to Mariandyne in Mysia. Here, they helped King Lycus to defeat the Bebryces, becoming battle hardened in the process and learning to work as a team. As a commemoration of the event, Lycus built the town of Hercules Pontica in honour of their leader.

By the time the group of heroes neared Amazonia, they were honed to perfection as a unit. This small band of men who as individuals were nearly invincible had become a mighty fighting body acting as one, each able to rely fully on the other as never before in their collective experience. The confidence and well-being they felt in each other's company was immeasurable and never had any of them been in better physical or mental condition.

When they arrived on the border, they paused and looked to Hercules who had been strangely silent.

"Shall we issue an ultimatum?" Theseus asked. "Attack the first town we see or wait for them to sally out for war?"

"No," Hercules said. "I don't think so."

"Go into the capital at night, hit Hippolyta's palace and make off with the girdle and a few hostages?" Theseus suggested.

"No, let's just find the border patrol and have them escort us in. All weapons such as clubs, war axes and spears put up, swords sheathed and bows unstrung."

"What?" Theseus cried, wide-eyed. "Against some of the deadliest warriors alive? I think we are good enough to take on anyone's army and win but not if we give away any advantages."

"Maybe we can just buy the thing," Hercules said, looking around at his bewildered comrades. "Or, well, sort of charm it off them."

"These Moon Goddess worshipping, men hating, warrior harpies?" one of their number scoffed.

"These backward, female barbarians who probably eat testicles as a delicacy on high holidays?" chimed in another.

Now, none of them thought their leader's idea a good one but they preferred to trust his judgement in the matter rather than jeopardize their unity. Anyway, it was his labour and making a challenge more difficult rather appealed to all of them. As they crossed the border, obviously unprepared to fight, they watched out for some sort of guardians of the territory to make themselves known.

Seeming to rise up from the very ground nearly as soon as they entered Amazonia, several large dirt smeared, grass- and hide-covered women popped up to challenge them. This well armed party eyed them so closely as to make the men become a little uncomfortable, but neither side offered any violence.

Hercules politely asked to be conducted to their queen. The woman in charge nodded from beneath her camouflage and instructed two of her subordinates to do this.

Word of their approach must have also been sent ahead, for everywhere they passed seemed deserted. At last they walked along the empty streets of the principal city of the Amazons' domain and into the palace of their queen. Once inside the palace walls they got their first glimpses of the people, or rather women, and such women. The strong palace guard impressed the band of heroes as much for their beauty as their obvious fitness and the easy way they handled their weapons. For their part the guard stared open mouthed at the heroes and their eyes followed them wherever they went. By now the border watchers who had acted as their escort had removed their camouflage and revealed striking figures, muscular feminine physiques and tough but comely faces.

The men were taken into the main hall which was also the throne-room. More guards arrived and, as Hercules stepped forward, the murmuring in the great room increased to a low roar. And then there she was, Hippolyta, raising her head to look at him. Suddenly her eyes widened and her jaw dropped, then slowly an enormous smile spread across her handsome features.

The truth was that none of the Amazons had ever seen such men. Their own were a scrawny, submissive rather coy sort whom they cossetted and looked after. Their enemies might muster one man in a hundred anything remotely like this group of obviously elite warriors. Hercules, their leader, was obviously the most magnificent specimen of them all.

For their part the Greek heroes were incredibly impressed with the Amazons. All were strong, forthright looking, bold and direct, as interested in the accoutrements of war and adventure as themselves, and, from the sparkle in their eyes, much more besides.

Everyone in that large well-armed company of aggressive, violent and daring individuals was desperate to get to grips with his or her opposite number, but no one was thinking about fighting. The tension in the room was palpably sexual.

"Why have you come to our country?" Hippolyta asked in a husky voice.

"I am here to somehow acquire your girdle, ma'am," Hercules smiled awkwardly but with all the roguish charm he could muster.

"Well," the queen smiled again. A worldly woman in her late thirties, muscular but shapely, she looked him up and down. "A bauble like that doesn't come cheap, you know. You don't seem to be carrying any sacks of gold."

"No, ma'am."

"How do you propose to pay then, dear lad, for a priceless thing like that? A fellow would have to do quite a lot to earn it, wouldn't he?"

"I imagine so, ma'am." Hercules gave her his best saucy grin. "I have a reputation as a very hard worker, though."

"I'll just bet you do, my boy," Hippolyta said breathily. "Let us go and see if we can strike some sort of bargain. The court is dismissed. See that our other guests are entertained," she told her troops. "But, I warn you, none of your coarseness. Take no unseemly liberties with them. Show all proper respect for their sex."

With a wink at Hercules, she held out her hand, which he took with enthusiasm and they withdrew to her private quarters. As soon as the queen had gone her attendants and guards moved in on the heroes with wicked looks and sparkles in their eyes. Silently all on both sides had established contact with someone and each pairing made for couches while serving boys and girls brought food and drink, which would be largely ignored for quite a while yet.

Both parties were equally pleased and taken aback at just how easy the other side seemed to be. There was no talk of respect in the morning, commitment, or having children. There was no coy behaviour or pretend delicacy or modesty, no need for flowers, flattery and pretence. The Amazons had never had it so good, and the heroes very rarely. Sadly, though, it was not to last.

By morning Hera was among the Amazons, disguised as one of them, starting rumours and spreading false reports.

"Why do you really think they are here?" she would whisper to one or two of the guards or attendants of the queen the next morning. "You cannot believe the girdle story. What could be more ridiculous?"

"Isn't it a little unlikely that such well armed and obviously well seasoned soldiers should come amongst us, all good looking and on such a spurious mission?"

If any of the Amazons demurred or said anything about the fine time she had had, Hera replied. "And you think that fine lad's head was turned by your pretty face, an old war horse like you, all of twenty-five and veteran of three campaigns? What could he really see in you? Wake up."

"Well, some men like a woman with ..."

"Isn't everything a little too good to be true? Has any of them asked for money after giving you their favours? Have they held out for marriage? When did men ever just give it away?"

"Ah, well, that's true enough but ..."

"You all know you always pay for it, somehow."

"That Theseus, though, is such a sweet ..."

"I tell you they are a bunch of tarts, especially trained in war and they are up to something."

Then Hera would start speculating.

"They are here to taint our own dear, gentle men. To teach them their ways of easy virtue and fast living, to rebel against the wise control of a wife or mother. They wish to teach our girls subservience. They would subvert the Goddess and introduce the worship of Zeus and the phallus, mark my words.

And, finally, she simply said she had actually overheard Hercules and his companions plotting to kidnap Queen Hippolyta. That was enough. Though there had been no let up in their enjoyment of the heroes, everyone certainly had gradually become more suspicious as Hera's lies had spread. Now the Amazons became enraged.

After arming themselves the Amazons rushed to the room that had been given to the heroes to rest in during the day. Hercules was telling his friends that the queen was insisting on one more instalment before giving up the girdle. Though expensive, it was not really magic and she deemed it a small price to pay for the fun she was having.

Just then one of the Amazons burst into the room, not simply carrying personal weapons as usual but very heavily armed. In a trice they had killed a couple of the utterly surprised heroes. The others began to scramble for their weapons, or picked up furniture with which to defend themselves. Thinking themselves betrayed by those they had come to trust, they went berserk with rage, particularly Hercules.

Dodging a sword thrust from the first Amazon who came at him, he grabbed her arm and broke it like a stick, taking her weapon. With this sword he flew into the midst of the Amazons and slew them furiously. They were good warriors, some even excellent, but none was a match for such a hand-picked band of heroes, most of whom were in some way or the other touched by the gods.

At last Hercules and Hippolyta came face to face. Their eyes lit up at sight of each other and without hesitation they converged at once, swinging their swords for a killing blow. The blades clashed and a furious duel began. Hippolyta was not queen by heredity but because she was the greatest warrior of her generation. Any heroes who crossed swords with her were in a fight for their lives, even Hercules.

Nevertheless, as they fought, and all around them battled too, Hercules was aware of an Amazon standing behind Hippolyta. This woman took no part in the action, in which so many of her comrades were dying, but to whisper advice in the queen's ear and call out for his blood. A hatred of this odd woman grew in him. Perhaps to delay coming to real death blows with Hippolyta, whom he admired more and more by the second, he determined to kill the other one first.

Feigning to move left, he went right and came around the queen, in a flash striking a blow that should have cut the woman in half. Instead his sword went through her without resistance, leaving her standing there, laughing. Seeing this, he paused for only an instant, but he had exposed his left side badly and as a blow fell towards his head, which would have split it to his shoulders had it landed, he ducked and rolled. The roll was inwards, towards his attacker. Dropping his weapon, he took hold of the queen and threw her to the floor.

Beneath them lay the body of an Amazon with a broken spear threw her chest and this is what Hippolyta landed on. The spear pierced her lower back and with a scream she stopped struggling and looked up at him and the woman beside him. All this had taken no time at all. She had seen the sword pass through the woman but so intent on her attack had she been that it had not registered. Now, as death drew near, the significance was plain to her. Hera appeared as herself and the image of the carping woman who had started it all faded before their eyes. Everyone stopped fighting, including the few Amazons still alive.

"My," Hera said, looking fully herself now. "I haven't broken up the party again, have I? You all seemed to be having nearly as much fun as you were thrashing about with one another in a different fashion. What a betrayal of principles that was. Shame on you all. It had to be put a stop to."

"It was you," gasped Hippolyta.

"So?" Hera shrugged. "I'll be seeing you Hercules. Another time another place, I will defeat you." With that she disappeared.

Struggling with the buckles of her girdle, gritting her teeth against the pain of moving with the spear deep in her back, Hippolyta reached up to hand it to Hercules as he knelt beside her.

"Take it," she said, smiling weakly. "You were the best f...f...fight I ever had."

Smiling back at her, he took the girdle and her hand.

"You too," he told her.

With a slight gasp and a tighter grip on his hand, she died.

"It's all bloodstained and a little torn," Eurystheus complained, looking aghast at the girdle as he held it in his fingertips. "Oh, who wants it anyway." He tossed it aside. "Why did you delay returning, Hercules? What was the meaning of all that faffing about in Troy?"

"I slew a sea monster for King Laomedon," Hercules sighed. "But he cheated me of my reward."

"Serves you right," sniffed Eurystheus.

"I'll pay him out later," Hercules smiled thinly.

"Well, in the meantime, you are still working for me," Eurystheus said with a sneer. "And as it happens I have hit on a most unusual and very special labour for you this time."

"Yes?" Hercules mumbled, not hiding the weariness in his voice.

"I want the Cattle of Geryon. Don't know why exactly, but I must have them. Simple as that. Leave now," he smiled wickedly. "And mind how you go."

Now this labour was monumental and epic in scale of time, deed and distance. The island of Erythia, where Geryon lived, was literally at the end of the earth, beyond the ocean. Geryon himself was a three-bodied monster, his herdsman a giant and his dog a vicious two-headed hound.

Only with divine help did Hercules succeed in crossing the ocean from Tartessus (Spain) and back again, after killing all the monsters and taking the cattle. To commemorate his achievement he built the pillars of Hercules at the entrance to the Mediterranean and from there he drove the cattle to Greece, having other adventures, founding cities and doing wonders all along the way. When at last he delivered the cattle, Eurystheus sacrificed them to Hera. Thus ended Hercules' first labour that was, in fact, a battle with death itself and forces well outside the mortal realm.

The Apples of the Hesperides were the next prizes Eurystheus sent him after.

"Where are they?" Hercules asked.

"How should I know," Eurystheus shrugged. "Just go get them." He scowled. "Right?"

Hercules nodded resignedly.

The Hesperides were three daughters of Atlas and Hesperas who lived far away, again like the land where Geryon had dwelt, to the west. They guarded a tree upon which golden apples grew. Originally a present from Gea to Hera when she wedded Zeus, the tree had been put in the fabulous garden of the Hesperides. Here a serpent called Ladon helped the sisters watch over the apples.

Simply finding out where he had to go was the first obstacle in Hercules' way. Heading north in the first instance the nymphs of the River Eirdanus advised him to ask the sea-god Nereus. Eventually, with the mischievous god changing into many different shapes and being generally difficult, Hercules had literally to lay hands on him to make him talk. Then the real journey began.

While passing through Egypt he was taken prisoner by the king, Busiris, who was in the habit of sacrificing a foreigner each year in hopes of ending a terrible famine. Hercules was chosen as that year's victim and taken to the temple, where he succeeded in throwing off his chains and escaping, after slaying Busiris and his son Amphidamas.

Arriving next in Ethiopia, Hercules killed another king and replaced him with a better man before travelling on once more. In the end he could not bare to confront yet more females in a mission of thievery.

Earlier, while in the Caucasus, Hercules had shot the eagle that fed on the liver of Prometheus, and rescuing that long suffering individual, he was given yet more valuable advice. Acting on this eventually, Hercules found his way to the realm in which Atlas stood balancing the world on his shoulders. Here they made a bargain.

Hercules agreed to relieve Atlas of his burden for a time if Atlas would go and pick the golden apples for him. As it happened, Atlas was so grateful for the break that when he returned, he had second thoughts about resuming his awesome responsibility.

Masking his dismay, Hercules had to think fast.

"Oh, Athene," he laughed, for she from above was assisting him in this present feat of cosmic strength. "Who would have thought it would be so easy."

"What do you mean by that?" Atlas demanded.

"Never mind," Hercules grinned. "You can go now, and be quick about it."

"Exactly what are you trying to pull?"

"Oh, nothing, nothing at all."

"You weren't after my job all along, were you?"

"Well," Hercules winked. "Did you really believe that yarn about the apples?"

"Wait a minute. I'll have my world back, thank you very much," Atlas began to fume. "You can't pull the wool over my eyes so easily."

"All right," Hercules smiled. "Catch."

As Atlas dropped the apples and struggled to get his grip and balance on the world, Hercules scooped up the golden orbs and left in a hurry. When he finally got back with them, Eurystheus told Hercules he could keep the apples. This uncharacteristic gesture was almost certainly due to his fear of bringing divine wrath upon himself. Hercules then gave the apples to Athene, who returned them to the Hesperides.

Drunk at the time and sick of always being bested by Hercules, Eurystheus thought he had come up with something truly impossible for the final labour. Hercules, he said, was to bring him back Cerberus, the three-headed hound that guards the gates of hell.

For this mission, Hercules first had himself initiated into the infernal mysteries at Eleusis and then, guided by Hermes, made his way down a subterranean passage descending from Cape Taenarum. For a while everything he encountered was more afraid of him than he was of it. Everything fled at his approach, except the ghost of Meleager, whose sister he promised to marry, and the Gorgon, whom he overcame.

Farther along he found Theseus and Pirithous chained up for the attempted kidnap/rescue of the fair Persephone. Freeing Theseus, he was prevented from helping Pirithous by a sudden earthquake. Wounding Hades himself, he forced the god to allow him to take away Cerberus. The only condition was that he must subdue the beast without the use of any weapon other than his bare hands.

In a monumental struggle Hercules brought the hellish animal to heel by nearly strangling it. Then, dragging the awful beast by the scruff of its neck up to the surface of the earth, he brought it to the utterly flabbergasted Eurystheus. At long last, his labours were over.

From here on for the rest of his mortal life Hercules continued killing harmful beings, avenging wrongs done to himself and others, and conquering and replacing bad kings. Often he was assisted both by the divine Athene and his nephew Iolaus. He also kept getting into trouble.

King Eurytus of Oechalia announced he would give his beautiful daughter, Iole, in marriage to any man who could best him in an archery contest. When Hercules emerged the victor, Eurytus went back on the deal, the hero's lamentable record as a husband being given as the reason. But Hercules loved Iole and never forgave him. Soon afterwards he killed the king's son, though the young man had come to him for help. Once more Hercules went to Delphi to be purified. The killing had been done in a fit of madness, but the Pythian priestess was so perturbed by his behaviour that she turned him away. Enraged, he stole her tripod. A bitter dispute with Apollo resulted and Zeus himself was forced to intervene. In the end the oracle sentenced Hercules to a year of slavery.

In contrast to his servitude to Eurystheus, under Queen Omphale of Lydia it was rather enjoyable. She had paid only three talens for him in an open slave market and at first did not know who he was. Aside from giving her pleasure and spinning wool for his own long robe, while sitting at her feet, he found time for more adventuring: fighting demons, killing a king who forced travellers to work in his vineyard then cut their throats, dispatching a giant serpent and another monarch who was in the habit of making strangers labour in his fields before beheading them with a scythe.

Omphale was so impressed with all this and his unstinting service at home that she gave him his freedom. He then sailed with the Argonauts, but being rather too senior in rank and too experienced to be subordinate to the other heroes, he soon dropped out of the expedition. He took part in Zeus' battle with the giants and killed the terrible Alcyoneus.

Not long after returning from the underworld, Hercules had kept his promise to the spirit of Meleager to marry his sister, Deianira, daughter of Oeneus, king of Calydon. This promise was not so easy to fulfil, however. He had to wrestle the river god Achelous and defeat him first. Horned like a bull and capable of changing himself into various shapes, Achelous gave Hercules a supremely difficult contest. In the end the river god lost both the match and one of his horns, which Hercules returned.

When going to Tiryns afterwards, Hercules and Deianira had at one point to make a troublesome river crossing. Hercules, encumbered with their baggage, asked the assistance of a centaur, Nessus, who agreed to convey Deianira across. This traitorous creature attempted to ravish the poor woman upon arrival on the far bank, while Hercules struggled in the current. Outraged, the hero flung off his burden and shot the centaur with an arrow, mortally wounding it.

As Nessus died, he asked Deianira's forgiveness and told her that the blood flowing from his wound would make a charm for her that would prevent her husband from loving any woman more than he did herself. It would be many years, after they had settled and had children, before she felt she needed to use it.

Unbeknown to Deianira, Hercules was still angry at King Eurytus of Oechalia and in love with Iole. Fatefully, he determined to go back, have his revenge on the king and win Iole for his second wife or concubine. Only when he mounted an expedition with these objects in mind, did Deianira find out.

When word of his triumphant killing of Eurytus and the sacking of Oechalia reached her, along with the news that he was sending Iole and several women captives home, Deianira really begin to worry. Hercules himself was lingering abroad a time and had asked her to send his white cloak back with his messenger. He wished to wear it in a great thanksgiving sacrifice to Zeus he had planned.

Coating the inside of the cloak with the long hoarded blood of the wicked centaur, Nessus, Deianira sent it on to Hercules. Of course, the dying centaur had lied to her. When Hercules donned the cloak in preparation for the sacrifice, he was suddenly wracked with excruciating pain, as if his flesh were on fire. Learning the truth later, poor Deianira killed herself with a sword. In his agony, Hercules was so maddened as to fling his friend Lichas, the messenger who had brought the cloak, into the sea. Suffering horribly, Hercules next pulled down whole pine trees in a nearby forest. Building his own funeral pyre and lying upon it, he begged someone to light it. No one would at first, but the man who finally did was given as his reward Hercules' own bow and arrows.

As the flame grew and all fell back from the conflagration, the mortal part of Hercules was consumed by the fire. His soul, however, ascended to Olympus where he was at last reconciled with Hera, who allowed him to marry her daughter, Hebe. Here, for all eternity Hercules was granted rest at last and enjoyment of the blissful life of the Immortals.

Doctor Li
Hollow Eyes

Chung-tsu, the most distinguished follower of the founder of the Taoist religion, Lao-tzu, wrote: "Confucius walks within society whilst I walk outside it." These two approaches to life are evident in this story which seems to blend the Confucian emphasis of social duty with the notion of individual salvation. There are strong overtones of sorcery here too, reflecting perhaps the influence on Taoism of the animist-shamanist religion brought to China by the nomadic tribesmen of North Asia. The sheer but believable goodness of Doctor Li is what I find most striking and it explains why he is so well-loved a legendary figure throughout China.

Doctor Li was a portly man of dignified, gentle and intelligent countenance. Now, for professional and spiritual reasons it was his habit to occasionally leave his body. When he did this his ghost would search the mountains of the west and other realms of interest where few mortal men can go. In these out of the way places, beside icy streams and in sunny meadows on distant plateaux, on cliff edges and sheer slopes, he would gather wild flowers and herbs with medicinal properties. From these he would draw nectar and put it into his spirit bottle, which was rather like a simple leather flask.

The doctor was hardly up to such steep climbs and long journeys in his physical self, which he would leave soundly sleeping in the charge of one of his trusted disciples. It was vital for this young man to guard the doctor from evil spirits, for such creatures might try to occupy the temporarily vacant body, putting it on and running off with it as a thief might steal a coat. This was a dreadful prospect and one that troubled the doctor considerably. Indeed, he left orders to his guardian-disciples to cremate his body after one week, if for any reason his spirit had not returned to it by then.

The day came when one of Li's spirit journeys gave cause for grave concern. It was the fifth day of the doctor's journey and there was no sign of his return. Usually the doctor was back within two or, at the most, three days. The very best of Li's disciples sat watching over his body, and he was more than a little worried.

Then a messenger arrived with word that the disciple's mother was seriously ill and might well be dying. A man of considerable medical knowledge himself, having learned so much from Doctor Li, the disciple felt he might be able to help her but he was honour-bound to continue his vigil. Torn and miserable, he waited, hoping that Li would return at any moment and release him.

By the morning of the sixth day the doctor had still not returned and another messenger came to say that the disciple's mother had grown worse in the night. She was not expected to survive and her fondest wish was to see her son once more before she died.

The disciple passed the next few hours in an agony of doubt and indecision. His anxiety intensified when only 12 hours of the deadline remained. If his mother should die now and the doctor still did not return, his vigil would have been in vain on two counts. He looked closely at Doctor Li's body. It was stiff, cold and lifeless in a way he was sure it had not been before. The disciple made up his mind, and with great reluctance but much ceremony, he burned the doctor's body.

The doctor's spirit returned shortly after the disciple left for his mother's sickbed. All it found was a pile of ashes, still warm and intermixed with the remains from the funeral pyre. A terrible sense of urgency struck Doctor Li. He must find a body to occupy before his spirit faded way on the wind. Rushing to a nearby forest he searched for the body of any dead creature he could reanimate. The first dead things he found were an ant and a bee. He passed on – he could not practice medicine as either of these, nor as the parakeet he came across next. In the few moments remaining to him, he was willing to gamble, though. His spirit was growing dimmer and he knew his time had almost expired. Desperation mounting, he pressed on. Then he glimpsed something that made him start with joy. In a ditch beside the road was a human body, partially covered in leaves and dust.

The body was that of a beggar recently died of starvation. There was no time to examine it. The doctor raced towards the cold flesh, and settled into it with only a few seconds to spare, sighing with relief. For several minutes he simply lay inside it, experiencing the sensation of fleshly existence. After a while he began to move the arms, legs, hands and feet. Warming and revitalizing his new shell, he discovered that it was intact, just, and that it was male and not so very decrepit as to be useless.

Shakily climbing to his second-hand feet, the doctor swayed momentarily before setting off determinedly. He knew as an absolute certainty that if his disciple had burned his body before the agreed deadline it must have been done for nothing less than a dire emergency. Doctor Li had a good idea of the nature of this emergency.

Moving his now thin, bowed and twisted carcass as quickly as he could, he hurried off to give assistance where he was sure it was needed. The eyes of his new body were deep-set, dark and glinted as new minted coins, yet they shone too with the doctor's former gentleness and care for others. His future was as his past: to continue his work as a much loved and greatly respected man of medicine.

Mamadi Sefe Dekote

This is a legend of Sudan, whose rich tradition of heroes,
damsels and adventure is much like that
of medieval Europe.
The story of Mamadi Sefe Dekote is no children's fairy-tale,
however, and has a particularly bitter
and sharp battle-of-the-sexes edge to it.

Everyone agreed that Sia Jatta Bari was beautiful, but to the warrior known as Mamadi Sefe Dekote, 'He Who Speaks Little,' she was the most beautiful woman in the world. The virgin Sia herself was fully aware of her stunning looks, even somewhat perplexed and rather spoiled by them. Certainly she too felt that she was clearly the most beautiful girl of her generation in their city, capital of the Soninke people of Sudan. And this, a very truly blessed city, prosperous and populous, had officially agreed with both of them.

The provider of the city's wealth and fertility was a serpent named Bida which surfaced periodically from its lair in the bowels of the earth through the well in the main square. Here it bestowed its bounty upon the people, thrice yearly causing a rain of pure gold to fall in the streets. All the Soninke had to do in return was to feed the serpent a particularly exquisite virgin every now and then, as suitable candidates appeared. Bida would not be satisfied with just any old virgin and had long ago, quite perceptibly, begun to lean towards quality rather than quantity.

Now, Mamadi Sefe Dekote was not stupid and was assuredly a very single-minded man. Usually his mind was focused exclusively on what he did best. He was a highly skilled fighter, the foremost warrior among his people, their best horseman, swordsman and tactician, brave as a lion and swift as a leopard. Lately, though, his mind had been taken over by a need to come out best in another sort of battle, one for the heart of the beautiful Sia. Fortunately for his fellow citizens, there were no wars to fight at the moment, no feuds to pursue or quests to embark on. If Mamadi's skills had been required just now, the Soninke would have found themselves short of a hero, for the warrior was not to be distracted by anything.

So it was that for some time he had been paying diligent court to the young maiden, trying to attract her, seduce her, lure her to his rooms, but all his efforts had ended in dismal failure. The young couple were social equals, yet he felt that she considered herself too good for him. Him! Had he compared notes with his peers, they would have assured him that they fared no better, and in many cases were treated worse, but that would have been no consolation to a man used to getting his own way. In truth, when all was said and done, Sia did indeed feel she was too good for him, or for any other man in the city. Indeed, far more than most beautiful women, she felt she was a little too good for the world as a whole. She knew it could just never quite measure up to her.

This state of affairs was no secret to anyone, especially the wiser heads in charge of official matters in the city, who wondered how the matter might be resolved. After much thought they came up with a solution which they hoped would bring the obsessed and deluded Mamadi back to his true vocation. They appreciated the fact that warriors had the desires of ordinary men, but ordinary men were usually content to satisfy them with ordinary women. The solution devised by the elders was very much to the taste of Sia herself, it must be understood. So, it was with pride, satisfaction and a calm sense of justice being done that she accepted the high honour duly offered to her.

Anybody else in town could have seen it coming. Sia's own family had expected as much since she was twelve or so. However, 'The Man Who Speaks Little' had been listening even less of late. For one thing he had not been going out much – he was a man with a mission and saving money had become central to its completion.

For a native of a city that had gold rained upon it, Mamadi Sefe Dekote was not wealthy. Honourable public service seldom pays, and even honest loot from raids and successful campaigns is often given out as largesse, to pay retainers, feed slaves, buy equipment, the best weapons and horses. Saving and selling off a few valuables were the only methods open to him of raising a large sum of money quickly.

The family of Sia Jatta Bari were in no better financial position themselves. Perhaps in a city that has gold rained upon it, everyone spends too freely. Between showers, money can get a little tight. The idea had come to Mamadi, in desperation it has to be said, to offer Sia gold to come to him, to spend the night with him, in short to lay with him. In those pre-Islamic times this was not such an impossible notion.

Mamadi bided his time and when he had amassed a suitable sum, he approached Sia as she was strolling in the public gardens. The particularly aloof and serene expression on her lovely face changed when she felt a gentle touch on her arm and she saw who it was.

"What?" she snapped.

Ever a man of few words, he said, smiling "Come to my bed and I will give you this bag of gold." He opened the large leather sack he had brought with him and showed her the considerable amount he had saved. He tried to be appear calm as she perused the contents of the bag, swallowed hard, and braced himself for the stinging rebuff he felt sure she would deliver.

Sia looked as though she was fighting to concentrate, to ward off distraction, and bring her thoughts back from a very long, long way off. At first she looked through him, then at him.

"Yeeees," she said vaguely. Then she added, "In advance, of course."

Now Mamadi's sudden good luck surprised him, for he had regarded this latest bid of his as a last-ditch effort. When his jaw could be persuaded to stop hanging loose, he agreed at once. It was only after Sia had snatched away his moneybag and disappeared in the direction of the milliner's quarter that he wondered if she planned to cheat him. No, he reasoned. She had obviously wanted him all along. She had simply been too proud to admit it. The money was only an excuse, a decider which had tipped the finely balanced scales in her feminine mind.

It was with both keen excitement and some trepidation that he went home to anxiously await her arrival that evening. The atmosphere here was hardly soothing, though. He had only one slave left to his name and many of his finest possessions and decorations had also been sold. Sia was worth all his sacrifices, he told himself fiercely, pacing up and down his bedroom.

As the evening turned into night and Mamadi was on the verge of fury and despair, she came. When he saw her he felt a great wave of relief wash over him and instantly relaxed. Oddly his excitement waned a little, or rather became a slow-burning sense of sweet anticipation, the enjoyment of a longing soon to be fulfilled but not rushed at.

He gave her wine and they talked haltingly of family and friends they had in common. She spoke of the fine gown she had bought with the money he had given her and how it was finer than any that had ever been seen in the city. She was lucky, she said, to have found the material, just in time. His kind offer of money had been so opportune.

He smiled and reminded her that his offer was not merely an act of kindness, that they had made a bargain.

"Of course," she nodded without so much as a maidenly blush.

Standing up he held out his hand. She took it, still looking at him directly and smiling. Slowly he led her up the stairs to his bedchamber where he began to disrobe, inviting her to do the same. She shook her head. Thinking this was at last a sign of modesty, and liking the idea, he stepped over to undress her.

"That was not part of the bargain," she said firmly, backing away from him, her slender hands held out in front of her.

"Right," he said grimly. It was going to be like that, was it? "Very well."

Mamadi Sefe Dekote leapt into the bed and with a wicked grin patted the space beside him. "Come then, lawyer."

Walking over to the bed she looked stonily at him and lay down beside him stiffly.

"Huh," he grunted, shaking his head and reaching out for her breast.

She slapped his hand.

"No," she barked. "That was not part of the bargain, either."

He groaned angrily and thrust out his hands to delve beneath her skirts, but she crossed her legs tightly, pushing his hands away and tugging down her clothing.

"Not part of the bargain?" he snarled, only to see her nod smugly. "How then are we to keep the bargain, woman? How am I to make love to you?"

"Make love?" she raised her fine eyebrows and looked curiously down her fine nose. "Who said anything about making love?"

"It is just that one wonders how it may be accomplished, with all these conditions placed upon ..."

"I did not mean that there is no question of making love, but that it is not in question. I mean it was not mentioned. You said nothing about it. Making love was never part of the bargain. I agreed to lay with you. To spend the night, as it were. To sleep with you, if you wish. Nothing more."

"Is it marriage you want?" Mamadi asked, jumping from the bed and stalking up and down upon the now carpet-less floor, for the carpet too had been sold. "Well, when was that ever in doubt really? I am in love with you. Everyone knows that. Our families would not object. There is no problem. I wish it, in fact, and you know that. We can make love now and marry tomorrow. You have my word. And I do keep bargains, in letter and spirit. As I say, I love you."

"I realize that," she said sadly, pitying him a little now. "But I cannot make love or marry. Bida the serpent is my destiny and I desire no other. I go to him tomorrow morning. That is why I wanted a particularly fine gown, shoes and a bit of new jewellery."

"And what will you say to him," Mamadi snapped in his exasperation, hardly taking in the full import of what she said. "'You may eat me, but not my new dress and shoes, they are not part of the bargain.'"

She smiled serenely and shook her head in pity for him still.

"Shall I stay?" she asked after his silence had gone on too long.

"No, get out," he sighed, angry and confused.

"We have been friends," she said, stroking his face as she left. "But nothing lasts forever." With a groan he turned away.

At first only in fury he took up his sword, finding comfort in the feel of the weapon in his hand. Then a little absently he began to practise a move he had invented. It was a way of drawing and slashing all in one movement, perfected, unknown to him, by the Samurai of Japan but unheard of among the swordsmen of Africa, Europe or Asia Minor. Repeatedly he went through the action, gaining in swiftness each time he executed it. Then, sharpening the sword and testing it and the movement together, he split a grain of barley in mid-air.

In the morning Mamadi Sefe Dekote went to the deep well in the square on the east side of the city where Bida the giant serpent would appear. Here, with most of the town turned out to watch, and all the city fathers, her family, and visiting dignitaries, Sia Jatta Bari stood calmly, resplendent in her new finery.

Going over to her, Mamadi Sefe Dekote experienced a greater sense of longing than ever before. He was moved by Sia's beauty as never before. The love in his eyes did not touch her, however, and like everyone else gathered in the square she felt a little awkward in his presence.

"I do not believe you truly want this," he whispered, but she ignored him.

Suddenly a hush went over the crowd, and from out of the well popped the head of Bida the serpent. On catching sight of Sia his eyes lit up and grew rounder, all but bulging from their sockets. Then his head disappeared again.

"Say your goodbyes quickly and stand back, Mamadi Sefe Dekote," cried the city officials. "It is time, it is time."

Bida appeared once more, rising a bit farther from the well this time, his enormous mouth opening, the dark pink of its wide interior gaping, salivating. But when the serpent saw Mamadi Sefe Dekote standing by Sia's side, he withdrew again.

"Say farewell now," cried the officials and the people. "Sia, bid your friend stand away," they shouted.

"Yes," she snapped in annoyance. "Move along, will you."

Sighing loudly, Mamadi Sefe Dekote stepped back a pace or two.

Again Bida reared his head from the well, and eyed Sia appreciatively. It was a very handsome head, for a giant snake, she had to admit, returning his gaze. His teeth, though sharp and long, were quite clean and neat, too. As more and more of the long neck slipped out of the well it was plain to see how many-coloured and elegant were the patterns of his scales. Slowly, Bida looped his gleaming neck and swooping down with his mouth opened, he came for his delectable offering.

When the serpent's head was only inches from Sia, Mamadi Sefe Dekote glided forward, drew his sword and in one swift motion swept its razor sharp blade through the neck of the giant serpent, spraying blood everywhere. A warm gush of the crimson liquid dashed across Sia's calm features, making her open her eyes. In that moment she realized she was not going to be gobbled up in sacrifice to the magical beast after all.

She and the crowd watched in horror as the head of Bida fell with a squishy thud and went bouncing and rolling down the street. As it came to a halt upright on its stump, the eyes popped open and its mouth began to work up and down, the forked tongue dancing

about. Then suddenly, incredibly, it spoke.

"For seven years," the head groaned, "seven months and seven days you shall be without golden rain." With that it toppled over and lay motionless in the dirt. Meanwhile the serpent's body had collapsed and slithered back down the well.

The deathly hush that had greeted the severing of Bida's head broke into a roar of anger and outrage directed at Mamadi Sefe Dekote. From every corner of the crowd came shouts for his head. Led by the city fathers, the townspeople surged forward, closing in on him, ready to tear him to pieces.

However, as we have seen, his killing of Bida was not a spontaneous act, and Mamadi had taken the precaution of having his slave, Blali, at hand with warhorses made ready for a speedy exit from the town. Leaping into the saddle, swinging his sword about him, Mamadi pulled the dazed Sia across his pommel and spurred his fiery steed into a gallop. Mounted as they were on the fastest horses in the town, they soon disappeared into the countryside and travelled onwards for many miles.

In the months that followed Mamadi came to regret his reckless deed. Penniless and in disgrace, having destroyed the greatest blessing of his people, the former hero fell very low indeed. They had settled in another town, among another people, and Mamadi could barely earn enough to keep Sia, himself and his slave by hiring out his sword to help guard a local potentate. Their social status as gentlefolk was all they had, and each other, alas.

Even now Sia remained aloof from him, would never come to his room and seldom spoke to him. Though they kept separate quarters, they were married, their lives completely linked in their misfortune. When he came to her, however, when he touched her or attempted to make love to her, she always claimed to have a headache.

She suspected that when the excitement of their escape had abated, she at least would be able to go home and not be blamed for what had happened. But while not wishing to be abandoned by Mamadi, she hated him too much to leave him. She was a woman with a taste for revenge and whereas from back home she would have been unable to do anything to harm him, here, in their current situation, she could. He had ruined her life, after all, interfered with her destiny. Her pride was too great to stand the insult of it.

One day, when his entreaties became particularly irksome, when his passion for her seemed eternal, she came up with a novel idea for curing it.

"Perhaps," she smiled innocently, "perhaps if you cut off one of your toes, you who love me so, and present it to me, so that I may rub my brow with it, this might relieve the pain of my headaches. It is a magic cure I have heard of."

Without hesitation Mamadi drew his dagger and slipping off his left boot severed the small toe of that foot. Bowing, he handed it to her.

"Leave me now and I will see if the magic works," she sighed, as if weary from the pain of her headache. "Come back tomorrow."

Once outside, with the help of his last, not very bright slave, Blali, he made his way to his lonely room and bandaged the wound, hope rising in his heart. The next night, trying to hide his limp, he returned to Sia's room.

"I am afraid the pain has not gone. My head feels as if it will split like a melon dropped on a stone. Perhaps though," she suggested, "I was wrong about the spell. Perhaps, if you were to present me with a finger instead, that will work. Yes, I believe that it was the severed finger of a true love ..."

Again, not hesitating for a second, Mamadi Sefe Dekote slapped his left hand down upon the table, drew his dagger and sliced off his little finger. Gritting his teeth, he fought hard and managed a smile, once more bowing to present it to her.

The next day, sure enough, Sia no longer had a headache, but when Mamadi Sefe Dekote approached her she only laughed at him, throwing him out of her room and then sending a note via his despised slave, to explain the way things now stood.

"I do not love people with only nine fingers and nine toes," she wrote. "Why would I wish to give myself to an incomplete creature like you?"

They were beyond the reach of their own people here, of course, and safe from the wrath of the city fathers, but Sia was convinced that word of Mamadi Sefe Dekote's humiliation would quickly get back to everyone who knew him. Sia was quite certain that their doings were the subject of eagerly received gossip back home, and she was correct.

At last the proud warrior was being made a total fool of, Sia smiled to herself with satisfaction. Indeed, now she lingered in this foreign town just to watch his unhappy progress, to see him wincing when he walked down the street or maladroitly dealing with anything requiring two hands.

There was another reason to remain, even after the foolish warrior's wounds had begun to heal. Sia's beauty and her now obvious independence had opened several possibilities. All the higher born men of the town had begun to show considerable interest in her. Soon, Sia re-established communication with her family and it was arranged that an income would be paid to her, but it was also agreed that she might stay away a while longer. The still-virgin Sia Jatta Bari, with the serpent no longer an option, and wealthy men she had not known from childhood in the offing, had suggested this herself.

Mamadi Sefe Dekote, however, had not disappeared from the picture. He had again been saving money and was selling off possessions that were not vital to him. The spare warhorse had gone, but he had decided to keep his lowly slave Blali.

With the money he had thus accumulated Mamadi Sefe Dekote went to a witch, the most renowned in the area. In return for his gold, she made him a love potion the power of which had seldom been equalled. This potion she mixed into hair oil, and, as part of her agreed role in their transaction, brought it to Sia. Posing as a hairdresser and offering a free sample of her ability in the hope of future work, she was allowed to give the beauty-conscious virgin a treatment.

After only half of the oil was applied, Sia jumped to her feet and flung a garment over her bare shoulders.

"Where are you going so suddenly, my lady" the witch asked.

"I hear Mamadi Sefe Dekote summoning me," Sia cried desperately, before hurrying from her house and running to his room down the street. "Yes," she breathed anxiously, as she burst through his door. "You were calling for me, and I am here."

"I didn't do any such thing," Mamadi said, raising one eyebrow disdainfully as he reclined languidly on his bed. "It is my understanding that you cannot love anyone with nine fingers and nine toes. Go away."

Confused and strangely unhappy, Sia returned to her house and allowed the 'hairdresser' to continue the treatment, but hardly had she applied a drop or two more of the oil than again Sia leapt to her feet and ran once more to Mamadi Sefe Dekote. Again, he dismissed her harshly.

Back home the witch went to work again, rubbing the last of the love potion into Sia's hair as the girl twitched and shivered with excitement and confusion. After dressing her hair nicely the witch pretended she would return if required, for a modest fee, and left. At once Sia felt driven to go to Mamadi again.

Arriving sheepishly at his door, she fought to retain some dignity as she stood looking at him.

"You must have been calling to me," she sighed. "All I can hear is your voice constantly in my mind. All I can see before my eyes, open or closed, is your face, your body."

"All right, I suppose I have been thinking of you," he replied with a yawn. "Come to me tonight. Not too early, mind you."

"I will come to our marriage bed tonight," she whispered huskily, wondering how she could stand the intervening hours. Then she blew him a kiss before departing.

No sooner had Sia gone than Mamadi Sefe Dekote shouted for Blali to prepare for the night's big event. If he did not follow instructions exactly, Blali was bluntly told, his life would be forfeit.

As soon after dark as she felt was reasonably proper, Sia went to Mamadi's room, where apparently he had retired without her. Seeing his shoes beside the bed as she entered, she smiled to herself. Closing the door on the darkened room, she felt her way across the floor and slipped under the blanket beside him.

He said nothing but turned to face her in the gloom.

"Truly you did not earn the name 'He Who Speaks Little' for nothing, but please, tell me now that you love me. I know you have reason to be angry but at last we are together …"

Wordlessly he took her in his arms and all through the night, lustily, in every conceivable position, many, many times and hour after hour, he enjoyed her, and she responded with equal enthusiasm. Finally, exhausted and satiated, she lay her head upon his chest, dozing at last as dawn broke and faint light showed around the cracks of the shutters and under the door.

At full light, the town already bustling, the door was kicked in and Mamadi's voice boomed around the room.

"Blali, you lazy thing," he shouted from the doorway. "My horse's stall is full of dung, and you have not cleaned it, nor groomed, watered and fed the animal."

"Apologies, master," muttered the yawning Blali from the bed, reaching up to open the window shutters above it. "But I have been occupied with this woman."

Outside, passers-by glanced in, drawn by the uproar, and went away giggling.

Fully awake now, Sia sat up clutching the blankets around her, looking from Blali to Mamadi. Jaw set, she rose with legs and knees like jelly. Dropping the blanket, she dressed quickly, though not fast enough to hide the bruises and bitemarks upon her neck, breasts, thighs and buttocks.

Walking shakily to the door, she paused as she passed Mamadi Sefe Dekote and said with grudging admiration, not looking at him. "You take a good revenge."

With that she went home. It is said that she died of shame not long afterwards. But who knows?

The Knight and
the Lady of Loch Awe

*This tale has a theme common to many
of the cultures whose men went off to the
Crusades. Aside from the nature of the far-off campaigning,
though, it takes a gentle, reflective line,
and Black Colin does not exact the grisly vengeance
one would find in other Highland stories.*

Breathing heavily and sweating profusely in his padded leather jerkin and chain mail, Black Colin looked down at the dead Saracen at his feet. The fierce Mediterranean sun was taking its toll, but on this particular day in what had been a long campaign it was the enemy who were in full retreat, leaving the field to him and his comrades. In a flash his mind went back to his home in the cool, green glens of Scotland. There he had land, wealth, status and family but, above all else, a beautiful wife whom he had left for the Crusades. They had been married a very short time before he had ventured off. He had taken the decision to go so lightly, so thoughtlessly and without a backward glance. Now, as he removed his helmet and wiped his forehead, it sickened him to recall it.

Visions of home itself were less painful, and remembering his proud heritage while surrounded by so many foreigners, some of very high birth in their homeland, cheered him a little.

It had been during the wars between England and Scotland in the reigns of Edward I and Edward II that his father had made his name. As one of the leaders in the cause of Scottish independence, Sir Nigel Campbell had served boldly. The Knight of Loch Awe, as he was generally called, had been a school friend and comrade of Sir William Wallace, and a loyal and devoted adherent of Robert Bruce. As reward for his heroism in the war of independence, the Bruce gave him the former lands of the rebellious MacGregors. This included Glenurchy, the great glen at the head of Loch Awe through which the river Orchy flows, in a wild and isolated region of the Highlands. Sir Nigel Campbell had had a fight on his hands before he was able to expel the MacGregors and settle down peaceably in Glenurchy. Colin was born soon afterwards. As the years went by he earned the nickname of Black Colin, on account of his jet-black hair, dark skin and his temperament.

Over time the boy's fierce temper and rashness were beaten, reasoned or loved out of him by his tough father, kind foster-father and devoted foster-mother. As all Highland chiefs did in those days, Sir Nigel Campbell sent his son to a farmer's home for fosterage and so the boy became a child of his foster family as well as the son of his father.

Young Black Colin ate the plain food of the clansmen, oatmeal porridge and oatcake, drank the milk of the cows and occasionally enjoyed the beef from the cattle herds. He ran and wrestled and hunted with his foster-brothers and learnt woodcraft and warlike skills, such as broadsword play and the use of dirk and buckler, from his foster-father. Most importantly of all, he won a devoted following in the clan. In these times a man's foster-parents were almost dearer to him than his own father and mother, and his foster-brethren were bound to fight and die for him and to regard him more highly than their own blood relations.

The foster-parents of Black Colin were a couple named Patterson, who lived at Socach, in Glenurchy. In every conceivable way, they fulfilled the trust placed in them. Indeed, in Black Colin's case they did more than was strictly necessary, and became closer to him as a consequence. With his mother dead and a father who was unusually cold, the Pattersons were in his heart his first family. In some ways he came to regard his title and future responsibilities as a duty and a burden.

Sir Nigel Campbell died in his forties, leaving Black Colin to become Knight of Loch Awe, lord of Glenurchy and all the surrounding countryside while he was still only in his late teens. Colin was already renowned for his strength and handsome face and by virtue of this extra slice of good fortune he became the young man all the girls in the district wanted to capture. By luck, for a young man's fancy can seldom be trusted, advice from his foster-mother and the wit, charms and merit of the young woman in question, he married the best, brightest, and truly loveliest of all the girls in the area.

The couple dwelt happily enough together on the Islet in Loch Awe but it was not long before Colin became restless. He had yet to perform great feats of arms, and, sadly for him, the peace in the land then looked like lasting. He was too young, too well schooled in war and too brave to be content with the life of what amounted to little more than that of a gentleman-farmer. Soon, a cause would inspire him to leave his responsibilities as clan chief, husband and landlord.

One day a traveller arrived at the castle on the Islet with fascinating tales of the many places he had been. This fellow was a palmer just returned from the Holy Land who had visited all the holy places in Jerusalem. He eloquently described his experiences, the customs and religious sites of the various distant lands, all of which interested Black Colin's wife.

"The Saracens rule the country with a fist of iron and hinder men from worshipping at the sacred shrines," the palmer said. "But soon this may be remedied, for coming home by way of Rome, I heard most wondrous news. It seems the Pope has just proclaimed a new Holy War."

"What's that?" Colin cried, coming quickly out of his daydream of what he might have done had he lived in former times, during the last Crusades. His attention was captured by the word 'war'.

"The Pope has declared that his blessing will rest on the man who would leave wife, home and kinsfolk, and go forth to fight for the Lord against the infidel."

The palmer's words greatly moved Black Colin, and when the old man had made an end he raised the hilt of his dirk and swore by the cross it formed.

"I swear by all that is sacred that I will obey this summons and go on crusade."

The fair Lady of Loch Awe turned pale. They had barely been married for a year and already he was to leave her alone for what might be a very long time, if he survived the journey and the battles and illnesses he must face. She tried to master her emotions as she turned to her husband.

"How far from me will this errand take you?" was all she could manage to say and still be in command of herself.

"Why, all the way to Jerusalem, if the Pope bids me."

"And how long will you be away from me?" she whispered with difficulty.

"It is hard to say," Black Colin barked excitedly. "It may be many years if the heathen try to continue to hold the Holy Land against us. In the end, the warriors of the Cross must prevail, but I can not return before that time, of course."

"What shall I do during those long, weary years," she asked, growing stronger as the inevitability of it all sank in.

"Why, my darling," Black Colin responded, waking up a little from his ecstatic dreams of war and victory. "You shall live right here on the Islet and manage our affairs as lady of Glenurchy until my return. Our vassals and clansmen will obey you as they do me, and the tenants will pay their rents and dues to you. You will hold and control the land in my place." He had thought she would be just as excited by this prospect as he was over the Crusade, for she was a clever young woman and he knew she had her own ideas and longed to influence their affairs.

"I see," the Lady of Loch Awe said with a sigh. "But if you should die so far away in that distant land ..." her voice nearly broke and she stopped, cleared her throat and tried again, pretending to be cool and practical. "How will I know? What am I to do if eventually I hear that you've been killed or carried off by some dread disease? How am I ever to know for certain?"

"Yes. We must think," said Colin, a touch sobered by talk of his mortality. "Wait seven years, and if I have not returned by then, you go ahead and marry again. Take a good brave husband to help you guard your rights and rule the glen, for I'll be dead in the Holy Land."

"No," she said gently, her heart breaking. "I will be the Lady of Glenurchy until I die, or perhaps a bride of Christ, hoping to find peace for my grieving soul in a nunnery. I'll let no second husband have me or hold your land. Please," she said, no longer acting and desperate to avoid the awful uncertainty so inherent in the campaigns of those times, especially such distant ones. "Give me some token that we can share between us, something that on your deathbed you can send to me. That way, if I get it, I will know that you will never come home and that you have died."

"I will do as you ask but I may have no deathbed as such," Black Colin answered, both touched and amused. He understood her need, however, and so he went to the clan's blacksmith and had him make a very large gold ring. On one side of it was engraved Colin's name and on the other that of the Lady of Loch Awe.

Breaking the ring in two, Colin gave his wife the piece with his name and kept the one with hers.

"I vow to wear this near my heart," he solemnly told her, "and will only part with it if I am about to die, in whatever circumstances."

Nodding and weeping bitterly, his lady also swore to keep her half of the ring, which she put on a chain round her neck. Then, with heavy hearts and great mourning from the whole clan, Black Colin and the sturdy band of Campbell clansmen who had volunteered to go with him, marched away to the swirl of the bagpipes, plaids fluttering in the breeze. Many looked back with a lump in their throat, and those who were older or wiser feared to find themselves supplanted when they came back after God only knew how many years.

Colin had not shared such doubts at the time, but they had begun to plague him recently. How could he have abandoned her with such an easy mind?

Some men's courage rose as the miles lengthened behind them, while others became homesick or sentimental. By the time they had reached Edinburgh and boarded a ship at Leith, many were already thinking of home as an abstract ideal and looking forward to the joy of battle. All were also eager to see Rome and the Pope. Later, they believed, would come Jerusalem.

Black Colin now remembered that all he had dreamt of then was glory and how he would fight with such valour as had seldom been seen in all the battles in all the world. These days all he dreamt of was home and his lady.

Journeying up the Rhine, he and his Highland clansmen had made their way through Switzerland, then over the passes of the Alps. Coming down into Italy, they were astonished at the splendour of the cities, which surpassed their wildest imaginations. At last, with many other bands of Crusaders, they reached Rome.

Here the Knight of Loch Awe was lucky enough to have an audience with the Pope, who was touched by the devotion of these tough warriors come to do battle for Christ so far from their homes. Later, after years of blood and struggle, Colin would remember that day with pride and a certain ruefulness.

They had been dispatched at once to Rhodes were they would fight in the service of the Knights of St. John. Often in the years to come the bravery and skill of Black Colin and his men would be praised by the Grand Master, but the dream of going to reclaim the Holy Land was never realized. All their fighting, and there was much of it, took place elsewhere.

Early on Colin had sworn that he would liberate and then worship at all the holy sites in Jerusalem. Over the years, as his men died around him, he began to regret the oath as an impossibility. He came to a decision, that he would keep as much of his promise as he could, and if he could not reach the Holy Land as a triumphant warrior he would go as a pilgrim, risking his life in the process if need be.

For his sad and lonely wife the seven years passed slowly indeed. She dwelt in the castle on the Islet, ruling in all gentle ways, but fighting boldly when raiders came to plunder her land and clansmen. Every year she claimed her husband's dues and took good care to see that he was never cheated. Hawk-eyed as she was in defence of her husbands rights, in times of trouble she was the best help her clan ever had. There were none who did not sincerely bless her name for the kindness she showed and the good she did.

Of course, such a lovely and wealthy woman as the Lady of Loch Awe was bound to attract the notice of single men of her rank. Certainly there would have been no shortage of suitors had she been a widow. Indeed, even before the seven years had passed, there were men who would gladly have tried to convince her that Colin was dead and that she was free to look elsewhere.

"When he left," she said, steadfastly refusing to entertain the vaguest notion of a remarriage, "my husband promised me two things: one that he would return, if possible, within seven years; and, secondly, that if he should fall, he would have sent to me a sure token of his death. The seven years are not yet over, and I have never received the token of his death. By Heaven above, and my own heart's desire, I am still the wife of Black Colin of Loch Awe. Who will say that I am not?"

This firm resolve and unshakeable determination eventually daunted all her suitors except one, who would not be dissuaded. Baron Niel MacCorquodale had reasons other than love or admiration or clan alliance for pursuing this lady. His lands bordered on Glenurchy, and he had long cast covetous eyes on the glen and its contents. The fair lady was prize enough, he had to admit, but she was only a part of his goal. The wealth she was reputed to possess and the power the marriage would give him were the prizes he was most intent on winning.

At midnight seven years from the day when Black Colin had gone to the Crusades, his lady wept miserably and awoke with a terrible feeling of emptiness. Bright and early that very morning the Baron MacCorquodale arrived again to pay court to her. Hiding her sadness, she received him reluctantly but did not respond to his references to her 'freedom'.

"Until I have the token of my husband's death, I will be wife to no other man."

"What is the token, my lady?" asked the Baron, already thinking of sending a false one. "What exactly does it amount to?"

"I'll never tell anyone that," replied the lady. "You wouldn't dare to ask about such private things between a husband and wife, would you? I will know the token if it comes."

The Baron was at pains to hide his rage over this. Nevertheless he decided that even if he could not discover the secret, he would wed the lady and her wealth by hook or by crook. Dispatching a trusted messenger to Rome, he set about forging a letter that would convince the lady that Black Colin was dead.

On the day the Baron arrived at the castle in the company of a palmer to bring this news to the lady, she was gazing out the window and saw them coming. The sight of the palmer filled her with both excitement and dread, for she believed he might have word of her husband.

"Lady," the Baron said with a solemnity bordering on the excessive, even in the circumstances, "this palmer has tidings for you of a most saddening kind, I fear."

"Well," she said, turning pale, a wretched flutter in her stomach, "allow him to give these tidings then. Palmer, what news?"

"It is bitter, fair lady, very bitter," said the palmer. "Your husband has fallen in battle, slain by the Saracens while in the service of the Grand Master of the Knights of Rhodes. This letter gives the details and the condolences of many officials of the Church." All these individuals were in the pay of the Baron, of course.

"But is there any proof?" the lady demanded, taking the letter.

"My poor dear Lady, I am myself acquainted with the wounded soldier who brought the news," the palmer said with arms outspread and a doleful expression.

"Is the soldier one of our people?"

"No, my lady. But this man saw him die with his own eyes. The last of your clansmen also perished with the Knight of Loch Awe. I was told that as he lay dying of his wounds your husband bid one of his last surviving followers to take from him a token, to withdraw from the battle and return with it to you, but alas the man was killed before this could be done. A sudden onrush of the enemy forced the Christians back and when once more they retook the ground – forgive me, Lady, but war is an ugly thing – and came upon the bodies of their comrades they had been stripped and plundered of all that was precious or even useful. I am sorry, but whatever your husband wished to send you was lost. They wrapped his body in a plaid and buried him on the field of battle."

Without any real reason to doubt this news, the lady began to grieve at last. She dressed herself in mourning and wept anew for her lost husband. Nevertheless, some part of her did not give up hope. She still wore the broken half of the engraved ring on the chain round her neck, and she could not help but cling to the notion that the promised death-token had never come.

Naturally, the Baron now redoubled his efforts to wed the Lady of Loch Awe, courting her more openly and ardently than ever. The Lady herself was not uninterested on one level, for it would be a good match for the clan. But in her heart she did not like him, although she was hard put to find reasons for refusing him.

The fact was that she had to keep him on good terms, because from his lands bordering Glenurchy, he could easily make war on the people in the glen, who had been psychologically weakened by the news of the death of their chief. The lady was forced to turn to trickery, like Penelope of old in similar distress.

As the Baron's persistent wooing grew more sickeningly romantic, although always with a sinister threat underlying it, the Lady of Loch Awe seemed at last to come to terms with her loss and, from his perspective, she began to see sense.

"Yes," she replied to his hundredth proposal. "I will marry you, now that I know that Colin is dead. You understand, though, that it cannot be at once. It would offend the clan and cause trouble to us both, and I need a period of mourning for myself."

"I quite understand, my dear," the Baron crooned, bursting with self-satisfaction at finally winning his prize, or rather both his prizes.

"To commemorate my husband and for many practical reasons, I must first build a castle to command the head of Glenurchy and of Loch Awe. The MacGregors chose the best place for a house there on Innis Eoalan. You know where the ruins of MacGregor's White House still stand?"

"Yes," the Baron smiled indulgently.

"I will build my castle there. When the building is completed my mourning will end, and we may set the date of our wedding."

The Baron now felt contented, having secured this promise. The building work on the castle began at the head of Loch Awe. Progress was painfully slow, however, for the lady had secretly instructed her men to build feebly. Surprisingly to the casual observer, often the walls fell down, stone cutters fell ill and labourers fell and injured themselves. The construction of the new castle was taking a very long time indeed, even with the Baron supplying encouragement, advice, doctors and workers whenever he could. Slowly and inexorably, however, the completion date drew nearer.

Meanwhile, everyone who loved Black Colin mourned, distressed at the knowledge that the Lady of Loch Awe would marry again. The absent knight's foster-mother grieved most of all, instinctively feeling certain that her beloved Colin was still alive. The death token had never arrived, and her nose for a scoundrel told her to fully mistrust Baron MacCorquodale. Mother Patterson was convinced that the palmer's message was a deliberate lie. Finally, unable to bear it any longer, and concerned that the new castle was almost complete, she called one of her sons to her.

"Go to Rome," she said. "Find out for certain if Colin is alive or dead. If he is dead, do all you can to be certain of it. If he is alive, get word to him that he must return at once, and tell him why."

Secretly, the youngest of the Patterson boys set off for Rome. His mother would always be grateful to Colin for not taking any of her sons to the Crusade, including her eldest – the only one of them who was not much younger than Colin – who at the time was married with two small babies and, everybody knew, was a much better farmer than a fighter.

In Rome, the traveller's enquiries after his foster-brother led him directly to Black Colin himself, just returned from Jerusalem. The knight, much changed by his experiences, was at last on his way home. The seven years had gone in sprints and crawls, he had seen much fighting, lost all his old comrades and all the new ones of other lands. He had been captured once and had escaped thanks partly to his dark complexion and black hair. He had been wounded in battle many times and suffered illnesses that had carried off less sturdy men. He had beheld the places where his Saviour had walked, preached and died, and all these things had made him a different man from the one who had set out for the wars so many years before.

The frustrations of his service had been many, but despite these he had felt he must fulfil at least part of his vow. That is when he had gone as a pilgrim to visit the holy places, so that he might honourably return home. He missed his wife more with the passing years and the gaining of wisdom, but he did not worry overmuch about her. He knew the death token had never been sent and he trusted that she would be loyal and patient and give him the time he needed.

Meeting his foster-brother and hearing the news of his supposed death and the betrothal of his wife galvanised Colin into action, however. Nothing could have more horrified the tired, homesick, love-starved knight than the news brought to him by his clansman. As time had gone by, his faith in God and in his wife were all that had sustained him through the horrors he had witnessed.

Colin and his clansman started for home at once. Their fellowship was warm but silent over the long miles they travelled by land and sea. Both were men of few words, and Colin was largely lost in thought. He knew his lady could not wait forever and that the crafty Baron MacCorquodale must have been convincing. He had been gone too long, leaving not just his wife but his clan vulnerable.

Black Colin understood that his wife had only very reluctantly promised to marry the Baron and had delayed her wedding by some stratagem. Now, as he and his foster-brother trekked north, he vowed that he would return to Glenurchy in time to thwart MacCorquodale's wicked plans. Not pausing for longer than was absolutely necessary in their journey, Black Colin and his faithful clansman at last drew near to Glenurchy.

"Go on ahead, speak to no one about my coming," he told his young foster-brother. "Find out how things stand and come back here to tell me the news."

When the youth returned he brought word that the wedding had been fixed for the next day. He was then treated to the horrible sight of the old Black Colin in a fit of fury. The Baron was roundly cursed and a terrible vengeance sworn upon him for being such a forging, cheating thief and liar. Then, just as suddenly as he had erupted, Colin calmed down and quizzed the boy gently.

"Is he such a bad man, the Baron? Can my lady actually wish to marry him? Perhaps he simply knew he had to trick her out of her hopeless loyalty to me in order for her to live and not waste her life in waiting. I am not seven years gone to the wars but, by now, more like nine or ten."

"He is wicked," the youth swore. "And greedy. She cannot wish to marry him."

"We shall see," Colin said thoughtfully." Perhaps some self-sacrificing part of this warrior longed for nobility, to stand aside and find the simple, spiritual solace of a monastery. He did not want to burst back into his wife's world, which did not yet seem his own, and take everything for granted. He was not the man who would once have welcomed the chance to avenge himself on the baron and show how mighty and stern he could be to his clan and family.

"Shall I raise the clan?" young Patterson asked. "Shall I find us horses and weapons and ..."

"No, just go to your mother, and say nothing about me. I will be along directly, but pretend that I'm a stranger."

Doing as he was asked, the perplexed young clansman showed no sign of recognition when Colin appeared at the farm in the glen. There, an hour before, the anxious Mother Patterson had awaited the return of the wanderers. Seeing her son alone, her heart tightened in her chest, and she concluded that her foster-son would return too late to stop the wedding.

Later that day the Knight of Loch Awe, looking like a beggar, came down the glen and saw the smoke from the old castle on the Islet. For a moment he lost his breath at the sight of it and he gasped a sob of happiness. "I see smoke from my house," he said to himself. "And it's the smoke of a wedding feast being prepared. Oh God, who sent us light and love, I pray that I may reap the fruit of the love that is there." In this moment he knew he did not want to repair to a monastery or start a lonely journey back to the Holy Land. This was his home and in that old castle was his wife, whom he loved. But a question remained in his mind: did she still love him?

The knight then knocked at the door of his foster-mother's house and, playing the beggar, humbly asked for food and shelter. There were things he needed to know that the love and loyalty of his people might prevent him from learning.

"Come in, good man," said Mother Patterson despite her cares. "Have a seat in the chimney corner, and I will bring you your fill of oatcake and milk."

Colin sat down with a heavy sigh, as if over-weary and watched as the farmer's wife moved about slowly, putting before him what she had. He could tell that she had recently been weeping. Clearly, too, she did not recognize him. He was a little astonished by this at first, then hurt, then amused. It was what he had hoped, after all, for the moment.

"I can see that you're very sad," he said. "What, if you don't mind a stranger asking, is the cause?"

"I'll not confide in or burden a wandering stranger." She replied with a shake of her head.

"Perhaps I can guess what troubles you," he persisted. "You've lost some dear friend ...."

"Much worse," she said, her voice breaking along with her resistance to this stranger, in whom she felt compelled to confide, as one might to a holy man. "I had a dear foster-son who went crusading. I loved him just as much as I do my own sons, but now it seems he is dead in a foreign land."

"That is indeed sad," Colin whispered.

"But it is not all," his beloved foster-mother went on, weeping openly. "His wife, the Lady of Loch Awe, is meant to marry another man tomorrow."

"A hard thing for a mother to bear, when a son's widow marries again.".

"She waited ever so long for him. All of three years past the seven he had asked her to. Even now, she would not be marrying again but that a letter came to assure her of her husband's death."

"I am sure, it were best to be certain."

"Even yet she is fretting because she has not had the token he promised to send her. As it is, she is only marrying the Baron because she dare not delay any longer."

"What token was this?" asked Colin.

"She has not said," replied his foster-mother.

"Do you see the lady? Can you say with certainty that she does not wish to marry the Baron and that she loves her husband still, that she would surely prefer him alive and home?"

"I do not know the lady. It would not be proper," Mother Patterson declared. "But if my Colin was here there would be no question of who she preferred. She would have him and so would we all, and then none need fear that Glenurchy should fall into the hands of such as the Baron MacCorquodale."

"If Black Colin were here, would you know him by sight?" asked the beggar with a smile.

"Know him? Did I not say he is my own dear fosterling?"

"It has been many years though, and war makes many changes."

"I should know him in an instant," Mother Patterson insisted.

"Tell me then if perchance I resemble him at all."

"Well," she began doubtfully, not in the mood for games. "Not much …."

"Look more closely then, oh my mother, for I am indeed Colin of Loch Awe, home and alive."

Grabbing the beggar by the arm, the mistress of the farm pulled him out into the light and eagerly studied his face. After nearly a minute she let out a hoot of joy and threw her arms around him.

"My dear son, home at last. Oh Colin, Colin, how I have missed you. The years have been long and sorrowful since my nurseling left us, but you are home now and all will be well again." Hugging him she kissed his brow and stroked his hair, remarking on his even darker hue and his very ragged attire.

"There is something I must know," he said when the ecstasy of their reunion subsided. "Does my wife still love me? It has been so many years, far more than I ever intended to be gone. We have had no word of each other and the Baron, as I recall, is a handsome and clever man."

"I am sure she does not wish to marry him, but is compelled by circumstance and the danger he poses to her people. She could never prefer him."

"A mother would say so," Colin smiled sadly.

"Yes, that is so," she allowed. "I see you would know her true mind and be sure in your heart that she loves you."

"Yes, I long to know it."

"Perhaps there is a way," the knight's foster-mother considered for a moment.

"Please advise me, mother."

"Very well. Stay here tonight, and in the morning go in your beggar's clothes to the castle on the Islet. Stand at the kitchen door with other beggars, and refuse to go away until the bride herself brings you some food and drink. She is very kind and considerate of both beggars and her servants. Eventually, if you persist and they insist, she will come. When the Lady of Loch Awe hands you something to drink, put your token in the cup. Her reaction will show you if her heart is in this marriage and whether she still loves you."

Thanking her, he agreed to abide by her plan. Meanwhile, the young man who had been to Rome to find Colin had been quietly sending the rest of the family to the farm to be reunited with their foster-brother. One by one they came home and were greeted by their long-lost kinsman, and all swore not to reveal Colin's presence to anyone else.

Early the next morning Colin went alone to the castle, dressed in his beggar's rags. Even at that hour all the servants were up and busy and the whole place was a-buzz with preparations for the wedding. Vagabonds of every kind were already hanging round the doors in honour of the day, begging for food and money, and he took his place among them.

The big newcomer looked little different from the others but he behaved much more boldly. From the start he planted himself right in the open doorway and begged for food and drink with scant humility and no shame. Indeed, his lordly manner impressed the servants and soon one of them brought him what he asked for, oatcake and buttermilk.

"Here you are. Now, on your way."

Colin drank the buttermilk, tucked the cake inside his clothing, ostensibly for later consumption, but still would not budge from the doorway, making it impossible for the servants to enter or exit without hindrance. Their testy comments would not make him move, so one of the servants tried bribing him with more food and a horn of ale.

"All right, take this second gift of food and be off with you. You are in the way standing there."

He thanked the servant but yet again did not move.

"Will you please go before you get us and yourself into trouble." one of the exasperated servants cried.

"No," he said standing more firmly than ever with his stout travelling-staff planted on the threshold. "I will not go."

"Go now, or it will be the worse for you. You have had more than enough for a single beggar."

"I won't go away until the bride herself, with her own fair hand, gives me a drink of wine," said the disguised knight. Sure enough, he would not move, no matter what they said or did, yet he was not offensive and they could not find it in their hearts to treat his courtesy with outright anger and aggression. There was also the question of his size. Despite his appearance, he was strong and agile and clearly could be dangerous with that staff. In the end they just wanted to be rid of him and, after whispering among themselves, agreed to fetch their mistress to indulge his fancy. Doubtless he wished to say a few obsequious words of congratulation in hope of some other gift, and then finally go away. They hoped she would not mind too much, on such a day as this, being asked to help get rid of the fellow.

Hearing of the problem with the importunate beggar the Lady of Loch Awe took it with her usual good grace.

"It's a small matter on my last day in the old house," she said, laughing, and asked a servant to bring a large jug filled with wine and accompany her to the door.

In fact, the Lady was glad of the distraction from her own concerns and the opportunity to delay her personal preparations for a few minutes.

When she came out to the beggar, he bowed his head in greeting.

"You've travelled far, good man," she said, glancing at his travel-stained attire.

"Yes, lady, from distant lands."

"Would that others also gone to distant lands had returned," she said wistfully. "Well, if you desire a drink from the bride's own hand, here I am. You may have your wine now." Holding a bowl in her hands, she asked the servant to fill it. "There you are," she said, managing a smile.

"I drink to your happiness," said he, draining the bowl. As he gave the bowl back to her, he dropped his half of the engraved ring inside it. "Lady, allow me to return this cup a little richer than I took it."

Her curiosity aroused, she looked into the bowl. When she saw the token she gasped and snatched at the small piece of gold, dropping the bowl which fell to the ground and broke at her feet. Now trembling violently, she examined the token. When she saw her own name engraved upon it, tears welled in her eyes. Looking long and intently at the token, she pulled a chain from around her neck, and held up her half of the ring with Colin's name engraved upon it.

"There is no hope now," she whispered in despair, tears flooding down her cheeks. "But, stranger," she said, grasping his sleeve. "Please tell me, did you know him and does this truly mean my husband is dead?"

"Dead?" he said with gentle warmth, looking tenderly at her. "No, it simply means he's home."

Hearing his tone more than his words, she stared hard into his eyes and then fell into his arms.

"Colin, my husband," she cried holding him tightly against her pounding heart, prayers of thanks racing through her mind.

Flabbergasted the servants stood staring in bewilderment, until after a few moments their mistress turned to them, beaming.

"Run, bring everyone in the household, bring all the clan, Black Colin of Loch Awe, your chief and my own wonderful husband, has come home to us."

Soon all in the castle knew the great news and amidst tremendous excitement and rejoicing, they feasted on the already prepared wedding banquet. In mid-celebration, and while the glowingly happy wife sat beside her long-lost husband, holding his hand as if she feared to let him leave her, the distant sound of bagpipes was heard.

The Baron MacCorquodale was coming for his wedding, which in their joy the people of Glenurchy had entirely forgotten. They looked at one another in amusement and then at the Lord and Lady of Loch Awe.

"Will someone kindly go and tell the Baron that I will take no new husband today, as my old one has come back to me. And say that there will be certain questions asked of him when the time is right."

A group of gleeful clansmen fell over themselves to deliver this message, but one man was ahead of them all. He set out in a rowing boat, and pulling for all his worth on the oars sped towards Baron MacCorquodale's great wedding party of relations, henchmen, vassals and pipers who were making ready to enter the boats that would take them across to the Islet.

"What can this be," the Baron wondered as the man – a spy he had placed in the Lady of Loch Awe's household – approached. He took the man aside to hear his message. The news of Colin's return was unexpected to say the least and put him in a fury of frustration.

With a frantic gesture the Baron ordered the pipers to cease their music.

"There will be no wedding today. We must be off at once, Black Colin is home again," he cried. The astonished party looked about them in confusion, but the Baron's haste told them all they needed to know. Everyone soon followed his example, fearful of the terrible vengeance the long-lost chieftain might take. All reached their homes out of breath but safely.

In the days that followed, Colin had many things to tell his wife about his travels, the wars and his pilgrimage. He was also curious about her life during all these years alone. They told each other everything and Colin read the forged letter that had been sent to his wife. Like everyone else, he knew who must have been behind it.

His anger, or so it seemed to all who heard him that morning, was white hot against MacCorquodale.

"That evil man, who has wrought this wrong and so nearly gained his end, must pay in blood," he vowed.

Sympathizing with him but deeply concerned that a terrible war might result, his wife calmed him. Finally, in front of many witnesses, she got him to swear he would take no grisly revenge on the Baron, whom she felt she had made a fool of throughout, and who must now be living in fear. In the end everyone, especially the Baron, credited her with preventing the wrath of Black Colin from descending on his head.

"What have you done with the rents of Glenurchy all these years?" Colin asked his wife one day not long after his return, wondering if his long ago hunch about her interests and abilities was well founded.

"With some of it I lived," the happy lady replied. "With some I've guarded the glen, and with some I made a cairn of stones at the head of Loch Awe." By now she knew from his foster-brother that Colin still did not know the particulars of her stratagem to delay the Baron's wedding day, only that she had done so.

"A cairn of stones?" Colin asked with a smile.

"Come with me, and let me show it to you," she said.

Deeply puzzled, Colin rode with her to the head of Loch Awe.

Grand and white, shining in the rays of the sun, the new castle which now stood on the site of the former home of the MacGregors, struck him as truly marvellous.

"Well," his proud wife laughed, "do you like my cairn of stones? It took a very long time to build."

Leaning out of the saddle he put his arm around her waist and kissed her rapturously, lost in admiration.

Black Colin was indeed pleased with the magnificent castle she had raised for him, and renamed it Kilchurn Castle. Staying true to his vow, and to his own hidden nature, which his wife soon happily fathomed, he took no warlike vengeance on Baron MacCorquodale. However, there came a time when it became necessary for that gentleman to resign much of his lands to the Knight of Loch Awe, which were united with those of Glenurchy. It was the reverse of what the Baron had hoped to accomplish by dishonesty, achieved fairly and through clever plans largely conceived by the Lady of Loch Awe.

Izanagi and Izanami

*The worship of the forces and forms of nature was central to the ancient
native religion of Japan, Shintoism. Over time this developed into
a kind of polytheism (the worship of numerous gods)
and there was little scope for the formulation of
spiritual ideas. Izanagi and Izanami are the last of the seven generations
of Japanese gods, and it is they, according to Japanese myth,
who are responsible for the creation of the world.
The mythology and legends of Japan were preserved for centuries
through an oral tradition practised by the Katari-be, or 'reciters'.
Much later, in the seventh century AD, they were written down
and incorporated in the first history of Japan.
As a pair of bickering, sibling-lovers, Izanagi and Izanami
have spoken to people down through the ages.*

Below the floating bridge of Heaven there hung a thick, impenetrable mist. Nothing lay within that mist and nothing existed but the Heavens. Upon the bridge stood twin deities, in whom burned a powerful desire both to fully experience one another and to create. As Izanagi, 'The Male Who Invites', watched by Izanami, 'The Female Who Invites', thrust his jewelled spear into the nothingness and slowly stirred it, a thrill ran through them both. From the mist arose a great bubbling, a further thickening of the mist and the strange sound "Koworokoworo".

Izanagi withdrew his spear and the two deities watched as its point dripped curdles of brine. The brine fell below, forming an island. Down to this solid ground the young god and goddess descended and here, with a grand burst of creative energy, they set about causing to appear a great hall whose central feature was a giant pillar. All the while, however, both were aware of another very startling new fact. In making this physical world, they too had become physical. From around the pillar, they eyed each other shyly.

Suddenly they realized they could not communicate with one another except by speech. Mouthing words and thoughts with difficulty, they discussed the slight but obvious deviations in their two bodies. While one had soft hemispherical mounds on her upper body, the other had one pronounced appendage on his lower body. Closer examination revealed other fascinating features, but what exercised most of Izanagi's attention was a strategically placed niche in Izanami's body which corresponded in position exactly to that of the increasingly prominent protruberance on his own. He conceived the idea that one might actually be inserted into the other with interesting results, and with the usual difficulty of speech and by using gestures, he said so.

Incredulous at first, Izanami soon realized the possibilities and discovered a growing inclination towards the notion. To merge, to embrace without and within, had great appeal for them both. Instinctively, they felt, this might lead to further, better creating and in a new way. So now, just as Izanagi was assailed by a profound need to bury his strangely exterior organ in warmth, an equal need to fill a yawning, yearning void within herself overtook Izanami.

Sensing that a ritual of sorts was called for, that many precedents were being set, and subject to a sudden shyness, they repaired to opposite sides of the giant pillar. Stepping round one side of it and meeting Izanagi's gaze, Izanami cleared her throat and searched for the unfamiliar words of spoken language.

"Oh," she said at last, "what a handsome man."

"Oh," Izanagi, thus inspired, uttered in response, "what a lovely young woman."

Slowly they drew one another into an embrace.

Awkward, uncomfortable, especially for Izanami, their first coupling was unsatisfactory and all that came of it creatively was a bloodsucking water leech. An almost reluctant second attempt produced a small island of foam. A new approach was called for, though neither

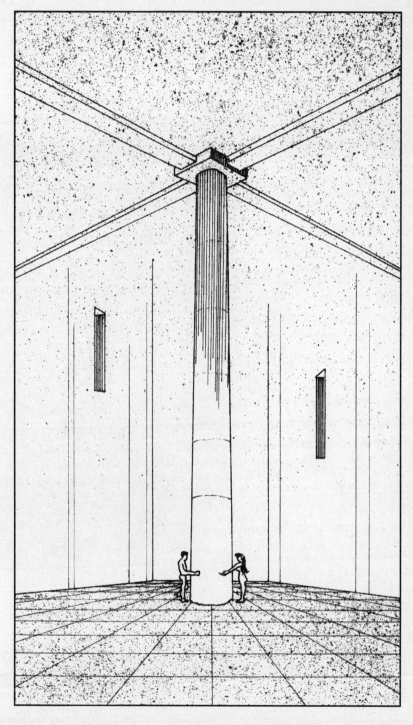

questioned the instinct that drove them to carry on with the experiment.

Meeting now on the other side of the giant pillar, Izanagi spoke first.

"Oh, what a lovely young woman."

"Oh," Izanami replied, "what a handsome man."

Falling into one another's arms, they fitted together more easily, less clumsily and with slightly greater abandon. The results were quickly recognized as being of a far more satisfying nature, and a grand creative flowering immediately followed. The seven islands of Japan were born, then the sea appeared, all the land of the world as a whole, the four seasons, wind, trees and mountains. Finally, issuing from its mother Izanami, came the flaming, leaping, male Spirit of Fire.

This last offspring was Izanami's undoing, however, for it so burned and damaged her that she lay down vomiting, giving life even by that to many lesser creatures. Soon, she died. Weeping, her brother and lover fell at her feet, stricken with grief and confusion. His tears ran down his face and from them the spirit who lives on Mount Kagu was born.

Taking up Izanami's limp body, Izanagi carried it to the boundary between Idumo and Papaki and buried her. Then, in his rage he drew his sword and decapitated the fire child, whose blood created countless wild animals and from whose headless corpse emerged many thousands more.

In his loneliness, Izanagi descended into the kingdom of the Night. Here, at the portal of the Palace of Darkness, his sister-lover waited.

"Izanami," he cried, "the world we created, the living things you gave birth to are yet incomplete. Please return with me to the light and air."

"I wish I could go back with you," Izanami said sadly. "But it may already be too late. You should have come before this. I have already eaten and drunk in this dimension but I will go inside and speak with the spirits who dwell here. Please, do not follow me there."

For what seemed an age to him, Izanagi lingered but impatient with love and worry he pulled from his hair one of his two ornamental hair combs and set it alight to use as a torch. Cautiously he went through the door where his twin sister had gone. And there she lay, rotting and eaten half away by maggots inside and out.

Great was the horror he felt at the sight but worse was the terrible knowledge that something had been violated, some rules of the place and the power and nature and divinity. Words of warning seemed to ring in his ears.

Loud-thunder in her skull,
Burning-thunder in her bosom,
Dark-thunder in her belly,
Crack-thunder in her womb,
Young-thunder in her left hand,
Earth-thunder in her right hand,
Resounding-thunder in her left foot,
Reposing-thunder in her right foot.

From the decayed body itself came the scream: "You have shamed me!" And up rose the monster that the dead Izanami had assumed in all its frightfulness, howling. It chased Izanagi through the gates of the Palace of Darkness, out of the kingdom of the Night, into the upper world. Here, in this still-fertile land, where all grew at his slightest inspiration, he threw down his headband as he ran. At once a bunch of ripe grapes sprang up and these, as he had hoped, the monster stopped to gobble up. Soon it continued its pursuit, running with the Eight Spirit Thunders beside it.

Now Izanagi tossed aside his second hair comb and it became bamboo shoots, which once more the monster stopped to rip up and devour hungrily. This time it created and ordered ahead fully 1500 long-fanged soldiers of the night, which Izanagi desperately fought off with his sword.

Still fleeing, he came to the pass between the physical world that can be seen and touched, whose mysteries can be largely understood and the other dimension which is unknown. Here a mystical peach tree grew and Izanagi, weary and out of breath, stopped to rest. As his enemies appeared, he threw peaches at them and all except the monster itself retreated before this magical onslaught. With a mighty effort, Izanagi pushed and rolled an enormous boulder into the pass, blocking it.

On the other side he heard his sister-lover gasping for breath from her exertions. He shouted out his anger and outrage. Forever, he cried, he would deny her. They were no longer one. He would divorce her.

"Ah, but if you do that," she screamed back at him, "my handsome brother, my lover, if you do that, every day I will eat alive a thousand people of the land you still so care for."

"If so, my lovely sister-lover," he retorted grimly, "I will cause fifteen hundred women to give birth each night."

Thus, the human condition was forever set.

Amaterasu and Susanoo – The Sun and the Seas

*The word 'Shinto' means 'the way of the gods', and Shintoism –
the original religion of Japan – involves the worship of many gods.
The most important myths of Shintoism involve the Sun
goddess Amaterasu, from whom the ruling family is said to be descended.
There are several shrines to Amaterasu in Japan but the principal
one dedicated to her is at Ise. Until the first century
BC she was still worshipped in the imperial place itself,
but as the power of the emperor grew he began to resent the
curb on his authority exercised by the priestesses through the oracles
of the goddess, and the decision was made to move her
shrine to a less politically sensitive place.
Interestingly, in the mythologies of most other cultures the sun is
invariably a god and not a goddess. As myths go,
I found this one irresistible.*

After Izanagi and Izanami – the seventh generation of self-created gods to exist in the heavens – made the world and many other deities, they fell out with one another. Some of their creations were the result of the god and goddess breeding, some came about during and following their dispute. One way or the other all were due to their shared fruitfulness.

Izanami had died giving birth to the god of fire but had not liked it when Izanagi had intruded on her life in the underworld. Izanagi had felt unclean after escaping her wrath. He discarded his contaminated clothing and cleansed himself by diving into the river Tachibana. Two gods of different ills came forth from this and so he made two more gods to set such ills right.

He dived into the sea, causing creatures and gods from this realm to come into existence. While bathing his left eye he gave birth to the goddess of the sun, Amaterasu, and while bathing his right eye, he created the god of the moon, Tsukiyomi. Washing his nose caused the birth of the god Susanoo.

Izanagi ordered his eldest daughter to rule the plain of Heaven and gave her a necklace of jewels. To the god of the moon he entrusted the realm of the night and to the god Susanoo, the kingdom of the seas. The deities of the sun and the moon obeyed Izanagi and left at once to assume their responsibilities, but Susanoo lingered, weeping and groaning so that his father asked what troubled him.

When Susanoo said he wanted to be with his dead mother, Izanagi became furious. Perhaps he preferred to suppose he had created all things since his wife's physical death by himself, or it may have been that he had simply not forgiven her for their quarrel. He banished Susanoo, who wished only to say farewell to his elder sister before going to the underworld.

In Heaven Amaterasu was unsure of her brother's intentions and right away he made such a lot of noise, shaking the mountains and rivers and making the earth quake, that she took precautions before meeting him. Slinging a quiver of arrows on her back she held a bow in her lap, tweaking and vibrating the string as he approached.

"Why have you come?" she asked.

"I have no evil in my heart," he assured her. "I wanted to visit you awhile and to say goodbye before I go to the faraway place where our mother is."

"You can be very loud and disruptive ..."

"But I have come to be friendly and creative," he told her, and as a sign of this made a proposal. "Let us make some children. I will create boys and you girls. What do you say?"

"Very well," she nodded. "Give me your sword."

Susanoo did as she asked and Amaterasu broke the sword into three pieces and put them into her mouth. Chewing them up, she then spat them out in the form of a fine mist and this mist became three new goddesses.

Impressed but not willing to be outdone, Susanoo asked his sister for the five strings of jewels around her neck. She gave them to him and he too popped them into his mouth, chewed them up and spat them out in a mist. This mist turned into five new gods.

Amaterasu declared that all the children were hers because the five gods were made from jewellery that belonged to her. Susanoo did not protest or point out that the sword had belonged to him. He was too pleased with his creations and the welcome it provided him in Heaven. The trouble was he got carried away with his celebrations, even going so far as to play very mean and destructive practical jokes, such as destroying rice fields prepared by his sister. He also filled in irrigation ditches and threw dung into temples built for the festival of the First Fruits. To begin with, Amaterasu tried to make excuses for her brother, but in the end he went too far. One day, while she was weaving clothes for the gods in the sacred house, Susanoo made a hole in the roof and dropped a completely skinned piebald horse through it.

This horrific sight caused such a panic that in the confusion one of the weaving women pricked herself with a needle and died. Amaterasu was so terrified that she ran away and hid herself in a Heavenly cave high among some rocks and blocked the entrance with a boulder. Below and above, the world suddenly went dark.

The darkness naturally proved a great help to the wicked gods, much to the consternation of the good ones, confirming in all minds that something had to be done to bring the sun goddess back. The eight hundred gods of all kinds gathered in a dry riverbed to decide what steps to take.

Upon the advice of the god of 'Hoard-thoughts', they brought offerings to the mouth of the cave, such as strings of jewels, a large mirror, a bright sword which were hung, along with banners, in the branches of a Sakaki tree facing the cave. They also brought many cocks to announce the dawn. They spoke ritual words and played music.

The goddess Ama no Uzume, who was thought by some to be a

little vain, dressed herself ornately and further embellished her appearance with different plants and bamboo leaves. Then she mounted an up-ended tub near the entrance to the cave where Amaterasu was hiding, and began to dance upon it, drumming rhythmically with her feet, swaying with the music as the cocks began to crow. Soon she was in a state of divine ecstasy and got so carried away that slowly, one by one, she began removing her plants and leaves, then her actual clothing until she was dancing completely naked.

All eight hundred gods began to applaud and laugh so loudly that Amaterasu became curious. First there had been the crowing then the music, now such laughter – she wondered what was going on outside. Moving the boulder aside just a crack, she shouted out to ask what was happening.

"Just that a better, brighter goddess than that of the sun has been found," taunted Uzume.

Intrigued, and maybe a touch jealous, Amaterasu poked her head out of the cave to see better. As she did so she caught a glimpse of her reflection in the mirror. This was indeed a shiningly beautiful goddess. Almost instantly she realized she was looking at herself. She came a little closer to admire her reflected image, then suddenly the god of force grabbed her and pulled her away from the cave. Some of the other gods shoved the boulder back and threw a straw rope, or shimenawa, across the mouth of the cave so that she could not hide herself again.

And so the sun was restored to the heavens and light returned to the world. Amaterasu was forbidden to go away again and Susanoo was to be punished. The other gods fined him heavily and his beard and moustache were cut off. They even tore out his fingernails before tossing him out of Heaven.

Susanoo became a god of fertility much associated with serpents, as well as the god of thunder, storm and rain. He had a good spirit, which did good things but a bad spirit too, and in that guise he never really learned his lesson. However, in killing a snake that had been devouring an old couple's daughters, he found within it a sword, which he gave as a present to Amaterasu. After that he married and built a palace at Suga, where he and his new wife had a son who became Lord of Izamo.

Roland

The real Roland on whom this legend is based was a Frankish soldier who commanded the emperor Charlemagne's army at the battle of Roncesvalles in 778. The Franks had been withdrawing from a campaign in Spain and were on their way back through the Pyrenees to put down an uprising among the recently conquered Saxons of Germany when their rearguard was attacked by Basques. Some 300 years later the death of Roland in this action would be woven into the Chanson de Roland *('Song of Roland') from which the soldier would emerge as a Christian hero, nephew of Charlemagne and staunch enemy of Islam. Aside from its historical inaccuracy (the Franks had been in Spain giving military assistance to a group of Saracen princes), there is a fundamental truth at the core of this story: pride almost certainly does come before a hefty fall.*

The Saracen King Marsile of Saragossa ground his jaw and looked around at his advisers. The emperor of the Franks, Charles the Great, also known as Carlos Magnus or Charlemagne, was ravishing Spain, carrying all before him in battle and doubtless even now plotting the conquest of Saragossa itself. At this thought a shiver ran through Marsile. It was not just concern for his city, for his people, family and wealth but for his very soul. His greatest fear was that, in defeat, facing whatever unknown pressures, perhaps hideous tortures, he might be forced to renounce Islam and become a Christian.

Thus far, and with much courage, Saragossa had held out, but it was clear that even the resistance of the people of this mountain stronghold could not last much longer. The faces of his most able councillors looked as mournful as he felt his own must appear. Sitting as he was on a seat of blue marble, in the shade of an orchard, all in seeming peace, he sighed and prepared to address his advisers on perhaps the most painful subject a king can possibly contemplate. Surrender.

"My lords," he began, "you know our plight, you know the enemy's great strength. Advise me, if you can, upon what course it would be best to take to spare my people and realm from disgrace and death."

All hung their heads and remained silent except Blancandrin, the wily emir of Val-Fonde. Wise, courageous and loyal, he had been the one man the king had most been counting on. In the past he had given invaluable service to his liege-lord.

"Do not despair, Sire," Blancandrin said, coming forward with a bow. "Send to the proud and arrogant Charles a message promising fealty and true service. Give him magnificent gifts of rare wild beasts, lions, bears, and speedy hounds, hundreds of camels, birds of prey, mules and gold enough to fill fifty carts."

The king and his other advisers looked shocked. Blancandrin continued.

"Yes, gold, my liege, gold enough for him to pay his vassals. Gold enough to please even men wealthy with all the loot of the north of Spain and elsewhere. Gold enough for much honour. And, above all, say you will take the Christian faith."

At this the king nearly choked, but Blancandrin carried on.

"Say you will follow him to Aix and be baptised there. Say you are even now a believer but that you must further prepare yourself and your kingdom for the change."

Pale and hardly breathing, Marsile waved one hand in protest and pounded the arm of his chair with the other.

"You will not go, of course, Sire. You will never go," Blancandrin said quickly, kneeling at the feet of his sovereign.

"But ... but ..." the king stammered.

"What if Charles demands hostages?" asked one of the other royal advisers.

"As surely he will," muttered yet another.

"Yes," Marsile nodded, coming to himself once more. "What then?"

It was plain that the clever emir had something in mind, however.

"He shall have hostages," said Blancandrin firmly. "The best we have, my own son among them. Aye, and the sons of every man here, and daughters if they have none."

"Yet you say I am not to go to Aix," the king said, puzzled. "That I will never be baptised as I am to promise Charles."

"You shall not."

"Then what of the hostages?" cried another emir. "They will have been taken to France as pledge of His Majesty's word."

"They shall surely die," Blancandrin replied solemnly. "But I am willing to suffer this. I am willing to give my son for my king." He turned to the assembly. "Will you, my lords? Is it not the only way? Charles will have left our country, his army will mostly have disbanded, the rest going into winter quarters. They have been here and elsewhere on campaign for many, many years. Charles is growing old. Maybe he will tell his people he has conquered us anyway. He will have much of our wealth and our beloved hostages. Perhaps he will never return to Spain. And if he does, it will not be for at least a year, probably longer. We will have bought much valuable time."

The king bowed his head and raised his arms helplessly.

"Well," Blancandrin addressed his fellows. "Are you willing?"

"For the king," said one of them. At the back another voice agreed, then another. Soon, all had promised to provide a hostage for certain sacrifice.

"Very well then," Marsile nodded slowly. "It is the only way." With that he dismissed all but his inner council, which consisted of ten trusted men. Principal among these was Blancandrin.

"Go, my lords and take this offer to Charles at Cordoba," he commanded them. "Bear olive branches and other tokens of peace. Take all pains to reconcile me with him. Beseech him to have pity on me and say that I will come to Aix within a month to be received into the Christian faith and to swear fealty to him, to become his vassal in love and loyalty. Do all this and I will reward you exceedingly well."

So it was that the ten men soon set off, carrying olive branches, riding white mules, with reins of gold and saddles of silver. Passing through Charles' army, which was resting after the taking and sacking of Cordoba, the envoys realized that none of the Frankish soldiers seemed surprised to see the deputation from Saragossa.

They found Charlemagne situated as they had left Marsile, in a pleasant orchard, his Twelve Peers nearby. The difference was that Charles was at the heart of a great and victorious army. It was the state of that army, especially those closest to Charles, that most worried Blancandrin, giving him doubts about the likely success of his plan.

Charlemagne sat on a throne, surrounded by wise nobles and enthusiastic young men, watching the fencing bouts and games of chess going on around him. No one needed to point out the king to the newly arrived members of the embassy. With a flowing beard, grey head and stately carriage, majesty written in every aspect of his appearance and manner, they knew him at once.

Having been announced and brought before Charles, the ambassadors paid homage to him and to his God.

"Peace be upon you from God, to whom you are devoted. These words are those of our brave King Marsile, who has been secretly converted to your faith, the way of salvation, and he only wishes to be baptised."

"But this is marvellous news," cried Charlemagne. He paused then looked to heaven and gave silent thanks while all around his nobles, knights and men twittered in amazement.

"Peace for all is his fondest desire," Blancandrin went on. "Your armies have long been in Spain. You are triumphant and we are weary of war. You, Your Majesty, may now return to France in full glory, having conquered all. My liege lord will follow you to Aix in due course and there be baptized. He will become your vassal, with you holding the kingdom of Spain in your hand. Many gifts have we brought to lay at your feet, fine treasures, splendid objects and rare beasts, for our king will share all he has with you."

These wondrous things were then brought forth and spread before Charles and the Twelve Peers and the officers and soldiers round about.

"It is well," Charlemagne nodded with satisfaction. Nevertheless, he held off saying more. He was a prudent man and never hasty when a decision was not a matter of urgency. He considered everything he had heard before he spoke. "Yes, it is well," he repeated. "Yet, forgive me, how am I to credit this wonder? Marsile willing to accept Christ, to swear fealty to me ... to give these treasures, and more, I take it?"

"Much more, Sire."

"Yes, and yet Marsile is my greatest enemy. How am I to believe he will keep his word to me if I take my army back to France?"

"Naturally, many assurances, word of honour first among them, will constitute the king's bond, but he will also give twenty of our most noble youths, including my own son, as hostages. These, our beloved offspring, will be the King's absolute guarantees of good faith. Marsile will follow you, after preparing his nobles and people for the changes in himself and our country. He will join you in Aix-la-Chapelle on the feast of St. Michael and receive baptism at your court."

On the face of it this unexpected news of Marsile's peace offer was an occasion for rejoicing and a pavilion was erected in the orchard, where the ambassadors were guests of honour at a merry feast, full of companionship and the expression of fine feelings.

After mass the next morning Charlemange called together the Twelve Peers, principal nobles, knights and officers. Chief among these twelve heroes were Roland, his friend and brother-in-law to be Oliver, and the Archbishop Turpin. Standing a little to the rear of another group of nobles was Ganelon, Roland's stepfather. A deep and abiding enmity divided him and Roland. In the bold, young warrior there could be found perhaps too much arrogance and stubbornness; in the mean spirited and sly Ganelon, alas, blind selfishness and downright treachery.

"As all of you must know by now," Charlemagne began, "a delegation from Marsile of Saragossa arrived yesterday with gifts and offers of still greater gifts, with a plea for peace from their king and assurances that he wishes fervently to accept our faith and become my loyal vassal. All this on condition, mind you, that I take the army out of Spain and return to Aix. Who among you thinks I can trust him?"

"Trust him, my liege, my uncle?" Roland cried, leaping to his feet. "Trust him, yes, by all means, to betray us at the first opportunity. It would be insanity to believe him, his ambassadors or his troops in so much as a local truce to bury the dead. I have campaigned with you here in Spain these seven years, won you many cities and well I remember the last time you and the French foolishly trusted him. He sent an embassy then, holding olive branches and speaking soft words, and when our own messengers were sent in return, they were beheaded, murdered. I say avenge those two counts, prosecute this war to the end. Bring Saragossa under siege, take the place by storm, put it to the torch and punish Marsile for the two-faced evil he has already amply shown."

After this outburst silence descended on the assembly and Charlemagne looked grave and deeply thoughtful. The young hero spoke truly enough and fairly. It had been foolish to trust Marsile before, impudent though it was for his nephew to say so.

"Sire," Ganelon said, stepping forward through the throng. "My step-son is to be applauded for his zeal and his past service in these wars. For such his youth and boldness are of inestimable value."

The look the two exchanged at this point all but burned those standing between them. Their hatred was palpable.

"However, recognizing opportunities for making peace and settling matters of state are best left to older, cooler heads."

"Perhaps so," Charlemagne smiled.

"And yes, my liege," Ganelon went on. "Of course, Marsile betrayed us before. Who has forgotten? But things were very different then. He yet had hopes of defeating us in battle."

"That is true," the king and others around them allowed.

"We must be practical, though to younger heads it seems tame and tiresome, womanish even. We older men know better. The Franks cannot stay in Spain forever. We have beaten our enemies. When God places in a wise man's path such an opportunity as this, it is foolish and impious to refuse. Marsile, Sire, offers you peace and treasure, to place his realm in your hands, to accept Christ. Why, any man who would urge you to refuse such terms is careless not only of his own life but yours and that of many others, careless indeed of God's good grace."

Only the distance and press of bodies separating them kept Roland from rushing at Ganelon, that and the restraining grip of Oliver. The moment passed, too, because the most respected and experienced soldier amongst the assembly spoke up in qualified support of what Ganelon had said.

"This is good advice Count Ganelon gives," said the venerable Duke of Naimes, "if taken well. Marsile is desperate. He has few men to fight with and fewer still willing to do so. His allies are defeated, his chance of receiving help from elsewhere is gone. It would be a sin to fight on if there is no need, if Marsile is sincere, if there will be important hostages, if he will, in fact, take the faith. Yet be cautious too. Risk only a single one of us as ambassador to be sent back with the Emir Blancandrin to settle the peace and make the necessary arrangements."

Everyone applauded the duke's wisdom and when the murmurs of approval had died down the king posed the obvious question.

"Who shall undertake this task? Who shall we send to Marsile of Saragossa?"

"I will go, of course, Sire," the Duke of Naimes said matter-of-factly. "Give me your glove and your staff and I ..."

"No," Charlemagne barked. "I'll not be deprived of my chief adviser at such a time as this. Someone else."

"Me, uncle," Roland stepped forward. "I will do this for you, Sire, and I will not be fooled by any of his tricks."

"You cannot do this work," cried Oliver, shaking his head and throwing an arm around his friend. "You are too quick tempered, too impatient and blunt. I would be afraid you would fail in your office and be killed as well. I will go, Majesty."

"No, neither of you shall go," Charlemagne waved his hand dismissively. "No Peer shall. Thus would we give them a hostage. Who else is willing?"

"I, my King," said the Archbishop Turpin. "Give me your glove and staff and I will take the message to the heathen. I will also see how Marsile's heart is truly disposed regarding Our Lord."

"No, no, not you either," Charlemagne snapped. That would be too tricky, as well he knew, if Marsile was having a delicate time justifying his conversion to his court and people. Turpin was too great a prize for the enemy if treachery was afoot.

"What brave knight of France will undertake this deed? Choose one of yourselves to perform this task and defend the honour of his king if necessary, alone among the heathen."

The obvious distress of the king, who knew this mission might well mean suicide for the man who undertook it, angered Roland. Charlemagne did not wish to order a man to his death, yet none who had volunteered thus far was suitable. It was the fault of Ganelon, Roland believed, that things had come to this, yet he was noticeably silent now. Before any other knight or noble could speak up, Roland again sprang to his feet.

"Sire, if the honour cannot be mine, then surely no man in all the army is a better choice than my stepfather, Count Ganelon. He is wise, experienced, and inspired in this cause, as we have already heard."

Another fiery look shot between the two men. Ganelon's face had gone very pale and his lips trembled.

All around them the justice and wisdom of sending Ganelon was repeated and heartily agreed upon. Men slapped his back and shook his hand and as the king beckoned to him, he was proudly propelled towards Charlemagne.

"Come, Ganelon," Charles said. "And take the glove and staff, for the voice of the flower of France has cried for you."

"No," shouted Ganelon before he could stop himself, fear and anger taking control of his tongue. "I am the victim of a conspiracy of Roland. He, Oliver and the other Peers are my enemies. I will never forgive them and here before you all I swear it." Ganelon snarled.

"Calm yourself, Ganelon," Charlemagne said. "You are too unjust and angry. You will go because I wish it."

"Yes, Sire, I will go," Ganelon ranted on. "I will go and be murdered like your last two messengers. Oh, remember that I am your sister's husband, that my son will be a brave hero one day if he comes to manhood." Nearly in tears now, Ganelon continued. "Let him inherit all my lands and fiefs and please watch over him, Sire, for I will never see him again."

"Your thoughts are too dark, Ganelon," Charlemagne said more gently. "I command you to go to Saragossa and perform this duty, and you must go."

Rage once more flared within Ganelon's heart and he flew at Roland, struggling with the men around them.

"Lunatic!" he screamed. "Everyone knows that you hate me for marrying your father's widow, and now you have thrown me to the wolves. You have contrived to send me to Marsile and my certain death."

"Sire," Roland laughed. "I care nothing for these ravings but should not a cooler head be sent on this errand and not a raging idiot? Ganelon, if the king allows it, I will go after all."

"No, I will do my own work. The king has commanded me and I will obey." Ganelon said, growing more controlled as he made his way through the throng towards Roland. "I go to Saragossa, knowing the dangers, for my king," he said loudly, but as he drew near Roland he leant towards him and added, so that only Roland and those nearest him could hear, "Perhaps there I will find a way to be avenged on you."

At this rashness and wild talk, Roland started to laugh, and so incensed Ganelon that he howled in rage and cast aside all discretion.

"I despise you and it is you who have left me with this horrible decision. You will pay," he growled. "My king," he said, turning to address Charlemagne. "I stand before you ready to perform any office you wish. I willingly go to Saragossa."

"Excellent Lord Ganelon," the king said, like the others not taking seriously the count's threats against Roland and thinking him at last himself again. "Take these terms to Marsile: he is to become my vassal, and be baptised; half of Spain will remain in his hands, the other half will go to Count Roland. If he refuses, tell him I will besiege and capture Saragossa, make him a prisoner, leading him through the streets of Aix in shame, where he will die in torment. Take this letter with my seal and place it into King Marsile's own hand."

With that Charlemagne held out his right-hand glove for Ganelon to take. Such was the latter's reluctance to accept it, that it fell from his grasp onto the ground between them. All around the surprise and shock at this bad omen softly rumbled in gasps and whispers.

"What ill-fortune will come to the Franks from this business?" men asked of themselves and each other.

"You will be sent detailed news as soon as possible, Sire," Ganelon said. "And now I must hurry. There is no time to be lost if peace be the prize; and, if death, no point in dallying."

As Ganelon bowed low, Charlemagne made the sign of the cross over him and enjoined him to go for the honour of Christ, and for his king.

Back at his quarters, while preparing to depart for Saragossa, Ganelon refused to allow any of his retainers to accompany him, saying there was no need for good knights and men to die for nothing. He preferred to face the ordeal alone but beseeched them to look after his wife and son, Baldwin, and to guard his fiefdom. In tears they said farewell to him and he rode from the Frankish army's encampment with his heart in his mouth.

Riding hard, Ganelon soon overtook the Saracen ambassadors, who were returning to Saragossa at a deliberately leisurely pace so that he might catch up. Blancandrin greeted the nobleman warmly and invited him to ride by his side. As they rode on, each sized up the other.

Both made handsome speeches and adopted a friendly tone but behind this façade they were full of purpose, wishing to read the other's thoughts. The two envoys quickly saw in the other a skilful, cautious opponent and mutually enjoyed employing their guile in the mental fencing that occupied their journey.

For Ganelon, the challenge was to try to ascertain what his fate would be at the court of Marsile. Could Charlemagne trust the Saracen? Was he, Ganelon, going to be killed out of hand in some act of pure savagery, as part of some desperate attempt to draw the Franks into a rash attack? Were the Saracens stronger than was thought? Largely, too, Ganelon was desperate to find a way to revenge himself on Roland, and to do this he had to proceed with just as much, if not more, caution.

Blancandrin for his part needed to understand the Franks, to judge what they would do in the circumstances of the treaty being broken. It was on this point that the true meeting of their minds occurred. All their skill at deception and diplomacy could not hide this, one from the other.

For his mission, his life and his revenge, Ganelon was at pains to quite truthfully emphasize the danger the Franks posed, if crossed. He stressed Roland's talent and enthusiasm for war, and the loyalty to him of the Twelve Peers.

All this, while not being music to his ears, Blancandrin accepted with the good grace of a man whose pride did not allow him to underestimate his enemies. In his conversations with the Frankish envoy an unexpected truth emerged which he quickly saw could be used to advantage by his side. Ganelon, as if attempting at first to conceal it, let his hatred of Roland show. It was this seeming indiscretion that cheered Blancandrin, and it was Blancandrin's not too well concealed curiosity that cheered Ganelon.

Eventually, after a particularly vehement remark about Roland, Blancandrin laid his cards on the table. The plan of delaying, getting the Franks out of the country and then reneging on the agreement (in the hope they would not return soon or at all) was now in tatters, if what Ganelon said of Roland was true. The emir might have been more incredulous if he had only Ganelon's word for this – Ganelon, whose very life depended on Marsile believing it. However, his own observations, spies' reports, and the fact that Roland stood to gain half of Spain, told him the same story.

"Do you have something personal against Count Roland?" Blancandrin asked in lowered tones, leaning a little out of his saddle towards Ganelon.

Ganelon remained silent but his face burned with rage and he would not meet the emir's eye.

"You desire revenge upon him." Blancandrin suggested.

"'I hate him," Ganelon snarled, nodding reluctantly at the same time, as if unable to withhold his fury at the mention of his stepson's name. It required no fine acting.

Even now they wordlessly entered into a conspiracy to destroy Roland, each in his own mind feeling the other's certainty. It was only a matter of time before it came to be openly discussed, details worked out and measures taken. At this juncture neither man wished to risk speaking aloud of it. The matter had to mature within them and between them, and the emir would have to discuss it with his king. Ganelon knew that, too, of course.

At Saragossa Blancandrin and the other ambassadors brought Ganelon before King Marsile, praising Charlemagne's gracious reception of their message to him. Formally they presented the Frankish envoy.

"Speak, sir, and I will listen," Marsile nodded.

After a flowery and pious greeting, Ganelon spelt out Charlemagne's terms.

"You will be received into the Christian faith. Charles will allow you one half of Spain as your fief, the rest he will give to his nephew Roland." Ganelon announced, adding as an aside, "And an arrogant fellow ruler you shall have in him."

Ignoring the king's look and growing hostility among the assembly, he went on.

"If you refuse, Charles will conquer this city and bring you as a prisoner to Aix, where you will surely meet a miserable and humiliating end."

Furious at this galling message, Marsile leapt up and would have skewered the Frankish envoy on the spot with his golden javelin, but that Ganelon, half expecting such a move, had nearly drawn his sword in self-defence.

"I die gladly for my king," shouted Ganelon. "Yea, and die in noble company with a king, covered in his royal Spanish blood."

Thus given pause, and impressed with Ganelon's ferocity, Marsile allowed himself to be calmed down while all praised the Frank's courage in standing up to the monarch in the name of his own king. When order had been restored, Ganelon repeated Charlemagne's message and handed Marsile the sealed letter he had been given.

Reading this, Marsile's face went red and uproar ensued when it was found to contain a further condition. Marsile's own uncle, the Caliph, who had been responsible for the deaths of the two previous ambassadors, was to be given up as a prisoner.

Now, not only the king but every nobleman present was angry and Ganelon was forced to place his back against a tree and draw his sword, ready to defend himself to the death. Once more, largely due to Blancandrin's intervention, violence was avoided. Marsile adjourned the audience and went away to confer with his advisers.

Soon Blancandrin returned and conducted Ganelon to the council. "Forgive my former anger," Marsile told him. "Please accept this gift as a token of my regret."

An attendant presented Ganelon with a marvellous robe of marten's fur which he graciously took, hoping that he was correct in believing that he knew what would follow. If he read the look from Blancandrin correctly, they were about to woo him, to try and tempt him to treason.

"You understand that these negotiations and my sad position go hard with me," Marsile continued. "And I am still a relatively young king, a little rash still, I confess. Great Charles of course is very wise and full of years."

"That is so," Ganelon agreed.

"It is the only advantage I have over him," Marsile smiled. "In that way only do I pity him. To be so old, so weighed down with age and responsibility. He surely must grow weary of it all."

"Charles is yet full of power and strength and has no trouble governing his empire."

"Yet how much longer can he sustain it?" Marsile sighed. "Yes, as to age I pity him. I doubt not that death holds no fear for Charles, brave and pious, but to wonder and worry over the fate of his domain ..."

"As long as Roland and the Twelve Peers yet breathe," Ganelon insisted, "Charles need never worry or wonder, nor trouble himself over any power under heaven. He has them, and in the Franks he has the most valiant warriors alive."

"But without Roland?" Blancandrin prompted at last. "What if he were dead?"

"Will you have revenge on him through us?" Marsile suddenly asked. "If it can be turned to our advantage, we will help you destroy your enemy and I will reward you also with great wealth. All this will be done circumspectly, of course, that you may yet return to France with all honour. What say you?"

"Perhaps it can be done to the satisfaction of your cause and mine," Ganelon said thoughtfully. He had, in fact, considered little else since leaving the French camp. The trouble was convincing the Saracens, whom he now knew had intended to violate the treaty all along, that all was not lost.

"If Roland were dead," he exaggerated, "Charles would be thrown into deep melancholy and indecision. He would need to return at once to France to consolidate his power and look to the future succession. He would have little enough interest in Spain."

"Truly?" Marsile wondered turning to his advisers.

"It is possible," Blancandrin allowed. "But assassination would be difficult of execution and may accomplish nothing but ..."

"To make your situation worse," Ganelon agreed. "The Twelve Peers, Oliver particularly, would not rest until you were destroyed, even if Charles himself returned to France. For you to have a hope, they must all die."

"But how is such a thing to be accomplished?" Marsile enquired, shaking his head. "Would not the army of the Franks, in anger and for policy, still overwhelm us?"

"Yes, with more difficulty perhaps, but yes."

"Above all, the Frankish army must be got out of Spain," Blancandrin said.

"And Roland left vulnerable to us. To you," Ganelon nodded. "Here is how it may be done, with all your remaining troops and my manipulation back at Charles' court. Firstly, do as you have offered. Pretend to accept the terms of my message. Send gold and other treasure as agreed, send hostages and I will assure Charles that you are willing and happy to be baptised soon. Let the French depart over the high mountain passes, carrying this booty and all they have taken from the rest of Spain. Incite the people of the mountains against them and stress the presence of the treasure, but say it goes with the Peers, that only they can be trusted with it by Charles. This you may tell your own men, too.

I will see to it that, because of these mountain tribes and hot heads among your people, a strong rearguard is left this side of the passes. This will consist of Roland and the Twelve Peers, our finest men and the best ones for the job."

"This sounds promising," Blancandrin smiled, for what Ganelon suggested was an enhancement of his own plan. "And you are certain Charles will not turn and aid the rearguard, or quickly return and avenge it?"

"Once they are through the passes you and the local tribes will have little to fear from them. Without Roland and the Peers to lead and inspire them, in the difficulty and cold of the mountains, already nearly home in France with their new wealth, again as I say, the king needing to settle the succession, the Franks will not return. Not soon, perhaps never. And I will always advise against it," Ganelon declared grandly. "I will thwart the expedition at every turn if it is mounted, or even lead it myself and do little once here."

Looking at the faces of Marsile, Blancandrin and the other Saracen nobles, Ganelon knew they would agree to his plan, that they wanted to believe him when he said the Franks would not return.

"Defeating and destroying Roland and the rearguard will not be simple in itself," one emir with great battle experience and a good knowledge of Marsile's men commented. "If any portion of the Frankish force manages to return we may meet with disaster still, having risked all."

"I will tell you how it may be accomplished, knowing Roland and his flaws," Ganelon smiled broadly.

The traitor duly returned to the Frankish camp and presented the physical evidence of Marsile's willingness to accept Charlemagne's terms in full. Of course, this consisted of what seemed endless treasure and the most noble, well-connected young hostages. Alas, according to the testimony of Count Ganelon himself, Marsile's uncle had died at sea trying to leave Spain with several followers. The count was certain there was no doubt of it. He also attested to the sincerity of Marsile's

Christian conversion. All this seemed assurance enough.

Preparations were begun at once for the army's return to France, during which time nothing occurred to indicate any changes in the position of the parties to the treaty. Roland, while suspicious as ever of the Saracens, had forgotten – or so completely dismissed his stepfather's threats – that he looked for no danger from that quarter, though their enmity had not disappeared.

So it was that as the army moved off at last and entered the mountains, a messenger from Marsile arrived and spoke to Ganelon. None was surprised by the information the latter relayed to Charles. The traitor had already prepared the way cleverly.

"A few disaffected knights," he reported to Charles, "and the greed of the people who live in the mountains, may, King Marsile fears, lead to attempts to harass the rear of our column as we approach the high passes. There may even be an attempt to hold the passes against us for a time after most of the column has passed. They might hope thereafter to rally others who might turn against Marsile and defy France further. While Marsile's reign is secure, and these forces pose no major threat," Ganelon pretended to surmise, "he feels it best to warn us, to avoid misunderstanding, and to make sure we are not caught off guard."

"That is wise of him," Charlemagne said.

"We have left Marsile too weak to easily challenge these men himself or he would send warriors to do so ..."

"We can protect ourselves from a few marauders," Roland scoffed. "Had I not better form a rearguard for the column, Sire?" he asked his uncle, obviously keen to fight in this one last action of the war.

"Yes," Charlemagne smiled indulgently. "Pick your men."

Meanwhile, Ganelon smiled a different sort of smile.

Inevitably the courteous and valiant Oliver, the fighting Archbishop Turpin and the other Twelve Peers of France volunteered, along with the cream of the army. Roland decided to share the sport with the Peers, but in addition to them chose only a few hundred knights and men at arms to make up the main body of the force.

Charlemagne nearly vetoed this idea as rash, and considered ordering a larger unit of good veterans commanded by one of his excellent barons.

"Such a move, while wise in time of war, might prove counter-productive now, Sire," Ganelon said, even before Roland himself could protest. "In these circumstances it could provoke an even larger attack, seeming to signal to the enemy that we take Spain too lightly. These lands will be Roland's and he must stare down the die-hards and if need be dispatch them personally to leave his mark."

Charlemagne, preoccupied with his return to France, agreed, but later as he moved away with the centre of the column, after making a brief farewell to Roland and the others, his heart grew heavy. This feeling increased with each stride of his horse. What had he dreamt the night before? He tried to recall. And what was that which seemed to pass between Roland and Ganelon as they parted? Another argument, surely, but about what? And why just then? Ganelon was riding near at hand. He could ask him, but that would be foolish. It was their business and no doubt they always bickered. But what had that bad dream been about, the great king wondered.

Ganelon noticed Charles look in his direction but thought little of it. He was happily recalling his final exchange with Roland.

"Thank you stepfather for your words in my behalf," Roland had smiled a touch ironically. "Perhaps the role of wise adviser has come to suit you, after your survival as an envoy."

"My survival," Ganelon hissed in a low voice, "was thanks only to my own wit, which is your ill-fortune. But if you perhaps thought you would long regret my returning alive from Saragossa, you are wrong. You will regret it, but not long. Not long."

Now these words meant little to Roland, for he feared nothing Ganelon might do to him, but it was the smug, self-satisfied look in his stepfather's eyes that sent a chill through him. It was not what he might do, but what he had done and would yet be done with much help.

"You have betrayed me, you treasonous vermin," Roland growled. "But, unlike you, I will not whimper, nor bring an ill-omen to my errand by dropping from a shaking hand the symbol of my office."

Boldly, letting on to no one what he suspected, Roland stepped forward for the king's bow, swearing no harm would come to a single man or horse of the column while he guarded its rear. Only the guttural words and glares that he and Ganelon exchanged had signalled to anyone a hint of what had passed between them.

As Ganelon had guessed, again correctly, Roland's pride would not allow him to complain or explain, let alone ask for help. He also knew that even now, the Saracen host was gathering, armed with yet more well-judged information about Roland and the Twelve Peers. They would follow to the letter his advice about how best to destroy them, though it would cost more men in the process. It was too good and logical a plan to do otherwise. Ganelon's revenge would be most thorough.

As the army of the Franks wound its way through the high passes of the Pyrenees, and with glad hearts down towards fair France, Roland, resplendent in his gleaming armour, rode before the men of the imperilled rearguard. He well knew that his own honour, his men's lives and the safety of all the Frankish troops lay in his hands.

On the march as they were, in linear formation along the narrow tracks and defiles, inter-mixed with camp followers and the cumbersome baggage train, the army was vulnerable. A force overwhelming its rear could roll it up and cause many deaths and much damage to even so large and well seasoned a body of men as Charlemagne's. Calculating his betrayal, Roland, even better than his wretched stepfather, knew what a position the men of France were now in.

This bigger treachery angered Roland more than the idea that he himself had been placed in a dangerous position. That Charlemagne and his army, that the very point of these wars had been put in jeopardy over a personal dispute, enraged him. Alas, he cursed his stepfather under his breath and set about making the best of a bad situation. It did not cross Roland's mind to send back for more men, to have Ganelon arrested, to contact the Saracens and warn them of the consequences of renewed hostilities.

Roland would stand. He would endure. He would protect the Frankish rear, defying his personal and national enemies, and, he felt sure, win through or die magnificently. Either option was perfectly acceptable, both to Roland and nearly all the men at his command. Indeed, none was shaken even when a patrol led by his vassal Count Gautier did not return, but only the mortally wounded count himself.

Rushing from his bleeding friend to the top of a rise in the sloping ground, Roland joined Oliver. Here, through caution and a sense of military duty beyond personal glory, was the only man who would or could question him. Oliver had long been standing on the high place observing the enemy and hearing their shouts of self-encouragement and grisly plans for the Franks. Many cried out "Death to the Twelve" or boasted of his individual certainty of personally slaying Roland.

"We are going to have a very big fight on our hands, my friend," Oliver remarked.

"Good," Roland smiled grimly. "That is as it should be. Gautier shall soon be avenged."

"The enemy is in force," Oliver went on, "and manoeuvring to surround us."

"Even very good," Roland nodded. "We shall soon have them just where we want them."

"Hadn't we better increase the odds in our favour, though, old comrade?"

"Why trouble the king and the army with a duty we have sworn to perform?"

"Because," Oliver turned to his friend, a little impatiently, "we are betrayed. That is plain. The Moors cry out for us. They know already whom they face and there will be more of the enemy than these. Ganelon has done for you and all of us."

"Yes," Roland sighed, bowing his head. "I know it."

"Then blow your mighty war horn and alert the king and the army to our plight."

"No, that is not necessary. We can carry the day against these heathens and I will not dishonour our bold contingent by calling for help."

"But you admit we are betrayed by Ganelon. This will be far from the equal fight it seems. They are not as they appear merely twice our number but many more still. Ganelon has created this trap for us."

"Speak not of my stepfather now, he is my kinsman. I will not blame this on him. I am here for my duty."

The steady glare, the set jaw and cool words told his friend that Roland was determined and would not accept contrary advice. He could already see the action to come, already hear the cries of death and wounding, the songs of glory afterwards. Roland's pride would not allow him to seek assistance, or flinch from what was to come.

Walking somewhat stiffly down the rise, Roland went to address his men. Yes, he had been betrayed, his vassals killed, his men placed in danger, but there was only one reply and that was to smite the enemy and see to it that all was paid for in full. To fight so well, so boldly and with such disregard for his own life that nothing else mattered. He would lose his fears and doubts and guilt in battle.

As Oliver watched his friend mount his horse and take up his lance, he knew that unlike their comrades who even now were approaching France, Roland would not be going there, not be going home that way. Battle was his home and he would return only to that.

Catching up with Roland, he took hold of his stirrup and beseeched him once more to summon reinforcements.

"Roland, it may already be too late and you condemn all these men. Sound your horn."

"It would be cowardly and I cannot abide a coward," Roland growled, then suddenly he slipped from the saddle and embraced Oliver. "Please, say no more. The king has given us this task, these bold French comrades, and God, this time, this moment. Lay on with your lance and I will wield my sword Durendala and the pagans shall rue the day they thought to trick and overcome the likes of us."

Clapping his friend on the back, Oliver laughed with abandon and they sprang into the saddles of the horses their squires held ready.

"Death before dishonour," Oliver sang out, with only a light touch of irony.

"Noble Franks," cried Roland, riding before the rearguard, drawing his famous sword. "We fight for Christ, Charles and Glory. If we prevail, let all France sing of our valour and skill. If we die, let all know we fell as Christians, loyal vassals and the maddest, bravest sons of France."

"Aye, for the Faith!" shouted Turpin.

"The Emperor Charlemagne!" cried Oliver.

"And immortality. Charrrrrge!" screamed Roland. A roar went up from the French and the slow trot of the great warhorses began, soon growing into a thunder while on the flanks archers loosed arrows at the approaching heathen host.

The Saracen centre faltered for a second at sight of the Frankish charge. With every tactical advantage against them, facing numbers double their own and no escape in the direction of Spain, the wild Franks came on. It was incredible.

With a battle cry of 'Allah', the twelve champions of Marsile, led by the Saracen king's nephew, leapt ahead and thrust themselves at the Twelve Peers. The clash of steel, wood, horseflesh and human strength was mighty. A groan of ecstasy, agony, and relief arose from both sides. Battle had commenced at last, the waiting and fearful suspense was over. Nothing mattered now but the simplicity of killing an enemy, helping a friend, and surviving. In an ugly, complicated, demanding world, what bliss.

In the general haze of battle the individual combats largely went the way of the Franks, who bested Marsile's champions and tore into the Saracen army, killing many and losing yet a few of their own. All around the corpses of both sides piled up.

Roland was everywhere just when needed, seeing and filling a gap, rescuing outnumbered knights, driving back the enemy, reinforcing any weakened place in the line. The slaughter was great and the pagans' numbers dwindled, despite great acts of bravery, leaving the exhausted, battered and reduced French band in possession of the field.

With hope almost springing into their hearts, they saw yet another Saracen formation, larger than the first. Now, even the most innocent and optimistic of them knew they were finished, that their betrayal had been sure and complete. Cleverly, they had been shown just enough of the enemy host to stir them, just enough to prick their pride but not so many as to make any but the most prudent and cool-headed retreat and call for help.

The full realization of their desperate situation hit them all. Everyone had fought unstintingly, had seen comrades fall, repeatedly risked his body and his horse. Many were wounded and yet it had been a battle against the odds in which their superior skill and spirit had told, as they knew it would. Here was the proof, however, of their folly. Here was the first universally understood evidence that they were well and truly trapped.

That some would die was always accepted. That all might do so was liberally bandied about and even romantically dreamt of. To actually face this as a very distinct possibility gave them pause. Now, the real, desperate savage, body aching, hard labour fighting would begin. Thoughts of glory were fading rapidly.

Wearily, though no less bravely, they formed up once more to face the enemy. Turpin felt within himself the change and saw it in the rest. This was no time to speak of minstrel's songs, of poet's verse, of lad's awed respect and maiden's sighing regard.

"For Jesus' sake stand. For hope of Paradise and for salvation, with the power of God in your arms, the love of Christ in your hearts, meet these heathens now my brothers and smite them, the enemies of Heaven."

Bracing up with renewed fire in their bellies, they greeted the new onslaught, stopped it cold and cut down the Saracens as barley under a scythe. Personally led by Blancandrin, the emir who had conspired with Ganelon, the valorous Moors came on regardless, and slowly the French began to give ground and to tire. The Peers themselves went down in numbers, battling to the last, a swathe of slaughtered enemies at their feet. Blancandrin himself was among the Saracen dead.

Roland, Oliver and Turpin took a terrible revenge upon the slayers of the Peers, but more good French knights went down. Many died at the hand of the particularly valiant and swift-bladed Saracen warrior, Grandoigne, until he came face to face with Roland. A look of mutual respect and recognition passed between the two despite the chaos around them. No formal salute was needed, no words were exchanged and yet in that mêlée and at that desperate stage of the battle both knew and others sensed it and gave them room even while fighting for their own lives. Theirs was a single combat, a duel within a battle. One would die at the other's hand, perhaps both would be mortally wounded but this would be no fleeting passage of arms. There would be no escape, no turning aside to deal with others, to help a comrade, to give orders or rest horses or catch a breath.

Almost eagerly they met, exchanging blows, sword on shield, wheeling their mounts, flailing and striking solid or glancing hits, countering and blocking until their arms felt leaden. Finally, dropping their shields, horses alongside each other, they simply hammered two-handed blows upon each other. A chance, weary upper cut of Roland's blade found its way under the Saracen's right arm. The Frankish hero stood up in his stirrups and thrust down, driving the fairly blunt point of Durendala into the body of his brave enemy.

With a grunt Grandoigne stopped fighting and swayed in his saddle, then fell slowly like a great tree, crashing to the stony ground with a vibrating crunch that was audible above the general din and made men pause even in their own struggles to look for the cause. But the pause was not long and there was no rest for Roland, who at once rode hard for the hottest part of the surrounding action.

At last, though they had killed so many of the Frankish force, the exhausted and bloody Saracens retreated, leaving nearly all of their strength lying dead and dying at the feet of the enemy. The survivors of the attack rushed as best they could back to King Marsile and begged him to commit his last body of men to the assault, which would surely now prevail, but only with their help.

Marsile smiled and nodded. It had been costly but it had worked. Ganelon's advice and strategy was succeeding marvellously. Scouts reported that there was no sign of the main French army hearing of this fight, or turning around. Roland had been lulled by pride and design into thinking he could handle each Saracen force as it was revealed. Now, with a handful of knights left, it remained only to bring up the largest body of men yet, and finish him off at last. This time Marsile would lead personally, push his men to the end, and be there at the death.

As the remnant of the Frankish rearguard stood breathing hard, wiping blood and sweat from their eyes and resting weary arms, they counted the small number of men left on their feet and far fewer in the saddle. They spotted the new Saracen host arriving beneath their king's bright silken banner. Bigger than ever, royal guards to the fore, fresh and well mounted, there would easily be a hundred good, bold enemies to each of their own battered, broken band. They had expected and fully accepted their deaths, indeed believed the last attack would have been pressed until they were all down. Yet, suddenly, after the untimely retreat of the enemy, this all-new host had stepped up. It was almost bizarre.

Oliver stared with the others, amazed at the sheer effort and number the enemy was prepared to bring to bear on them and he began to laugh. From deep in his belly it swelled out loud, real and jolly, and other men joined in, until all roared together, save Turpin, who quietly prayed, and Roland who, at last, with this unwanted time for reflection, realized what he had done, to his men and to his king.

He looked round the battlefield and finally saw the bodies of his invincible friends and followers, of the very core of the king's power, of the lost future of France. He knew too that he was doomed and that his life was not his alone to give but the property of his sovereign, and that through his pride he had wasted it.

"I will blow my horn," he said desperately. "I will summon the king and the army."

"It was disgrace," cried Oliver, "when I spoke of it and when it might have been of use. Do not shame us now."

"Think of our king bereft of the flower of his chivalry, the security of his realm and conquests. I will call them ..."

"I cannot approve it. It is too late and you have killed us, risked the king's achievements and the nation's future. Do not play the coward."

"I must," Roland swore. "The king and the army will come ..."

"Coward," cried Oliver. "What of death before dishonour? If miraculously we live and see home once more, you will not wed my sister. I renounce you as my friend. Your valour without judgement is stupidity. You have undone your comrades, your king, and your homeland. I break with thee."

Turpin stepped between the shouting angry heroes and calmed them.

"This is no time to question but only to accept and to act and to die well. Let Roland sound the horn and summon Charles and the army to avenge us, to bury these brave dead Christians and let not the wild beasts feed on their bones. Let him blow the war horn and bring back the army to destroy at last the might of Saragossa, whom we have drawn out from behind her walls and so weakened, or all these heroes and we ourselves die in vain. Ganelon has betrayed the Moors just as he has us. Let that not be wasted, either."

"Yes," Oliver said. "That is true."

And Roland nodded, raising the magical ivory war horn 'Oliphant' to his lips. He blew so loudly that the sound was heard faraway by Charlemagne, who had recalled his dream and knew that it was of the loss of Roland and some symbolic trickery by Ganelon. It had troubled him all day and when the faint sound of the war horn came he pulled up his horse and harkened to it.

"Our men are in action. Hard action."

"Nay," Ganelon scoffed. "If anyone but the king had said so I would swear it a foolish lie."

When again Roland blew the horn, this time with such despair and self-disgust at his earlier folly that his mouth bled and veins burst in his forehead, Charlemagne heard it. Again he pulled up and listened.

"Roland is in battle. He would not sound the war horn else."

"But, Sire," laughed Ganelon with too much heartiness, "that cannot be, for Roland is too proud to sound the horn to signal danger. Nay, there is no battle. Perhaps he celebrates victory in some skirmish, or while hunting with his friends. Your worries but show your great age, Sire, the timid heart of the old. Let us ride on. Home lies far below us."

When faint and failing the horn sounded once more the king wheeled his steed around and his face grew grim.

"There is death in that sound."

"Sire ..." Ganelon began, riding up beside Charles.

"You," growled Charlemagne as he reached out a surprisingly still powerful arm and grasped Ganelon by the neck. "This is your work. You have sold them to Marsile."

"Majesty," the Duke of Naimes shouted, riding up at a canter. "Roland is betrayed, I fear."

Charging the men in the train about him to arrest Ganelon,

Charlemagne ordered the army immediately to turn around and march back into Spain. The prayer on everyone's lips was that God should preserve the rearguard until they arrived. Meanwhile, the kitchen staff beat Ganelon, chained his hands and feet, and set him bareback on a skinny old mule until Charlemagne should ask for him again.

Over the crests and through the passes and defiles, along the narrow tracks the French rode and ran, hastening to the rescue of their comrades in the rearguard. With blaring trumpets they hoped to hearten Roland's force and frighten the foe. Help was coming, coming swiftly but was it too late, too late?

As Roland let fall his warhorn upon its strap, he surveyed the grisly scene of battle around him where few Frenchman stood and everywhere was red with blood, limbs lay severed from bodies and brains spilled from battered skulls. Dying horses screamed and men moaned and wept or lay still and cold and lifeless. The smell was of a slaughterhouse.

"May god bless you all, my comrades, may every soul find its way into Paradise. Fair France is the poorer for your untimely passing and I am to blame. I alone have murdered thee. Please, God, take these men into your keeping."

Stumbling forward to the battle line he placed his hand on the nearest man and addressed the others.

"Brothers, come, let us attack the pagan horde and win a good death, or I die of grief instead."

With that he rushed at the advancing Saracens, aiming for the royal banner and those beneath it.

"Yes, attack," Turpin shouted approvingly, joining in the advance. "Give God a good death, ye Christian knights. Let the faint hearted be monks and cower in cloisters and pray for the souls of fighting men such as we. Show the heathen how we die for Christ."

"Come along ye martyrs for Christ," Roland yelled over his shoulder. "Sell your lives dearly."

Marsile had seen Roland's charge, seen him turn to meet the royal party within the Saracen line, Roland on his dying horse, his armour falling from him in places, his helm dented and his shield gone. The Saracen spurred ahead, hoping to have the honour of killing Roland himself. Beside him, however, his son of but fifteen summers rode. Lighter was the burden of the youth's steed, even armoured head to toe as he was.

Roland ducked a clumsy cut as they met, and sent a backhanded slash at the youth's kidney, knocking him out of the saddle and under the feet of the chargers around them. There he perished beneath the flailing hooves.

Incensed, Marsile flew at Roland, his deadly scimitar high above his head poised to strike at a bare spot in the Frankish hero's armour, where the buckles had given way. Despite his exhaustion Roland parried the blow and exchanged and blocked others of the furious king. Waiting his chance, he parried a slash at his face and then with a deft flick of the wrist, cut hard at the arm of the Saracen, neatly severing his hand before retainers and champions bore the wounded king away.

Marsile's withdrawal put a sudden panic into the Saracen host, many of whom fled in confusion. In this brief respite, Roland surveyed the carnage and counted his fellows. There were but two left beside himself. Turpin and Oliver, almost inevitably. The three exchanged a nod and a thin smile. Now, finally, was the time.

The king's uncle, the caliph, was rallying men and bringing up his newly arrived, fanatical volunteers fresh from Arabia. Again the Saracens advanced, emboldened by the sight of just three Franks left mounted and none still standing. All the rest were plainly dead or dying. From all sides they rushed in, the caliph himself thrusting his lance into Oliver's side, yet swiftly the courteous, judicious warrior, turned and with his sword 'Hauteclaire' severed the great caliph's head from his shoulders.

"With me, Roland," Oliver cried, knowing himself mortally wounded and wishing to die in action. Spurring one last time into the enemy's midst, swinging his sword and shouting the war-cry 'Montjoie', he slew yet more pagans as he slowly died.

At the sight of Oliver, slumped in the saddle, his side bleeding like a waterfall into a mountain stream, the broken lance protruding from two sides of his body, Roland wept with grief and guilt and came near to fainting. He was weakened by a hundred little wounds and sheer exhaustion. His horse was close to succumbing too. It stumbled beneath him, worn to nothing from speeding as it had from one point of danger to another. At last it fell, its heart giving out. Landing on his feet like a cat despite his state, but walking in a daze towards his friend, Roland dragged his sword behind him, his eyes glazing over and his head full of fog and horror.

Around Oliver the foe had fallen back to watch him die. Roland slowly approached his friend. His eyes filled with blood from a deep gash in his forehead, the dying Peer swung with all the might left to him and brought his trusty sword down on Roland's head. The blow cut through the helmet, but stopped short of cleaving Roland's skull, despite drawing much blood. Far from damaging Roland further, it woke him from his swoon in time to catch Oliver in his arms as the latter slid headlong from the saddle of his warhorse.

"Comrade," he asked gently. "Was that blow to kill one who loves you, yet has led you to doom? Would you take vengeance on me, Oliver?"

"Roland, I hear your voice but cannot see. I stuck at what I thought a Saracen's head. May God forgive me if I hurt thee."

"I but lost a helm I'll soon have no use for. But I am not harmed." The blinded warrior's hand felt the features of his friend's face then fell to his shoulder and gave a soft, parting squeeze. With a gasp, Oliver prayed for his sins to be forgiven, that he might be vouchsafed a place in Paradise, praying also for the protection of his king, and to preserve above all men his best-loved brother-in-arms, Roland. With that he breathed his last and died facing towards the east.

Roland wept, regretting all that had led to this and most of all that he yet lived himself. Looking up at last he saw that only he and Turpin were left, though the badly wounded Count Gautier, survivor of the lost patrol, had crawled forth, ready to expire but determined to die with his liege lord. He was finally snuffed out by the next shower of arrows loosed by the Saracens, who were wary of coming nearer the ground where Turpin and Roland stood back to back. Their leaders were dead or had retreated with wounds. They would not spare the Franks but were no longer willing to sacrifice themselves in order to dispatch them.

Another rain of arrows and javelins fell, hitting Turpin in many places. Two of the wounds were plainly mortal and so he charged the enemy, slaying many before he was finally felled, cursing the heathen in the name of Jesus.

Alone now and ready to collapse, his armour broken, his bare head pouring blood, new wounds being inflicted upon him all the time, Roland raised Oliphant to his lips and weakly blew once more. Charlemagne heard its faint notes and despaired.

"Faster," he cried to his knights. "Roland is nearly done for. Sound the trumpets that he may yet take heart and know we are drawing near."

At this, thousands of horns sounded all along the Frankish relief column and now the Saracens heard them and feared.

"Charlemagne is coming," they shouted in a frenzy of confusion.

"We must kill Roland or he will recover and he and Charlemagne will ravage all of Spain and our Saragossa will be sacked and raised to the ground." Thus they still believed Ganelon's lie that here lay their only chance of victory, that without his nephew Charlemagne would not prosecute the war.

Rallying forty men, a giant of a Saracen warrior led a final attack on the solitary figure of Roland, who roused himself for a last great effort while hoping for the death blow that would relieve his suffering. The Frankish champion killed several of his attackers and drove the remainder away.

As the moors retreated for good, hearing Charlemagne's war-horns grow louder and believing Roland's wounds to be mortal, the hero fell to his knees, calling for them to return and fight to the finish. With a sob he saw them disappear through the trees and down the mountainside.

With a Saracen banner he cleaned the blood from Durendala and sheathed the sword. Then limping and bleeding he went to the body of Turpin who was still breathing. Tearing off the Archbishop's battered armour, he tried to bind his friend's wounds. Turpin stirred, however, and waved him away as if to say he had no use of bandages now. Roland carried and dragged as many of the Peers and knights to surround Turpin where he lay, that he might bless and absolve them.

This struggle was as severe as his exertions in battle that day. With much effort he searched the field, looking into dead face after dead face. Painfully he brought the Peers and, last of all, his well-loved friend Oliver to Turpin, whereupon he fainted from loss of blood and utter exhaustion.

Fighting to get to his feet the Archbishop retrieved Oliphant, the ivory war-horn from round Roland's neck and stumbled to the stream nearby to fill it with water to bring to his friend. The effort was too much, however, and only feet from Roland's unconscious body, Turpin fell face first to the ground, the water-filled horn held out in both hands.

Awakening, Roland groaned to find himself yet living and slowly rose to his feet, looking for Turpin. When he found him he wept for pity, seeing what his friend had been trying to do even as he died. Commending Turpin's noble soul to heaven, he crossed the Archbishop's white hands and prayed over him for some time.

Knowing his own death was finally near, Roland, with sword in one hand and his war-horn in the other, took himself off a distance from the carnage, an arrow shot's distance forward of his men's last position. Up a small hill, he found two pine trees forming a V shape, with some ancient marble steps between them. Here again he fell, passing once more out of consciousness.

Suddenly from out of cover a lightly wounded Saracen who had been left by his retreating fellows, darted forward to claim a valuable trophy. Snatching Durendala from Roland's limp right hand, he raised it to the sky.

"The nephew of Charles is dead and I will carry this, his sword to Arabia."

Opening his eyes yet still dazed Roland looked at the Saracen. "You are not one of ours." he muttered, before smashing Oliphant against the man's head, killing him instantly.

This had been a near-run thing. The notion of his sword Durendala falling into unworthy hands horrified Roland so much that he found new strength, attempting repeatedly to break the blade on the marble steps. Again and again it only glanced away, chipping the stone, grating the steel but never breaking.

"Bright as an angel, my faithful Durendala, what victories we have won for our king, what champions we have vanquished. Let France not be disgraced by your coming into the possession of heathens." Again he swung the blade against the rocks, but succeeded only in shattering them completely while the sword vibrated and remained strong and complete.

Giving up and sensing the onset of death, Roland lay down upon the ground, his war-horn and sword beneath him, his body facing the enemy so that the French could see that he had died victorious and in possession of the field. He made his confession and prayed for mercy, crying 'Mea Culpa' and begging pardon for his sins large and small. Holding his right-hand glove up to heaven as a sign of submission, he felt the angels of God descend and stand around him. He felt Gabriel accept the glove and with bowed head and clasped hands the great hero died.

Soon afterwards, Charlemagne neared the scene of the battle, desperate for news of the rearguard's fate, his heart full of fear for his nephew and the Twelve Peers.

"Where is Roland?" he cried. "Where is Count Oliver, Turpin and the others? How many men survive?"

At the head of the army against all advice, he rode at the gallop into the valley of Roncesvalles where not an inch of ground was bare of pools of blood, severed limbs or dead bodies. By now all the wounded of both sides had perished.

Weeping and tearing at his beard, Charles lamented and everywhere around him the army mourned its fallen comrades and kinsmen. But when the tears dried, hearts hardened and but one thought settled upon them all. The revenge they would take would be terrible and swift.

With not a single wounded man to succour and no prisoners to deal with, the army's renewed advance was rapid. By the next day, the scattered and shattered forces of Saragossa were overtaken and overcome, though they had been aided somewhat by the force fresh from Arabia, which had arrived earlier on premature news of victory by Marsile. However, this unhappy king, lying mortally wounded in Saragossa, on learning of this final defeat, turned his face to the wall, cursed Ganelon and died.

Sated of revenge, Charlemagne turned his thoughts once more to mourning and he made his way back to Roncesvalles to look for Roland's body. He knew instinctively where this would be found. It would, he told himself, be at the head of his force, facing towards the enemy. On arriving at the battlefield he sought the higher ground in what had been the Saracen positions, and reckoned where an arrow shot from his own lines would have landed.

Here, overlooking the meadow full of the blood and dead flesh of his barons and peers, the king found his nephew, lying in the grass upon his sword and war-horn, facing towards Spain, the broken blocks of marble around him evidence of his final efforts.

Charles knelt to take Roland's body in his arms and wept for him anew.

"Lord have mercy on the souls of brave Roland, for France will never see again such a warrior and noble son as he. Slowly will my power wane with no kinsman or champion at my right hand. As age overtakes me, my days will be spent in grief for the loss of you, Roland. France is widowed with your death. Would that I, too, were dead, that my body might be interred with thine and join thee and the Peers in Paradise."

The French army buried their dead upon the field of honour, all that is but Roland, Oliver and Turpin whom they carried to Blaye. Here, in the great cathedral they were interred with much solemn ceremony before Charlemagne returned to Aix.

Learning of the death of Roland, her betrothed, and her loving brother Oliver from the king himself, the beautiful maiden Aude fell at Charlemagne's feet. Alas, she had not swooned as all supposed but died of a broken heart that very instant.

The trial of Ganelon was long, thorough and tiresome and ended in his much deserved execution. The traitor was torn limb from limb after being set between wild horses. But memory of his name did not die with him, and to this day it continues to live in infamy and disgrace.

Son of the Morning Star

All of the gods in the mythology of the plains Indians of North America
function as intermediaries between the supreme being,
the Great Spirit, and humankind.
The Morning Star is one of their principal heavenly deities,
ranking second only to the Sun. In this Blackfoot myth, all the heavenly
bodies are personified.

The Morning Star is imagined standing tall, a strong young man painted red, the colour of life, shod with moccasins, wrapped in a large robe and with a downy eagle feather stained red adorning his head. This is the image of the breath of life. To him the Great Spirit entrusted the Gift of Life, commanding him to spread it over the earth.

The Black Feet say he once fell in love with a lovely girl of their tribe, named Soatsaki. He admired her particularly as she slept on summer nights outside her tipi. She was flattered and honoured, and with her consent they married and he took her up to heaven. Here they dwelt with his father and mother, the Sun and the Moon.

In time, Soatsaki had a son whom they called Little Star. Her Mother-in-law, the Moon, gave her a pick as a present but warned her not to use it to dig up the turnip that could be found growing near the dwelling of the Spider Man.

But, eventually, overcome with curiosity, Soatsaki made her way to the spot where the turnip grew and, after digging and pulling, tore it from the ground. Light shown up from the hole. Intrigued, she leaned down. Far below she saw the Earth and her own family's camp. Clearly she could watch their doings and see their sadness and joy, and she began to grow terribly homesick.

At the height of her unhappiness the reason was discovered and for

313

the sin of disobeying her Mother-in-law, and digging up the turnip, the Sun decreed that Soatsaki was to be banished from Heaven with her son.

Down to Earth they were lowered, wrapped in an elk skin and there the poor woman, separated from her husband, became ever more remorseful and unwell until she died. Of course, no one believed their story about their kinship to the Morning Star.

Alone and very poor, Soatsaki's son, who also had a scar on his face, fared very badly. Called 'Poia', or Scar Face, he was treated cruelly by other children and when, as a young man, he fell in love with the chief's daughter, she laughingly rejected him because of his scar.

Torn between misery and outrage, lost as he was between two worlds and desperate both as a lover and lonely young man, Poia was determined to go to his grandfather the Sun and see if he could remove the scar. He trekked west, experiencing much and seeing many things on the way before he reached the Pacific shore. Here he stopped, and spent the next three days in fasting and prayer.

On the fourth morning, a glowing trail unrolled in front of him, stretching across the ocean. Without hesitation he courageously strode out upon it, following the magical trail all the way to the heavens. Near where the Sun himself lived, he found his father, the Morning Star, locked in desperate combat with three gigantic and hideous birds of prey.

Poia immediately waded in to help his father, killing the monsters with his arrows and war club. As a reward for his bravery the Sun took away the scar that disfigured his face. Then, teaching him the ritual of the Sun Dance, his grandfather gave him a gift of ravens' feathers as proof of his kinship with the Sun. Another present from his celestial family was a flute, together with the knowledge to play it to win the heart of his beloved.

Poia then returned to Earth by a path known as the Wolf Trail or the Milky Way. He taught the Black Feet the Sun Dance and married the chief's daughter he had long loved, taking her up to Heaven to live.

The Sacrifice of Countess Cathleen

*Probably Druidic in origin, this very old Irish legend
was taken up by Christianity. Where once a woman might have been
offered up to rapacious gods, to appease them, the sacrifice
on the people's behalf became more spiritual than physical.
One way or the other, sacrificing as opposed to doing battle was the
usual form of a woman's heroism in many legendary traditions.*

The fair Countess Cathleen had eyes of deep sea green and long flowing hair as golden as the ripe corn in her fields. She graced the very air she breathed with her beauty and charm, piety and dignity. The Countess lived in a stately castle set in a large forest, and scattered about her gates were the cottages of her people.

It was a happy time of relative peace in Ireland. The monasteries flourished where not long before warlike clans had held sway, and faith had replaced the blood lust in many hearts. Cathleen herself had come into womanhood soon after her people had embraced Christianity.

The young Countess loved the forests, fields and meadows beyond the walls of her home, and to watch the changes the seasons brought and the creatures living in the green woods and purple hills. She loved the legends of the old gods, the heroes of battles long past and, more than anything, she loved her clansmen and vassals. She prayed for them at all the holy hours, personally taught their children and gently looked after them when they were ill. Nowhere was there a more fortunate and contented people.

Then there came a disaster for all of Ireland and the bliss of these times passed into memory. Famine beset the land, seed corn rotted in the ground, rain constantly fell and mists filled the thick air, lying heavily on the sodden earth. Even when spring arrived at last, fields remained barren, cattle died in their stalls or in the bleak pastures. Oxen died at the plough and sheep perished in the fold.

As summer came and went, the berries failed in the sun-parched woods and withered leaves, fallen long before autumn had come, lay rotting on the dank ground. The small animals of the forest, the hares, rabbits, squirrels all died in their holes or fell prey to birds and larger beasts. These in turn died of hunger as the famine deepened. From mice and rats and hedgehogs to deer and foxes, all died, until hardly the sound of a fluttering wing disturbed the desolate woods.

The High King of Ireland declared a universal peace among those tribes still quarrelling, and raiders from abroad, with pickings so small, stopped plaguing their shores. None of this made much difference, however. Chiefs worked together, the wealthy aided the poor and all soon became equal in the misery of their terrible hunger.

Monasteries became deserted, their stores exhausted, their doors flung open, the brothers lying dead inside with no one to bury them. Hermits expired alone in their little beehive shaped cells or took refuge in some rich abbey that was still for a time able to feed its monks. And far from abating, the famine grew yet worse as each day passed.

No one suffered more than the lovely Cathleen, for although hungry like everyone else, she grieved too for the far worse plight of her people. She prayed constantly for their deliverance but no help came from heaven. Slowly, the Countess was wasting away, as much from worry and despair for others as from her own lack of sustenance.

Her attendants tried everything to restore her spirits, to no avail. The old stories and songs were no use, the glories of nature were but a bitter memory. The only thing that moved her now was the desire to save her people.

All along her house and stores had been open to supply the needs of the homeless, the poor and the suffering. She spent her wealth freely on food for the starving until supplies became scarce and then sent ever farther for them to keep feeding her folk. When all known sources failed she tried again, paying hugely for the hoarded grain of greedy farmers who had held it back for just such an opportunity. When this supply dried up she gave generously of her own winter provisions of wine and corn. No one left her castle with an empty belly. Soon her name was blessed far and wide, and from far and wide the poor and starving made their way to her gates. Now, not only her own clansmen looked to her daily for enough food and drink to stave off death until the pestilential mists passed from the land.

Any hope that the clean, cold of winter would clear the awful vapours was soon dashed. The poisonous yellow mists persisted and the famine yet gripped the feeble hearts of all and sapped the very springs of life. Everyone grew weaker, fainter and the winter frosts killed more than the heat of summer.

Finally, even in so saintly a land as Christian Ireland the sense of right and wrong disappeared. Respect for property vanished in the universal misery. Men began to steal and rob and trust to nothing but brute strength. They would stop at nothing to plunder others and survive. Conscience, mercy, and honesty were forgotten.

Bold, unashamed brigands cost Cathleen her remaining stocks of corn and fruit and the last few animals remaining in her flocks and herds. She was so filled with pity at the desperation of the thieves that she would not let her servants pursue them, eager though they were to do so and retrieve the lost supplies.

Now all the winter stores had been distributed and there was only enough left to feed her poor pensioners and her household on the shortest possible rations. Despite their earnest entreaties to take a little more for herself, she shared equally with them and would never have thought of doing otherwise.

Before much longer even this scanty fare would be expended and Cathleen's heart nearly broke as she watched her helpless dependants wither and die in front of her eyes. All looked up to her as an angel of pity and deliverance and yet she knew herself to be but an ordinary young woman, as helpless as the rest.

Each day she walked among them with her meagre dole of food, trying to give them courage, smiling and instilling hope by her very presence. In the privacy of her chapel however, in her fervent prayers, she could give vent to her fears and sadness. As she prayed to the Blessed Virgin Mary and all the saints for a way to save her tribe and all the people of her land, she ignored her own hunger and suffering.

One day while kneeling at prayer, overcome by her cares and weakness she fell into a faint and passed into a deep sleep. From within her troubled mind a thought emerged that seemed to come from Heaven itself and inspire her. On waking, she leaped up and skipped from the chapel with a light heart.

Her countenance was so changed, so relieved and gay that the servants stopped and stared. So wonderful was the happy glow of her face that her ageing nurse, Una, was overcome with a fear that the young Countess might be suffering from some form of enchantment by the old gods. Her worry that Cathleen might be bewitched away to Tir-nan-og, the land of never-dying youth, was palpable.

Seeing her anxiety, Cathleen took her hand and comforted her.

"Do not be afraid, dear Una. The Virgin has heard my prayer. The Saints have sent me a vision of what must be done."

Running to the door of her own room, she called for a servant to send at once for Fergus, her steward. Known as Fergus the White on account of his shock of pale grey hair, the steward had served Cathleen's family for many years. Foster-father to her grandfather, he had seen three generations pass away and witnessed the painful transition from heathenism to Christianity. And now, of all his chief's family to which he was devoted and supremely loyal, there was only this one girl left. He would have loved her as if she were his own child had she been a harridan and a miser. For her sweet self he loved her even more. Coming to her at once upon being summoned, Fergus paid homage to his liege lady and knelt to kiss her hand.

"What do you want of me, Countess?" he asked, smiling despite the hard times, just to see her. "Shall I render the accounts of …"

"No, dear Fergus, there is no need. But tell me how much I have in lands. The value in gold."

"Well, Countess," Fergus scratched his grey head and thought. "Your lands are worth something like one hundred thousand pounds."

"And what about the timber in my forests?"

"Another hundred thousand roughly, Countess."

"What would my various castles and other houses sell for?"

"I would say several hundred thousand," Fergus replied, wondering at her reasons for such talk when the famine made the value of such possessions meaningless.

"And in gold, how much have I stored within the treasure chests in your charge?"

"My lady," the steward answered. "There is over five hundred thousand pounds in gold."

For a time the Countess remained silent and lost in thought. Then setting her jaw, a look of firm resolution came into her eye and she spoke, though not without a slight trembling of her lips and a flutter in her voice.

"Fergus, please take the gold and go abroad, as far as need be to buy plentiful food. I will keep my jewels and some gold, for I still have hope of finding a little more grain hidden away by venial farmers and traders who may not part with it for love of Christ but will sell it for inflated prices. You shall also have my authority signed and sealed to sell all my lands, forests, fields, houses and castles, saving only this one where I must live. Most urgently send a man to Ulster where the famine is less severe and have him buy cattle to be driven here as quickly as possible."

Fergus stood astounded for a moment and then found his tongue. Desperately he tried to talk his mistress out of selling off nearly everything she owned. He begged her to keep her wealth and enjoy it fully when better times came once more, but she was deaf to his pleading.

"Fergus," she said finally, by way of explanation. "A cry is in my ears."

"Yes, Countess," he sighed at last and nodded.

"I cannot ignore it," she shrugged. "I must do something."

"Very well, my lady."

"Farewell, Fergus. God speed and look after you."

So, a good and reliable man was sent north to Ulster to find what cattle he could, weak and famine-stricken though they might be, and Fergus journeyed to England. There all was still prosperous and fertile, for the deadly famine had not touched that country and none even knew of that which afflicted Ireland.

Fergus spent the gold wisely and well and sold all the Countess Cathleen had told him to sell, everything but the one castle she dwelt in surrounded by her own people and the throng of dying folk about her gates and in her halls.

Loyal steward and friend, shrewd dealer and careful businessman, Fergus got good deals everywhere. It may even have been that Heaven smiled on the enterprise for the English merchants gave good prices. It may also have been that in their ignorance of Ireland's plight, they did not presume to take advantage of him.

One way or another Fregus did well on every score and bought grain, wine, fat oxen and sheep which were duly loaded aboard ships for transport back to Ireland. There was enough, he knew, to carry the starving peasants through the famine year until the next harvest. When the money was all gone and all ships fully laden and ready, they lay in the harbour and awaited a fair wind to carry them across the sea. Alas, none came.

A deadly calm persisted for days on end and the fleet sat with sails drooping and motionless, no hint of a breeze stirring them. Then fog came down so thick that no craft could set out all along England's coast. When at last the fog lifted, Fergus cast caution aside in his anxiety to return as soon as he could. The high running seas and bad weather, however, drove the ships back into harbour before they had gone far. Two vessels, indeed, were lost, striking rocks before sinking with their cargoes of food.

Fergus wept to see the wealth of his mistress so wasted and he dared not venture out onto the wintry sea until it was safe to do so. Two months were to pass after his arrival in England before he could sail back to Ireland, to his young mistress and their starving countrymen.

Meanwhile, the man sent to Ulster had also fared well in his trading and found surprising numbers of cattle to purchase. They were not strong, however, and driving them south was a slow business. Fodder was scarce, thieves had to be driven off and the weakness of the animals meant they could not be pushed very hard.

Cathleen knew none of this. No news came that food was on its way, though painstakingly. All she could do was wait in her remaining castle, filled with hungry mouths and growing desperation. Only her faith in God, and her own inspired vision, sustained her.

As the horror of death by starvation deepened, as the misery grew harder to bare, as grief and fear and death itself assailed the population, anger at Heaven seethed in many breasts. Christ and the Saints, they said, had abandoned Ireland, or they slept, or did not care. People remembered with longing the mighty old gods, for the new seemed powerless or indifferent. They yearned for the friendly 'good people' who had fled from the church bell, and some even began to secretly worship the old heathen gods once more. Love for Him was growing cold. Only fear of Christian Hell and its eternal tortures kept the majority from openly renouncing the One True God, and revolting against the Church. But, as ever, it was not the old ways and beliefs that were the real threat to righteousness.

At the same time that Fergus was setting out for England and

Cathleen's other retainer headed north to Ulster, a pair of mysterious and stately strangers appeared in Ireland. No one knew where they came from but they were first seen along the rough western shore. The few folk dwelling in this sparse region supposed they had been put ashore by some passing vessel or were the victims of a shipwreck. They were undoubtedly foreigners for they conversed between themselves in a tongue no one else recognized, and did not seem to understand questions people asked them.

As the strangers travelled inland they seemed to change. At the next sighting of them, at a village near Dublin, they were wearing magnificent robes and furs, and jewelled gloves adorned their hands, as did golden rings. Upon their heads circlets of rubies gleamed and the fine black steeds they rode showed no ill effects from the famine but were strong, sleek and spirited. Everywhere they went, they carefully noted the universal misery and despair.

Finally they came to the small hut of a forester's widow, who gladly received such a royal and lofty pair. Their bearing, equipage and language contrasted greatly with the humble hut in which they were accommodated but they did not seem to mind. The dead forester had been one of the Countess Cathleen's most loyal vassals and his holding was very near the castle. From the hut the strangers could observe the life of the village, the comings and goings of the castle and hear all the talk of the place.

When they had been around for a while, they haltingly explained to the widow that they were merchants from a far-off land. They claimed to be traders in rare gems, though they had no goods to sell or exchange. They made no enquiries after such things that others might sell them, bargained with no one for anything and were generally thought to be the oddest merchants ever seen in Erin.

Daily they ate without complaint the poor food their lowly hostess gave them. The black bread that was the best such terrible times could provide, they soaked in rich red wine from their private store, paying for everything lavishly in unminted gold. Naturally, it was a wonder to people that men who could clearly afford to go anywhere they wished should stay in a famine-ravaged region for no apparent reason.

Soon, oddly fluent in the Irish tongue, they started to gently question the widow and others about the country, the population and the famine itself. They wanted to know how people suffered and died, what they thought of life and faith.

They heard much about the generosity and kindness of the Countess Cathleen, who had saved so many lives and who was saving them still, though with greater difficulty as each day passed. To their interlocutors they expressed much admiration for this remarkable lady, but the sidelong looks exchanged between them at such times were dark and discontented.

Came the day when the royal merchants announced to the widow their true mission as friends of the poor and starving. Servants of a mighty foreign prince, they had come to help alleviate the suffering and fight the famine and death. Of course, it was obvious that they had no actual food with them, only wine and plenty of gold. With this they hoped people might, by searching, still discover food to buy.

Now the widow, knowing that there were indeed still some niggardly men who yet had mouldering hoards of grain to sell for exorbitant prices, fell to her knees and rejoiced. Blessing God, the Virgin Mary and all the Saints, she commended the strangers to Heaven, for if they would buy the grain and distribute it, people need not die of hunger any more. As she prayed for a blessing on the two strangers, they smiled disdainfully and grew impatient. The senior of them interrupted her and spoke with cunning.

"Naturally the evils of charity are well known and we would not wish to bring them down on a people already so troubled. For his honour, let each man or woman bring a single piece of merchandize to sell us."

"Oh, but Sirs," wailed the poor disappointed widow, all the hope she had felt a moment before fading from her heart. "Do you suppose that after all they have suffered that anyone has anything worth trading that has not long ago gone to buy one last morsel to keep body and soul together? No one will have anything left, I tell you, save the clothes on their backs and these only enough to keep themselves alive until better times return. You mock us in our misery."

"Nay, madam, we do not, I assure you," the elder merchant said. "Why, every person has the one precious thing we are prepared to buy and have come to find. All are still in possession of it, for none here have yet been lost or sold by anyone."

"But what precious thing can this be? The people of Ireland have nothing but their lives and only a very weak hold on these."

"Ah, but is there not something else?" the elder merchant enquired with a conspiratorial smile, alert for the first inkling of understanding. "Even folk so poor as the Irish have the thing we wish to purchase, if they will but sell it."

Still the widow looked blankly at them.

"Their souls," the younger merchant prompted. "Do you see now?"

"We are here," the elder continued, "to procure these for our powerful Prince and with what we are prepared to pay in pure gold we will surely save many lives until the famine passes."

"Why must men die a cruel and lingering death," the younger continued, "or live like a dog for so many dreadful months of ugly half-life when relief is at hand at the cost of a mere soul?"

"A thing no good to anyone," said the other. "Is it not only the source of fears and pain and regret, after all?"

"We take people's souls and free them from all that. And for this service we will pay them. We will pay much good money with which they can not only survive these hard times but find comforts and pleasure, as well."

Realizing that the strangers were minions of Satan come to lure the souls of men into Hell, the widow fled her cottage and ran to the village. Here she stayed, unwilling to return home, leaving the demons to themselves. She warned everyone about them, of course, but soon she died of famine. With her gone the strangers began to live a little better.

For some time though, people kept away from the place. Then, first wanderers reported having been there to no ill-effect, and finally even the local folk dared to go. Occasionally the strangers gave visitors food and rich wine, hinting that there was much more for those daring enough to earn it. When shyly asked how this might be done, they began the tempting proper and explained the comforts derived from the sale of a soul. One fellow had no qualms at all and struck a deal with them for his soul after very little prompting. Driving a hard bargain with the demons, he got three hundred crowns. Of course the younger demon felt this was a bit much for a soul they probably would have got for nothing eventually, given the man's character, but the elder demon knew his business.

The man became a tempter himself now, telling everyone about the wonderful food and wine he had sometimes got from the merchants and showing off his wealth. The most wonderful thing of all, he proclaimed to anyone who would listen, was that he had gained the liberty of knowing no pity, having no conscience and losing all remorse.

What had been a trickle soon became a flood as people beat an ever-widening path to the hut in the forest. Prices paid for souls now varied depending on what a soul was worth, what sins had already been committed. In enjoying the wine and food given out by the merchants, people did not worry about what any of this meant or where the endless supply of food and gold came from.

Everyone who dealt with the demons left with a full belly, a dizzy head from their fine wine and weighed down with bags of gold. The appeal of plentiful food, drink, gold and undemanding service brought more and more people each day. By night, knowing they were lost, that no hope of Heaven was left to them, they revelled and danced and caroused, intending to live life while they yet had it.

For a long while Cathleen was unaware of the activities of the demons because these days she never left her castle walls, so busy was she with the poor people who needed her. Any moment she was not with them she spent in prayer, first for the speedy return of Fergus and her man who had gone to Ulster and secondly for an end to the famine. Gradually the throng at her gates dwindled, however. The number of her own dependants seemed less somehow, though there were far fewer deaths. Soon the numbers of people arriving for the meagre allowance she was able to give out dwindled to several dozen.

The mists had not cleared and it was not the time even of sowing, let alone a new harvest. Cathleen began to hope that a miracle had occurred, that her prayers and those of so many others had been answered. Yet it was obvious this had not happened. The riotous and drunken behaviour of the villagers came to her attention finally, and she marvelled at the source of it. Where could people have got the money and the drink for so much carrying on? It seemed endless. She sent for an old peasant whose wife had died early on in the famine. He had longed to join her in death although until recently Cathleen had fed him each day.

He arrived deep in drink and reckless with it. His look was defiant and his manner insolent and rude. Though full of evil mirth, he tried to answer the questions she put to him as soberly as he could.

"Can you tell me why the villagers and strangers have stopped coming here for food? There is not much, but everyone in need is still welcome to share it with me and my household."

"They are no longer in need," the peasant smirked. "They have food and drink aplenty and money to buy anything else they want."

"Where in the world did they get food and drink? How have they acquired gold, now of all times?"

"They have everything from two generous merchants who have taken the residence of old Mari who died the other week, out in the forest. They keep open house in the old cottage day and night and are so rich they give bounteously to all. They are so powerful that they have no trouble finding good food and wine in great supply. More than enough for everyone who goes to them."

"This is quite incredible," Cathleen said, unable to understand how such things could be.

"Since Bridgit, your old servant, died her man and son have gone to serve the strangers and they encourage people to trade with them. I have done so myself and so have many others – and look, we are now rich."

He brought out from under his coat a bag of gold and showed it to her.

"We have food and as much wine as we can drink into the bargain."

"What can you all be giving them in return for such generosity? Are they so full of goodness of spirit that they ask nothing?"

"Oh," he laughed carelessly. "We give them something all right, but it is nothing we ever miss."

"And that is?" Cathleen asked archly.

"Our souls, lady. They are merchants who deal in souls, obtaining them for their king."

"God help us," the Countess moaned, her hands flying to cover her face.

"Yes, and they pay richly for the useless, painful things. I am glad I sold them my soul. I don't grieve for my wife anymore. I am happy and well fed. I get drunk when I like, which is all the time, if it please your ladyship, and I have gold enough to see out the famine and after, so there."

"But when you die ..." she gasped.

"I just will not have a soul," he laughed at her sorrow. "As I have none now. But I have no conscience to trouble me either. So what if I have no soul to trouble me later?"

She waved her hand for him to go and he reeled out of the room still laughing without joy, swearing to himself that he had made a fine bargain.

In her chapel later the Countess prayed to the Virgin and all the saints for assistance in defeating the demons and saving the souls of her people.

Going into the village the next morning Cathleen appealed to the local people and those who had come from far and wide alike, to return to sharing her rations. She admitted that she had only tiny portions of corn and meal, with a few drops of milk from the two starving cows her servants had somehow kept alive.

"But more is on its way," she told them. "I have sent to Ulster for cattle and to England for corn, wine and other livestock. Abundant supplies of everything are on their way, I can assure you all. You have only to be patient a while longer."

Of course she was only hoping, for there was no word from Fergus or the other man and she could but pray that what she told the people was the truth. Nevertheless, it did not matter because no one really listened to her. There were endless supplies at the forest cottage and no stinting in the amounts given.

The merchants themselves were naturally very active too in drawing new people to their door and stooges already in their thrall were only too ready to bring others into the evil fold. The wine they were so profligate with was heady stuff and helped dupe anyone who drank it and planted dreams of blissful, comfortable living once the famine was over.

In the face of seeming guarantees of good times now and tomorrow, Cathleen's appeal fell on deaf ears and the trade in souls became brisker than ever. The noise of the nightly drinking bouts increased as more people arrived and everyone grew riotous and reckless. Nothing mattered any longer to any of them and wildness of every sort abounded.

A sense of evil now pervaded everything for miles around, further depressing the stricken countryside. People laughed at death, laughed at the dying, even ones who had also sold their souls and passed away cursing the demons who had tricked them, horrified at what was to come. No one cared. The traffic continued unabated.

Summoning her courage and all her faith in God, Cathleen took the well-worn path to the forest cottage where the demon merchants stayed. As they saw her coming down the track they caught their breath and their evil eyes shone. Excitedly they rubbed their hands together, hoping that she was coming at last to sell her own sweet soul.

"Would the Countess be interested in doing business with such humble foreign merchants as we?" the eldest of the pair asked with a wicked grin.

"We are at your service in any way," the younger one bowed, leering at her, taking in her shape with glee. "Any way that is not contrary to the interests of our King, of course."

"I have nothing to trade with you," Cathleen replied. "for you purchase the souls of men for the Evil One, do you not?"

"Bluntly put, my lady, but yes that is our office. What may we do for you then?"

"I am here to beseech you to release my people from the bargains you have made with them. Give them back their souls and have pity on them."

"Why would we ever wish to do such a thing?"

"I still have some jewels and gold, please take them and leave my people be. Return their souls and leave our country."

The demons turned to one another and as their wicked, beady eyes met they burst into laughter, slapping each other's backs and doubling up with mirth.

"You mean, we are to undo all our labour, cease and desist forthwith, in exchange for some gold and gems?" the younger merchant scoffed, shaking his head in disbelief and smirking. Then, he said, with deadly seriousness. "Lady, don't you realize that we have unlimited gold and gems, and these people are nothing to us."

"Indeed," said the eldest petulantly. "This is our work, my dear Countess, not our sport. We buy souls for our Satanic master, to dwell with him in his kingdom and do his bidding. Our reward in rank and honour in his realm is equal to the success we have in this enterprise. No, we will not give up a single one of the souls we have bought."

"See by the circlets on our heads that we are as princes in his kingdom," the younger one said proudly. "We have brought him countless souls from all lands and will win yet many more. How can you come here and ..."

"Quiet," the elder said abruptly, holding up his hand. "There might just be one particularly valuable thing that might yet redeem the souls of the peasants of Erin. One thing that might count equal with them all in glory to our master."

"Tell me what it is," said Cathleen, "and if it is in my gift, or if I can acquire it, the thing is yours. Anything that will save my people's souls, I will give you."

"It belongs to you even now, Countess," the elder demon said smoothly. "A pure soul is more valuable than many, many, tainted ones. Our king would deem it a good bargain and commend us if we made such a trade."

"Yes," chimed in the other one, eagerly. "Your saintly soul, Countess, for all the others. You would redeem all the others with the sale of your own."

"And do not hold out hope," his crafty elder added, "for assistance from another quarter. Fool the people and yourself no longer with groundless promises of, what is it – cattle from Ulster and grain, wine and whatnot from England? There is none on its way. Both your emissaries have failed."

"That is so," the other merchant confirmed. "Believe us, we have sent to find out. One lays dying up north with an ague, the other is still in England, robbed and thwarted at every turn. The English much fear a famine of their own, you see, and sell no food. They pay next to nothing for worthless Irish lands and forests."

It seemed all hope faded from Cathleen upon hearing this news and turning to go she paused for a second, then left. The demons shivered with delight at their deception and felt good about their chances of securing her soul now, but time they knew was short. By diabolical means they had already seen the true state of the progress being made both by the cattle buyer, heading south at that very moment, and the ships full of food from England. There were but five or six days before they would arrive – five or six days in which they might win Cathleen's pure young soul.

Defeated and grieving, Cathleen entered her castle, now occupied by only a few loyal old servants. Alone in her oratory she stayed about her prayers for many hours, begging for enlightenment as to how she might save her people from the devil and starvation too.

Suddenly her orisons were interrupted by a loud thumping at the chapel door and the voice of Una, her foster-mother, calling to her. Cathleen left the altar and ran to the door.

'Thieves!" cried Una, as the door was flung open. "You have been robbed, my lady."

Going at once to the treasure chamber, Cathleen saw for herself that what little had remained was now gone. Even as she stood staring at the empty room more cries were heard in another part of the castle.

Dashing to the store house where the last of the mouldy corn and sacks of meal were kept, they saw that this too had been stolen. Only a few torn empty sacks littered the floor. The very last of anything edible was gone. Not a day's sustenance was left to them.

These new disasters seemed to lift a weight from Cathleen's shoulders. She had felt beaten and helpless before. Now a bright shining certainty grew in her mind and with it the knowledge that the salvation of her people must be accomplished at any price. Her prayers for guidance had been answered. So plain was her determination to sacrifice herself that it showed on her glowing features as she went once more to her chapel, surrounded now by weeping, moaning servants. Una knew at once what Cathleen planned and was so awe-struck by the appearance of her mistress that she could not muster the words to dissuade her.

At the Chapel door Cathleen looked one final time into her sanctuary, seeing its holy objects, remembering all her prayers. They had not been in vain – all had led up to this moment. Behind her the servants who loved her so well were still wailing and wringing their hands. She turned to them.

"I am forlorn, for I have had to make a terrible choice," she told them. "Yet do not despair for there is hope. Friends, be still. Our Heavenly father has not forgotten us."

Looking for a final time into the oratory, she sighed:

"Goodbye, Holy Mary, Mother of God and all you dear saints. Goodbye."

Closing the door firmly she turned and walked out of the castle, through the village and into the forest where she followed the well-trodden path to the cottage of the demon merchants.

Here business was as brisk as ever and food, gold and wine were quickly changing hands for the souls of starving peasants. Afraid of death and tired of suffering, people were selling to the merchants ever more cheaply in these hungry, lawless, and increasingly sinful times. Deals were being struck and prices bandied, while all around those who had already parted with their souls gorged themselves on food and drink. As Cathleen was seen coming slowly along the path, the peasants filtered away in ones and twos until by the time she arrived at the hut only the merchants remained to greet her. Sitting among their foodstuffs and bags of gold they watched her enter, rising only as part of their show of mocking deference.

"Lady, what brings you into our humble presence once again?"

"Merchants, are you still buying souls for the devil?"

"Surely Countess, and our traffic has never been better. People want to live through this famine and prosper in the times to come, to enjoy wealth and comfort. And why should they not when all we ask for is that insubstantial, feather-light touch of breeze, a nothingness that is called a soul?"

"Has the Countess by any chance come here to strike a bargain herself?" the younger demon asked mockingly with a sly grin.

"I have," Cathleen replied flatly. "But I will not haggle with you."

"What merchandize do you wish to sell, fair lady?" the younger demon asked, for he longed to hear her say it.

"Something so valuable that perhaps you cannot afford to buy it."

"Our purse is very deep, my lady – indeed, limitless," the younger merchant assured her, smirking and eyeing her greedily. "No price is beyond us."

"That is, of course, if the soul in question is worth having. If a soul be truly saintly, fit even to join the angels in Paradise, our king will authorize us to pay any sum you can name. Just whose soul are we talking about, Countess?" the elder merchant smiled, raising his brows in feigned curiosity. He too wished to hear it in plain words from her own lips.

"My people starve and die and so come to you. I hear their cries of anguish and despair ever in my ears," she said. "I want five hundred crowns in gold for the people to find food with, and more if need be, enough, in short, to see them through the famine. You must end your trafficking at once and I want all the souls you have bought to be freed and sent to God."

"Yes but …"

Swallowing hard Cathleen paused. Her hands trembled and her body stiffened, goose bumps covered her skin as if suddenly chilled by an icy draft.

"It is my soul that is for sale."

The demons could not restrain their joy and they danced about and punched the air, shaking hands as their jewels gleamed and their eyes flashed. To have won such a stainless and exemplary soul would bring them such honour and credit in Hell as had seldom been awarded to any of Satan's minions.

Laying out the documents excitedly they took possession of themselves long enough to watch with care as Cathleen signed her soul over to their master. Then they happily paid out the money she had demanded, already noting the change in her face, the dullness in her eyes that were harbingers of her coming early death. Gleefully they anticipated the imminent arrival of the food relief from Ulster and England which would show her irrevocable sacrifice to have been largely pointless.

With resolution and sadness in equal measure filling her heart, Cathleen left the hut in the forest followed by her grieving servants, who carried the bags of gold. As she went through the village everyone came out to see her pass, for the rumour of what she had done had spread quickly. The people too felt within themselves that their souls were once more their own and were overcome by remorse. All now lamented. Recognizing her great sacrifice, they wept, and wished they could die for her, help her, somehow redeem her poor soul, but there was no hope.

In the courtyard of her castle, Cathleen distributed the gold the demons had given her, and told everyone to use the money well so that it would see them though the famine.

"My steward will return soon and guide you in my absence, for I cannot stay among you. I cannot pray for you anymore, or for myself. I must go to the dark lord in Hell. I am his now."

The knowledge of her sacrifice spread though the country. People mourned. Feeling their own redemption, they prayed for her, barely hoping that it would do any good. They beseeched the Blessed Virgin and all the saints to have mercy on her, and all the souls in Heaven who had been saved by her also interceded for her on high.

As daily Cathleen faded, her life force ebbing from her, the demons, who had ceased trading, lingered. They wanted very much to enjoy the ironic return of her food-buying messengers and, of course, to catch her soul as it departed from her body, which it surely would before long.

Broken hearted, old Una nursed her mistress without rest and watched helplessly as the poor young woman grew weaker. Cathleen had resigned herself to the inevitable and did not struggle against the coming of death. She revived a little, though, on being told that word had at last come from the coast that Fergus had landed and was proceeding inland. Another message arrived about the whereabouts of the man sent to Ulster. He was within one day's march with seven hundred head of cattle.

Knowing her own folk were safe now, the Countess Cathleen breathed her last. She died with thanks to God for her people's deliverance on her lips and a smile on her face, regretting nothing.

That night an enormous storm blew up and swept the country with mighty winds and driving rains. It raged for the next day and night and then on the following morning people woke to find the pestilential fogs and poisonous mists had gone. New life began to appear in the woods and fields. The old forester's hut where the merchants had stayed had been crushed by a large fallen tree, and there was no sign of them anywhere.

When Fergus returned he distributed food and oxen to every family. Everywhere prayers were offered up in thanks for Cathleen's sacrifice and in blessings upon her. They grieved too at the knowledge that her spirit must now be in Hell. Everyone's heart was rent, for still there was no sign of her forgiveness.

Gloom shrouded the desolate castle as Una sat watching beside the body of her foster-daughter. Offering her own prayers the old nurse looked piteously at the face of her dead darling, pleading with Heaven, as were so many others, that Cathleen be spared. Suddenly she stopped. In a flash, a pure knowing, a vision that could only truly come from God, entered her being.

It was of Cathleen being received into Paradise surrounded by angels and saints. God had forgiven her, had known her clean spirited self sacrifice for what it was and understood it. The bargain with Satan's minions was void, and Cathleen was safely, joyously in Heaven.

Tlazoteotl and the Price of Temptation

The goddess Tlazoteotl is Mexican mythology's answer to Venus.
She was seen by the Aztecs as the driving force behind all types
of 'unclean' or immoral behaviour.
More positively, she would act as an intermediary for penitent
sinners with the all-powerful god Tezcatlipoca who could
take or give life. There may be a general lesson for the self-righteous
in this story, but on the whole it doesn't seem quite fair.

Perturbed, the Aztec goddess Tlazoteotl reviewed the situation and liked what she saw even less than before. Where would she be if such things caught on? She must lobby the other gods and force them to act. If she worked matters carefully, everything might even turn to her advantage. The trouble had all begun when some fool, to her way of thinking, had decided to become especially religious. She suspected the motives of this individual – whose name was Jappan – and she was inclined to regard his newly acquired religious devotion as the ultimate form of social climbing.

Since being overtaken by a yearning to be closer to the gods, Jappan had been able to think of little else. Middle aged and fairly prosperous, he had decided to leave his wife, family and all he possessed and make his way into the desert to spend his days contemplating the divine and doing all he could to demonstrate his piety. He had wandered for a long while before finding a suitable place to live and continue his attempt to commune with higher powers. His choice was at the top of a towering rock – a good spot for a hermit, he felt – which he had climbed with some difficulty, but once there he quickly became absorbed in his devotions and spent all his time in contemplation and prayer.

Abstinence from all earthly – and, especially, earthy – pleasures constituted a large part of Jappan's regime, hence the ill-will of Tlazoteotl, who was known colloquially as the Goddess of Guilty Love.

She, meanwhile, was trying to convince the other gods that it would be a good idea to test Jappan's virtue. She argued that a truly righteous man should be recognized and rewarded for his endeavours. Equally, fairness dictated that a man who only purported to follow a virtuous path should be punished. Not wishing to be seen to be condoning backsliding, the gods dispatched a demon, Yaotl, to observe Jappan and report to them of his conduct. Tlazoteotl had been very pleased with the selection of Yaotl – indeed she had done her best to assure it. She also had seen to it that the demon, whose name means 'enemy', was authorized to punish Jappan himself, if the man failed in his devotion. The demon relished such a task, as the goddess knew he would.

Among the temptations Yaotl sent Jappan's way were beautiful women. By the demon's own reckoning these were bound to be the most testing of his resolution to devote himself purely to worship. Many sirens came and stood beneath the high rock upon which Jappan sat. They called up to him in soft and gentle voices, talked explicitly to him with a come-hither gleam in their eyes, appealed to him as maidens in distress or as innocent but eager girls who wanted to learn of love in his arms. None of these lines succeeded in luring him down to ground level. Tlazolteotl watched with growing exasperation. Enough, she thought, and took matters into her own hands.

She went to the foot of Jappan's rock and called up to him. Wearily the hermit peered down at this latest temptress. His eyes nearly popped out of his head! There before him, in her full, divine splendour, was standing the most beautiful female in creation.

"Oh, Brother Jappan," the goddess whispered in a husky voice which carried surprisingly clearly to his lofty perch, "what devotion and fortitude you have shown. Such piety and sacrifice. Such restraint and wisdom."

All the poor hermit could do was stare at her, and marvel at her magnificence and other-worldly allure.

"I am Tlazoteotl," she said, knowing she needed no introduction. "Your virtue and suffering have touched me deeply. I long to console you. But please, how may I reach you and speak with you more easily?"

"I'll show you," croaked Jappan, who had not used his voice in some time, not even to reply in the negative to any of his other visitors.

A little stiff at first he climbed down to the goddess and, showing her the way, helped her to ascend to the top of his eerie.

"Well, let me look at you," the goddess said, making herself comfortable beside him, all the while gripping his hand which he had extended to pull her to safety during their climb. "Why, you are not simply a very pious man but a damned handsome one as well. Certainly your devotion deserves a kiss."

One thing inextricably led to another and there atop the high rock Jappan and the goddess coupled rapturously. That is to say, it was rapturous for Jappan. Tlazoteotl found the experience very satisfying in a quite different way.

As soon as the deed was done, Yaotl arrived and irately remonstrated with Jappan as the goddess faded away, a joyous smile lighting her serenely lovely face.

"What have you done, you who would be so holy?" the demon taunted.

"But she was a goddess and ..."

"That makes no difference," cried Yeotl. "It makes it worse. Far worse. And you a married hermit, at that."

"Have mercy, please," Jappan pleaded – but to no avail.

Bending the poor, kneeling man even further over, Yeotl cut off his head. The gods themselves then magically turned him into a scorpion. Ashamed and frightened of any further wrath, Jappan scuttled under the rock upon which he had committed his misdeed.

Then Yeotl went in search of Jappan's wife, Tlahuizin, which means 'the burning', and dragged her to the high rock, where he related the whole sad tale of her husband's downfall. She, too, was then unceremoniously beheaded. On his own initiative, Yeotl turned her into a scorpion, a fire coloured one, and she joined Jappan under the great rock. In time they had little scorpions of various colours.

The gods, however, deemed that Yeotl had overstepped his responsibilities and acted without authority. As punishment, he was changed into a grasshopper.

Tlazoteotl remained very much herself, and thought it all highly amusing, of course.

St. George
and the Dragon

*Christianity has spun a few myths of its own over the centuries
while attempting to destroy those of pagan peoples.
The dragon has long been a Christian metaphor for evil – St John the Divine,
St Margaret and St Michael, among others, have all been depicted
in Christian imagery slaying dragons. The Reverend Thomas Percy
included the myth of George and the Dragon in his book of ballads,
Percy's Reliques (1765), and kept to tradition in his treatment of the story.
I could not quite bring myself to do the same.*

The sun rose that morning no differently than it does most mornings and climbed slowly through the bright blue sky. There was going to be a monumental battle which only one of the duellists would survive. Neither of them was fully confident of victory and the hours leading up to their midday appointment could not go quickly enough. On the other hand, a dread of what might happen, and of much that was certain to happen, also nagged at both of them.

The dragon had woken early, which was not his habit. He lay abed awhile thinking on what the day held and how it had all come about. For the life of him he could not understand it. What did these humans expect? It wasn't as if he was eating them, just their enslaved animals. In his time he had eaten people, of course – who had not? But it took too many of them, once boned, to make a meal and they were difficult to catch, always put up an embarrassing and unseemly struggle and they had to be cooked just right or they withered to dry crust.

With people killing all the wild game though, or scaring it off and putting their own exploited beasts everywhere, what else was a fellow to do but develop a taste for mutton and beef? Humans could hardy expect to be the only predators on the planet, could they? What, get rid of all the big cats, the birds of prey, the wolves for heaven's sake? Dragons were another thing, of course.

He well knew that his own kind were few, sensitive, solitary and reluctant to cohabit and breed. Being extremely long-lived, wise and self-absorbed, this insularity had not mattered before. But now, with man having seen off his cousins the Neanderthals, breeding like rabbits and covering the whole surface of the globe with his progeny, the competition for food was getting ridiculous.

"Perhaps I should go to China," the dragon yawned, rising reluctantly to enter an alcove-like section of his cave. Here a small fissure miles deep into the earth and a spring babbling from the rock wall created for the fastidious creature a natural toilet and washroom. "At least there, the humans know how to appreciate a dragon. Why, they even consider us good luck."

And now here was this rather bolder, or crazier, human down there in the valley who wanted to fight him, to rid the local people of their rival. They had told the fellow that he, the dragon, was downright evil, of course. The fool had believed it, too, believed he had been eating people on a daily basis, devouring them in order of class, starting with the sons and daughters of the commoners, and rising ultimately to, horror of horrors, a royal princess. This had been too much for a passing hero to bear.

Evil indeed, the dragon snorted indignantly. The princess was pure bait, for him and the hero, a gutsy little so-and-so who knew exactly what she was doing. The dragon had learned all this by flying silently and slowly about on dark moonless nights and listening in at windows. As a snack the princess was hardly worth the bother of opening his mouth, though they thought he would not be able to resist her. It was the hero, of course, who could not resist her.

With a sigh the dragon knew he would have to show up that afternoon, and have a go at seeing off this champion. It might discourage the humans for a while if he won, though all they cared about was their prosperity. However, he had really no alternative but to starve to death. What else was a fellow to do? Lately there was nothing else but their livestock, though he was careful never to eat so many that he would bankrupt them. That would be as stupid as it would have been to have eaten all the wild animals in his own territory.

Evil, the dragon snorted again. Evil because he killed and ate what people were going to eat? Why, he even dispatched the poor creatures more swiftly and kindly than the humans did. No, to them, he and the lions were wicked and symbols of all that was bad in the world. Once dragons were considered the givers of life, of precious water, then the water became treasure they were said to hoard, and they had to be killed for people to get it off them. Humans never seemed to make up their minds about dragons. Until lately, the dragon thought sadly. Now we've become a certain evil that has to be overcome at every turn. And that, he knew, was what this was all about. It was a mere gesture, a show of righteousness.

The dragon knew the hero was going to try to prove himself to the others, mark himself out as different and more favoured by whatever strange forces or idols his brand of humans worshipped. The silly man had even succeeded in persuading, or coercing, a horse into carrying him not only to, but indeed in, the contest. This was a new innovation they had introduced in their wars in recent centuries. Formerly men had been drawn in wheeled chariots, the dragon recalled, but with the stronger backed horses they had produced (by interfering with the animal's natural breeding patterns), humans now rode right on the poor beasts' backs.

Again the dragon sighed. He had seen a lot in his life and had watched humans with a weary and curious eye ever since he could remember. As the only other sentient and intelligent creatures around, they interested him. He had seen early on that one day they might pose a threat, and knew, of course, that dragons had been killed by them, though it had always seemed one of those things that might happen to somebody else. He had assumed, too, that the dragons involved were troublemakers, or particularly feeble in mind or body.

It had been something of a shock for him to discover himself in this predicament. Yet there was little to be gained from running off to China or anywhere else. He had these people trained well enough, did not tax them too badly, no matter what they told the hero, and he was not about to let them get away with such a ridiculous attempt to deprive him of his life and livelihood. He had lived in this valley since long before their arrival. Let them pack up and move to China.

The George in this story was not a martyr of any monotheistic faith or even of the Roman Empire in which he was later said to have served as a soldier. This George was not thinking of glory or spiritual salvation, not his own or that of the town. No, all that was on his mind, apart from the will to survive, was a desperate longing to win the beautiful princess.

It would be a very fine thing if everyone else thought he was a hero, he told himself that morning, but it was the princess that he really needed to impress. He had no thought of becoming sacred to some future religion or the patron saint of countries not yet dreamt of. He was a young man in the throes of love, and no end of perfectly straightforward lust. The princess was, after all, a knockout. One way or the other, George freely admitted to himself, he was absolutely gone on her.

If he could not have this girl, then let the dragon have him, for he would not care to live a day, an hour, a minute, longer. It hurt to think of her, and all his considerable athletic ability, his co-ordination, quick wits and keen balance left him when she was around. As a consequence none of the attributes that had first singled him out as the man to tangle with the dragon had been much on display since his arrival.

Still, everyone had faith in him, it seemed, especially the princess. She was so kind and gentle, he thought dreamily, and so needed to be saved from that terrible creature. For a moment George dwelt on the rightness of parents sending their children out to be eaten instead of putting up a fight and mobilizing everyone to swamp the dragon with numbers. Many might die that way, but if, as the townsfolk declared, he was eating his way through the whole population anyhow, such a loss would be worth it in the long run.

How could parents, he mused, particularly the parents of so wonderful a girl as the princess, send her out to be roasted alive and devoured, just to save their own hides and property? Then he pulled himself up. It isn't right to second-guess royalty, he thought. The king and queen must know what they're doing. But did he?

George had done prodigious deeds in battle. He had slain some pretty impressive beasts of the more ordinary sort, such as lions, tigers and bears. A dragon was quite another thing, though. If it really had been eating two sheep a day, then two or more people, it must be pretty big. Much bigger than him at any rate, and able to fly and breath fire. This adversary would be a very tough customer indeed.

With a shaky hand George drank a little wine and looked out the window at the slowly rising sun. It was ages yet and he had not slept a wink. Young men in love and about to fight dragons seldom do. With a sigh, he remembered all that had passed between him and the princess and knew there was no way in the world that he could have her if he did not fight the dragon. He also knew there was little chance of him having her, or even of living, if he did not win. Setting his jaw, he went to see to his horse and his weapons, not for the first time that night.

To give the princess her due, she was unaware that the dragon was indifferent to her as fodder. He liked his food well done and to leave so slender a morsel as she was over the flame for so much as a breath would have reduced her to a flavourless cinder. She did not know either that the other things she and her fellows put such store by were also of no interest to him. He was unimpressed with either physical beauty or royal titles.

When they staked her out that day at high-noon, she honestly thought her life would be forfeited if the hero did not win through. It was an act of sacrifice and faith on her part and she was ready to face any eventuality. If her father's kingdom could be rid of the dragon and grow rich, then the risk would have been worth it.

A hero was not going to fight for the mere fun of it, after all, and a dragon was not going to venture out into the open to face one for just any sort of bait. They both demanded a prize and she was willing to play that role. Besides, she thought, that George is a beau-sabre, dream-boat and stud-muffin of the first rank. Wedding bells with that hunk or a luncheon date with a giant reptile, she thought with a toss of her head, oh how is a girl to decide?

With a brave smile she let them tie her hands to the stake she stood against and watched them run off to a safe distance. Over the next hill, she knew, George would be waiting, mounted and well armed and from somewhere else nearby, the dragon was bound to spot her, for his cave was known to overlook this gully. He would come for his offering and receive, she supposed, the surprise of his life.

Reluctantly, begrudgedly the dragon sauntered down the hillside, eyeing the princess with what would have been recognized by another dragon as a bemused expression. To her he only looked hungry and ill-tempered. That he did not even deem to fly hardly registered with her. If anything, she thought he was coming slowly in order to prolong her torment.

His progress was so slow that the prearranged signal was not difficult to make before her life was directly in peril. The shrill scream emitted by the princess would have broken glass had any been around. As it was it made the dragon jump and left him with an uncomfortable sensation in his ears. George and his horse, or rather George on his horse, came racing around the hill that had been concealing them to find the dragon stopped in his tracks, recovering from the pain in his head.

Now, the dragon was not large but the hero was not either, and the pole-thing he carried may have been sharp, but it looked rather flimsy. It was the horse that really attracted the dragon's attention. His fear of the hero was diminished now he actually confronted him. Yes, the fellow was armed and braver than the general run of humans, but human he was never the less. The horse on the other hand was good red meat and plenty of it. It was bigger than other horses he had seen or eaten before, bred up as a warhorse, he supposed, without thinking of what that might mean. As it was lunchtime, the one thing he did not want to happen was for the horse to escape while he was dispatching the silly humans and teaching their brethren a much-needed lesson.

As George charged at the dragon all he could think of, for his own part, was that it was disappointingly small, and then he remembered that it still outweighed him and his horse together. Dust boiled behind them as the din of clattering hooves blended with George's shouted war-cry, the girl's screams, which were now ones of encouragement, and the horse snorting and whinnying.

Only the dragon was silent, his mind occupied with the problem of how to sort the equine wheat from the human chaff. How could he deal with the hero, who was no doubt dangerous, and yet not lose the tasty looking horse? The answer, he realized, was simple. Do not frighten the thing off or let it throw the man from its back and become separated from him too soon. Let them get close, yes, but above all cut off their retreat. Then he spied the dry scrub around the entrance to the gully which they were just passing, and with a quick whoosh of fiery breath, he shot flames behind the charging horseman. The flames roared in the dry desert air. Horse and man felt their heat and then, from fear and instinct, training and breeding, far from pausing, far from thinking the next breath of fire had their names on it, they fled the flames but charged all the harder. The horse put on a sudden burst of speed, the man shut his eyes and gritted his teeth, while the dragon debated whether or not to spin and strike them with his tail, or singe them with his next breath. Then before he knew it, they were on him, far sooner than he had imagined they possibly could be.

The collision was tremendous and the noise of the combined thud and grunt echoed throughout the gully and all over the surrounding countryside. Tumbling and sprawling, horse, man and dragon rolled in the dust, the wind knocked out of all of them. The first to rise was the horse, which trotted out of the dust cloud and turned to look for its master. George was up next. Drawing his sword, he groped about blindly until the breeze took the dusty confusion away. And there, staring at the lance that fixed him to the ground, the dragon sat, wondering what on earth had happened to him.

George released the princess from her bonds and took the prize of a kiss, the first of many. Then he turned to the dragon, but he did not strike off its head as logically he should have done. Cruel and unthinking, supposing it a dumb beast and evil anyway, they harnessed it with the princess's girdle. Far from dispatching the dragon swiftly, shocked and subdued and suffering though it was, they led it stumbling, unable to fight them off or fly away, back to the town.

When they arrived, the whole populace turned out. Then, there before the town gate the creature was assailed and overwhelmed by the knife-wielding frenzied yet fearful mob. Seeing the dragon was helpless, the stay-at-homes darted in and attacked it, while George and the princess contented themselves with gazing into each other's eyes.

The dragon's thoughts as the blades went into his flesh were not fearful, and he endured the pain well enough, while deeming the whole sorry business as typical of the human race, his usual ill-luck and the correctness of his own predictions. Humans, especially ones raised west of the Ganges, wanted it all and would not let rare beasts or even the nature of life itself get in their way. Dragons and all they had symbolized, in the past, anywhere in the world, good bad and just plain magical, would be destroyed. Anything that challenged man, anything that ate what he ate, anything he feared and did not understand,

anything he respected but could not control, would be defeated and eradicated.

If that's the world these people want, the dragon thought, then I'm glad I won't be here to see it.

As for George, through the ages countless stories would be told about him. Different cultures and religions would adopt him as their own and everything would be adapted to purposes he could hardly have imagined or ever cared about. All that mattered to him, quite rightly, was that he had won the day, survived intact and got the girl. They married, had children, lived into old age and died as people do, in pretty short order.

Dragons are another story. They can, for instance, suffer multiple stab wounds and being thrown onto a town rubbish heap to be consumed by flames and smoke – much of them their own –, and manage to burrow under the ashes and sneak away in the dead of night to hide in a cave. Recovering their strength, they might even be minded to fly to China, there to be truly appreciated and live on for centuries.

The Adventure of Goroba-Dike

*Like the legend of Mamadi Sefe Dekote, this tale is also
from the Sudan, although of a more recognizably heroic
and romantic type.*

A swirl of dust, loud muttering and the pounding of hooves enveloped the village as the pair of horsemen raced about it, one overturning baskets and kicking out at people, ripping off shades and awnings, snarling and cursing. Behind him, the smaller, older man shouted flattering words, trying to calm the other, while smiling and whispering apologies to the scurrying villagers, rolling his eyes in wonder and embarrassment at each new outrage.

"You sheep," cried the infamous young warrior, Goroba-Dike, leaning down from his saddle to grab a melon from the frozen hands of a child and flinging it with precision at the grey head of the terrified chief of the hamlet. His less expensively dressed companion shut his eyes and shook his head, then removed his own scarf to wipe the globules of fruit from the old man's dazed face.

The horsemen were of the Fulbe tribe, black and tall and hardened by the rugged life of the African desert, one a highly spirited, hot tempered fighting man lost in a time of peace, the other his 'mabo', a poet and personal praise singer. This latter, Ulal, grimaced and spurred his horse to catch up with the furious Goroba-Dike.

"Once we Fulbe were herdsmen," the warrior shouted at the cowering, running, hiding villagers. "Then the cruel Fasa tribe conquered our traditional grazing lands and oppressed us. We became wanderers to escape them. We were strengthened by our suffering and we learnt to raid and fight and acquire new lands and to fear no one."

Goroba-Dike's warhorse danced in the tiny square surrounded by shabby huts of mud and sticks. Dirty children wailed and dogs barked from a distance but nothing moved.

"Come out and attack me. Drive me away from your daughters and your farms. Come on; send out ten good men. Twenty! Care you nothing for your women's honour, for the safety of your property?"

The hiding of a particularly comely maiden by her worried father had sparked off the incident, but there was far more than this to the whipped up passions of Goroba–Dike. Although a hero among his own people, he was, even at home, considered troublesome and prickly. A row with his wealthy family had brought him here, to the Bammama country.

A weaker tribe than his own, the poor Bammama suffered under his careless and violent temperament, and they longed for him to move on. He bullied them and made too free with their women and it was said among them that he liked to grind up Bammama babies to feed in mash to his warhorse. This slander was more than half-believed and it had the desired effect of making him less popular with the local girls. Somehow this tale had come to Goroba-Dike's attention and the restless hero was now more angry and fearsome than ever.

Suddenly, from nowhere, a small stone clanged against the warrior's helmet. Goroba-Dike whirled about, drawing his sword. He saw nothing until, looking down, he espied a few feet away the frightened but defiant figure of a boy of eight or so, his arm poised to throw again. Letting out a deep sigh, Goroba-Dike slowly turned his horse and rode out of the village. After a slight delay, Ulal followed at a trot.

Side by side they rode in silence for several miles, until the mabo suggested they might go back home and make peace with Goroba-Dike's father and brother.

"Never," the young hero grunted. "Just look at their tiresome existence. We are one of the very best of families, indisputably of the oldest, noblest blood, by heaven, and yet they have no idea how to live."

"Perhaps conditions are better now."

"Would they listen to me before, the only one with the sense to conduct himself according to our rank?"

"No, lord," the mabo nodded wearily.

"Indeed. We rule nearly all the Massina district and have great wealth but it is wasted on my father and elder brother. Wasted. No, nothing will have changed."

As the younger son it was also true that Goroba-Dike could expect to inherit nothing. Living under the thumb of his relations had galled him ever since he had come to manhood. A year or so before, in high dudgeon over some minor upset, Goroba-Dike had left, for good he swore, and with Ulal had come to live in these parts, on a small allowance, much to the discomfiture of the Bammama.

"But this life too is unworthy of me," Goroba-Dike conceded, catching a glimpse of the single arched eyebrow of his mabo. "Though of so noble a line, I live no better than a roving bandit."

"I had not liked to say, but it is hardly epic stuff, lord."

"Everything around me is petty and shabby and tiresome," complained the hero.

It was plain enough to one who knew him so well that Goroba-Dike was in pain, bored and unfulfilled, and was lately only lashing out in frustration.

Stirring the fire that evening and glancing at the listless Goroba-Dike lounging against his saddle, legs stretched out, Ulal fell to musing on a proposition the Bammama had made him that afternoon. The long and short of it was that they would make it well worth his while to lure his master as far from their country as possible.

With a little Fulbe hauteur of his own, the mabo had chuckled at their predicament and airily said he would consider the idea, hinting nevertheless that a far higher sum would have to be forthcoming than the figure named.

As the poet cooked (he was hardly more than a servant lately and the warrior's only retainer), he mulled the problem over. As a singer and teller of tales he had talent suited to the purpose in many ways and so it was that he began to spin yarns of far-off lands, of adventures in distant places, of the exotic wonders to be found beyond the horizon.

Goroba-Dike knew the old man nearly as well as the old man knew him, and could see he was being manipulated, but out of affection and some interest he listened and began to dream. However, a sort of listlessness had settled on the young warrior and nothing much seemed to excite him.

After weeks of seemingly futile preparation, a heaven-sent opportunity came Ulal's way. There was news afoot as strange as one of his own stories, and perhaps suited to his purpose. The darkness surrounding them, the stars sparkling above, Ulal chose his moment that night, as they sat facing the fire in companionable silence. With feigned nonchalance he imparted the tale as it had been told to him that morning, barely embellishing it.

"You have heard me speak of Sariam?"

"Lately of little else but such far-flung places."

"Apparently," Ulal went on, "the youngest and still unmarried daughter of the king there is making a very merry farce of her father's court. Both her elder sisters have married well from among the local nobles but she refuses to follow their example. It seems she has the most odd requirement of her husband to be. Most odd." Ulal smiled. "The girl has a very narrow ring and she insists she will marry no man but the one man that it fits. Is that not strange, Goroba-Dike, my lord?"

"Why strange?" cried Goroba-Dike. "It is an elegant physical attribute, a true mark of the best-bred of our own people." With that he held his fine hands before the glowing fire and admired the long, slender fingers. "Perhaps too she is not understood by her father and wishes to vex him for sport. It is a spirit I cannot bring myself to condemn," Goroba-Dike went on. "But this story is not new. I've heard the people around here whispering about it for weeks."

"Oh," Ulal sighed in disappointment, though he could see the story had captured his master's imagination like nothing else of late. It was true that the situation in Sariam had been going on for some time and that the king was losing patience, so it was logical that Goroba-Dike had heard something of it. Perhaps it was just as well, otherwise he might not have believed it. Ulal chuckled to himself.

"Have you not thought to go there and try on this ring and make your fortune?"

"In Sariam?" Goroba-Dike asked, more harshly than was his custom when addressing Ulal, whom he liked and respected above all other men, though he would never say so. "What would be the use of it?"

Ulal could see that it was with regret that Goroba-Dike said this and that the idea rather appealed to him.

"If I were a younger man and had such fingers ..." laughed Ulal.

"Have you no standards, no tribal loyalties?" snapped Goroba-Dike, before adding glumly. "Perhaps it is just that my position is greater, but no foreign princess ..."

"A very beautiful princess, I understand," whispered Ulal, though he had heard no such thing.

"It does not matter. It would be impossible for each of us," muttered the warrior sadly.

"You do not know that King Hamadi Ardo is himself a Fulbe? Have I managed to teach you nothing of the world?" The mabo asked, laughing.

"Has the bribe to take me away from the Bammama risen so high, Ulal, that you would betray me to earn it?" Goroba-Dike shouted.

"It has certainly risen to a very attractive figure," Ulal conceded.

This response took Goroba-Dike aback, and he stared at his mabo in astonishment. But Ulal was engrossed in thinking of ways to inspire and challenge his master and took no notice of his reaction. "In fact," he said. "I would have thought your own brother would have gone to try his luck if he had been warrior enough to brave the dangers of the journey, so full of brigands and thieves ..."

"That fool," laughed Goroba-Dike. "His fingers may be nearly as long and slender as mine, it is true, but what princess would look at his face?"

"Certainly it is not unlike that of a camel," Ulal conceded. "But women are perverse creatures and this one is inordinately spoiled, it would seem. There is no telling what will please such a one. Perhaps by this time some refined fellow of fair Sariam has at last come forward ..."

"Saddle the horses, Ulal," Goroba-Dike snapped decisively. "We ride tonight."

"Yes, lord."

"But only after you have received your bribe," the grinning warrior said. "It should just about cover our expenses for the journey."

Apart from the odd skirmish with robbers, a sandstorm or two and nearly perishing from lack of water, the two men arrived on the outskirts of Sariam in good order. What worried both now, aside from the inevitable court intrigue, was how they would deal with being in the strange and heady atmosphere of a proper town. In the younger man's case it would be for the very first time. That, and going amongst a far more opulent and sophisticated company than either had experienced, gave them pause for reflection.

Above all, feeling towards Goroba-Dike as a father towards a son, Ulal realized that his charge must learn to be a better, more thoughtful man. His arrogance towards strangers during their travels had embarrassed and endangered them more than once. In a place like Sariam such behaviour would not do.

Ulal himself was none too keen on entering the town. He did not like or trust such places. That the pair of them were very short of money was another concern. As they rested their horses on a hilltop, gazing on Sariam in the near distance, similar worries were going through Goroba-Dike's mind, although he would not admit to them.

Already the poet's mind was working on a strategy that would hopefully help assure their survival and prosperity, while giving Goroba-Dike some much needed humbling.

"We must not go in to Sariam as we are, especially you, lord," Ulal began. "It would not do at all."

"What do you mean? How else should we proceed? And why ever not?"

"We will be set upon by thieves ..."

"Do you think I fear thieves," Goroba-Dike laughed derisively.

"Those who come with knives and threats, lord, no indeed. But what of those who use soft words and who employ tricks and wiles the like of which we of the deserts and clean places of the earth know nothing? What of lawyers and officials, what of rivals for the princess's hand, and others at court, who, seeing you, will despair and send assassins by stealth? Think, lord, we could not trust the very food we ate in Sariam if we, lonely strangers, proceeded too openly."

"Perhaps what you say is true," the young man nodded sagely. "The jealousy my arrival will surely engender could well be dangerous, until we have the authority of the crown behind us ..."

"Exactly, lord. And, of course, there is a need for mystery. A man out of the story books, with no fortune, a fellow who would capture the heart of a princess must have more than slender fingers."

The great shoulders sagged and though Goroba-Dike did not reply, Ulal knew the young warrior had received his first lesson in humility.

Following the advice of his mabo, Goroba-Dike made his way into Sariam on foot, dressed in the clothes of a peasant, and looking for work. Ulal remained with the horses at the dwelling of the peasant they had bought the clothing from, keenly awaiting developments. He was glad of the opportunity to put his feet up for a while.

With his superior strength to recommend him, Goroba-Dike quickly found employment with a blacksmith and settled down to his labours. Encouraged by Ulal, he bided his time and was content to learn all he could about the town, its people and the doings of the court. Indeed, relieved of the responsibility of being himself, he began increasingly to enjoy the masquerade, the hard but simple work and the company of ordinary people who were neither afraid nor resentful of him.

At the palace, things were going from bad to worse. The king was losing patience with his youngest daughter, her mother was a nervous wreck and her sisters and their scheming husbands were making capital out of the turmoil. With no male heir the succession was uncertain, so the long-favoured, very intelligent younger daughter's choice of husband was a matter of great importance, and its implications for the others considerable.

The king's growing exasperation spilled over into anger after yet another suitor had presented himself and been found wanting. The whispered derision of his sons-in-law, who always subtly bullied him, added to his ire.

"At this rate she will never discover a man whose finger fits her marriage ring," they twittered in the background.

Embarrassed and outraged the king railed at his youngest daughter.

"Enough of this waiting and hoping," he thundered, and then and there ordered a convocation of all the unmarried Fulbe men of his kingdom. Every one of them must try the ring on and whomsoever it fitted must marry his daughter with no quibbling on either side, he declared. This was his last word on the subject, and such was the heat of his fury that none dared question him, even the princess.

The ceremony ordered by the king took place soon afterwards. Hundreds of bachelors arrived, no longer simply the high-born or optimistic. Those not of the better sort, the warrior class, were given short shrift by the court, however, especially by the husbands of two of the other princesses. However, none of any standing could manage to slip the little silver band past the second knuckle of his ring finger.

At Ulal's urging, for he was on hand at his master's side, also humbly dressed, Goroba-Dike stepped out from the throng, fresh from the blacksmith's forge.

"Mustn't let this one get away," muttered one son-in-law.

"A true blue blood, to be certain," hissed another.

"I am no warrior," Goroba-Dike said humbly, secretly thrilled by the deception. "But I too am a Fulbe."

"Present your finger," growled the exasperated king, who was about to turn away and dismiss the assembly. Anything was better than his daughter never finding a husband, he had decided.

Amidst derisive laughter, most particularly from the husbands of the other princesses, Goroba-Dike stretched out his hand. The princess regarded the unkempt stranger with disdain and only for form's sake did she put the ring on his finger. She gasped as the second knuckle presented no obstacle and the ring slipped easily into place.

"Right," cried the king. "Let the marriage take place at once." Laughter and ribald comments ran round the assembly, reaching a crescendo.

The princess burst into tears, humiliated at the prospect of wedding such a dirty, sweaty, lowborn specimen.

Goroba-Dike's act of faith in Ulal's plan and his own instincts were further tested when the marriage was performed. On the wedding night the beautiful and haughty princess refused to touch her new husband and treated him with utter disgust. Goroba-Dike exercised great restraint. He continued to play the part of the lowly blacksmith's assistant turned royal bridegroom for many days to come, and lived like an unloved palace house pet. Meanwhile, Ulal returned to the peasant's home. Many and varied were the slights and cruelties Goroba-Dike suffered at the hands of his brothers-in-law and others at court. Two of the brothers-in-law, however, surpassed everyone else in their meanness, tricking him into doing things that were demeaning to a real noble, making fun of him at every turn, indeed regarding him as a joke and no better than a servant.

Then, one morning it was excitedly reported that Burdama tribesmen had raided the cattle pens outside the town and stolen much of the king's livestock. Sariam's fighting men quickly assembled and rode off in pursuit, but Goroba-Dike refused to join them. Instead, he hopped onto the back of a donkey and headed off in the opposite direction, to the home of the peasant.

Ulal was feeling rather pleased with himself, because he had predicted such a happening. Goroba-Dike quickly changed his clothing before galloping off cross-country to catch up with the war party on the trail of the cattle raiders. He came upon them not far from the enemy's encampment, sitting on their horses, dithering about who would lead the attack. The men watched his approach and all were impressed with his heroic appearance. Goroba-Dike was resplendent in silk robes, well and expensively armed and bestride a horse of the best blood. None recognized him as the husband of the young princess but saw that he was a Fulbe warrior like themselves. They entreated him, so apparently a champion, to take command of their impending attack to recover King Hamadi Ardo's property.

"Has the king no sons or sons-in-law to fight in his name?" asked Goroba-Dike disingenuously.

"Three sons-in-law," said one of the warriors, leaning over in his saddle and spitting emphatically on the ground. "But one has run away and the other two are pretty useless as leaders or fighters. That's them on the hill over there, looking important, doing nothing and shivering in their boots."

"Well, it's like this," Goroba-Dike smiled, throwing one leg over the pommel of his saddle, resting an elbow on his knee and leaning towards the group of warriors. "Tell the two prince-consorts who are present that if they will both give me an ear, then I will lead this attack and give them a victory. They can take all the credit and pretend to have been honourably wounded in combat."

This was not part of Ulal's plan or predictions, but, if it worked, it might be useful and would certainly be very, very sweet to Goroba-Dike.

His brothers-in-law being both great cowards, certain they would die in the battle, unable to bring themselves to go back to Sariam empty handed, and loath to fight, jumped at the chance. Grimacing and whimpering, they had a servant cut off the right ear of one and the left of the other and these were presented to the strange champion from the desert. Although sad about their missing ears, they were pleased enough with the bargain.

The other soldiers enjoyed the spectacle, and found that the tough-mindedness of the stranger gave them heart. So it was that after a quick reconnoitre, Goroba-Dike drew his sword and led them in a thundering assault on the Burdama, who were busy gloating over their booty and dreaming of the profits to be made.

He was the first to reach the raiders and cut down several of them before coming face to face with their leader. This giant managed to mount his horse and meet him, as the rest of the king's men swept through the camp, driving all before them.

The clash of swords was ear-splitting as the two men squared off, horses turning, steel flashing, each seeking an advantage, assessing the other's ability. As his enemy's blade passed a hair's breadth from his nose, Goroba-Dike at last struck a telling blow at his enemy's head. The big Burdama could not parry quickly enough and, his head nearly severed from his body, he gaped in astonishment at what had befallen him. Goroba-Dike stood up in his stirrups, waving his sword in his lean but strong black arm and bellowing triumphantly as the dying enemy chieftain slithered from the saddle.

Bowing and laughing, he accepted the cheers of the warriors, who had scattered the rest of the enemy band and were recovering the cattle. Goroba-Dike bid them all farewell and very pointedly rode off into the sunset, leaving his brothers-in-law to slink out of the shadows now that the coast was clear. Desperately, they swore the warriors to silence about what had really happened.

Taking a roundabout route lest he should be followed, Goroba-Dike rode back to the peasant's house where Ulal was waiting for news. Together they groomed the warhorse, cleaned the weapons and discussed their next move. The young warrior then donned his humble clothes once more, mounted his flea-bitten donkey, and returned to the palace. Amidst the victory celebrations for the safe recovery of the king's cattle, no one took any notice of him.

Later that night he listened from a corner of the throne-room as his brothers-in-law crowed about their triumph. They told the king stirring tales of how they had been wounded – so ironically in a similar fashion – while in the thick of the fighting. Goroba-Dike smiled to himself and fingered the ears that he had placed in his wallet.

That night his wife not only rejected his timid advances but refused to share a bed with him, insisting he curl up on the floor like the dog he surely was. Her disdain had turned to contempt.

The next morning, howling for revenge and led by the equally large and bold brother of the giant Burdama champion, the raiders returned, but this time for more than cattle. Attacking and threatening to overwhelm the North Gate, the town itself was their target.

All the fighting men of Sariam massed together and rushed to the North Gate, all except Goroba-Dike who mounted his sorry donkey and rode out through the South Gate at a trot. Hooted at by the people, pelted with rotten fruit, he was called every filthy name in the Sariam language.

On reaching the peasant's house, he told Ulal what had happened. The mabo danced with glee and swore he had seen it all as if in a dream, or a song he had already composed. Then he urged the warrior to hurry and prepare himself. Goroba-Dike cleaned up before dressing in his own clothes, taking up his arms and mounting his warhorse. He arrived back in Sariam with not a moment to spare. Already the enemy had broken through the North Gate and were on the rampage in the town.

Goroba-Dike rode to the palace looking for the fight. He came upon a small party of the Burdama in the royal courtyard. On the steps of the palace, leading to the private quarters of the king's family, the youngest princess was wildly waving a sword at two laughing raiders, one of whom took a cut to the shoulder on purpose while the other darted in and disarmed her. Grabbing her slim body they hustled her towards the spot where one of their number stood holding their mounts.

Goroba-Dike urged his horse forwards, sword in hand. He split the skull of this third man, and then turned to face the other two. The horses the man had been holding scattered in fright. One of the Burdama released his hold on the princess and came at Goroba-Dike with deadly purpose, shouting a war cry, only to be spitted on the Fulbe champion's spear. The other Burdama slashed at Goroba-Dike as his charge carried him past, leaving a deep wound in the hero's thigh. Wheeling his horse, Goroba-Dike swung his sword down against the man's shoulder, cleaving him to the middle of his chest.

The grateful princess ran to him, not knowing him for her own husband, and flung one arm around his horse's neck, reaching up with the other to grip his hand. She babbled her thanks as she gazed tearfully at him. It was then that she noticed his wound.

Tearing off a strip of her gown, she quickly bandaged the bleeding thigh before he rode back into the battle that was raging in the streets of the town. Rallying men and repeatedly charging headlong into concentrations of the enemy, Goroba-Dike broke the invaders' momentum. Gradually the tide turned and the raiders were in full retreat. When at last the town was secure and the defeated enemy sufficiently punished not to contemplate another attack, Goroba-Dike disappeared back to the peasant's house and put on his rags once more.

By now addicted to this game of masquerade, half enjoying his ill-fame and degradation, deliciously anticipating the final moment of revelation, he needed little urging from Ulal to wait a while longer before showing his hand. As for Ulal himself, he was already at work on the epic poem that he felt sure would immortalize them both.

All over Sariam there were many fallen soldiers to mourn but a great victory to celebrate as well. By the king's reckoning they had dispatched enough of their enemies to make themselves safe from them for a whole generation. At the feast held in the great hall of the palace, all the surviving warriors were boasting of their deeds that day, as wives and sweethearts, children and elders listened rapturously. Even Goroba-Dike's brothers-in-law, who had made sure to be observed charging off in the direction of the attack (only to duck into a cellar unseen), could brag of heroics always performed in some other quarter of the battle zone than that served in by anyone in earshot.

All the women of the court, including her older sisters, teased the youngest princess, reducing her to a quiet rage and to tears she was loath to shed in public.

"Where do you suppose your husband was during the fighting?" they asked with false innocence. "Do you know?" Her sisters, and even the lowliest nobles, burst out laughing.

"I have married a coward, a filthy pig," she replied bitterly. All her efforts to discover the name of the warrior who had saved her proved futile, though many other people present also told tales of his fearlessness. Of course, the king himself was not unaware of this buzz, or of a certain song in which disparaging references about two of his sons-in-law and their part in the battle with the cattle raiders were made.

Following the revels, the young princess could not sleep and rising from her bed she stepped over to the window where a breeze moved the night air and stirred the muslin drapes. A snore startled her, for she had momentarily forgotten her despised husband, who was sleeping on the floor to which she had consigned him. And there he lay in disarray, beneath the window for coolness, bright moonlight streaming in on his recumbent form.

The princess nearly gasped in surprise at what she saw, for there on her husband's thigh was wrapped a bloody bandage. Bending low she examined it in the moonlight. The material was that which she had earlier ripped from her own dress. Lightly touching his forearm, she awakened him.

"Where did you get that wound?" she asked.

"That," he said sleepily, "is something for you to ponder."

"Who bandaged you?"

"That is something else for you to consider."

After a pause, she spoke again.

"Thank you for what you did today." She looked him frankly in the eye, showing true respect for the first time, put out her small hand to shake his, and smiled.

There was a long silence which developed into awkwardness when they became aware of their closeness and their position as husband and wife. She plucked up the courage to ask who he really was. He told her truthfully that he was the son of a king of sorts, but that he had nothing in the world beside his weapons, his horse and his loyal mabo.

"That is why I have had to deceive you," he explained. "As a lone, penniless warrior, married to you out of nowhere, I could not have survived here long. Your sisters' husbands, and no doubt others, would have seen to that. Without your full support and that of the king, I could still never be secure here."

"I understand. You are very wise."

"I am well advised by my old mabo," he smiled, "a clever fellow and not a bad poet, who also pointed out that as your good-for-nothing husband I would not be missed if I decided that the marriage, let alone the situation, was intolerable, if I had to go away, knowing I could not care for you or you for me, if I could never be master in my own home. Even now, I would rather be the despised cur I was than your loved but tame lap dog."

The princess studied her husband in the moonlight and slowly reached out to stroke his face, then she leaned forward to kiss him. He responded tenderly at first and then with increasing passion and no more words passed between them that night.

Having sworn his wife to keep his secret a while longer, the next morning, feeling as if he hovered light as air above his donkey's back, he rode to the peasant's farmhouse a final time. Still the object of derision, he made his way through the town, savouring his last moments of humility. Soon he was back for good in his fine silk robes, his loins girded with belt and sword. When he returned to Sariam as himself, Ulal was riding a respectful stride or two behind, and each was mounted on a splendid horse.

Recognized by many of the townspeople as the unknown hero who had performed great deeds in the two fights with the Burdama, his entry into Sariam could not have been more different from his exit an hour earlier. He was now followed by a cheering crowd and preceded by rapidly spreading word. When he arrived in the square, he was accompanied by almost the entire populace of the town. Here he and Ulal drove silver stakes into the ground to picket their horses and sat down cross-legged as if alone in the wilderness.

Hurrying from the palace with almost unseemly haste, the royal family and their retainers were not long in joining the crowd, agape at the prospect of seeing the fabled warrior to whom they owed so much.

The throng parted as the royals and their retinue appeared. The king, queen, daughters and sons-in-law looked in amazement at the warrior and his mabo sitting in the square. Nonchalantly, Ulal had started to brew tea over a small fire.

"Who is this fellow?" asked King Hamadi Ardo. "Who are you, sir?" he called to Goroba-Dike.

"This man," said the youngest princess, striding towards the two men, who rose to their feet as she approached. "This man," she repeated, clearly and loudly, standing by Goroba-Dike's side and taking his hand, "is my husband, champion and prince." Then she whispered, smiling. "I do not keep pets."

Uproar greeted the princess's public pronouncement.

The husbands of the other princesses demanded proof that Goroba-Dike was who he said he was. The attention he was getting from the people was far too enthusiastic for their liking.

""This fellow doesn't deserve any special honour," cried one of the brothers-in-law.

"What has he done, except learnt to act the part of champion and prince?" scoffed another.

"Are we not all sons of the king by marriage, and heroes too?" cried a third.

A silence filled the square, as all eyes turned to the king. Seeing Hamadi Ardo's embarrassed nod and his shrug, they dreaded that nothing would change.

"Heroes?" Goroba-Dike asked, taking out his wallet. He dipped his long, elegant fingers into it and drew forth the missing ears of his irate brothers-in-law. The court gasped collectively. Loud bellows of laughter issued from the crowd as the warriors among them shouted out the true story of the recovery of the royal cattle and the absence of the two cowards from the recent fighting.

And so it was that the influence of the husbands of the older princesses was washed away for good and Goroba-Dike and his wife became the official heirs and favourites of the king and the people.

The Example of Miao Shan

Miao Shan is a popular figure in Chinese mythology. Her story is not unlike Countess Cathleen's earlier in this volume. Buddhist, perhaps Taoist in earlier times, it is about sacrifice but also spiritual development. No doubt it serves as a cautionary tale in a culture notorious for underestimating daughters.

Blood sprayed across the room as the bandits burst through the door and instantly severed the head of the father of the family. Shouting and running through the humble dwelling, they came upon the wife and hacked her in two, then went on to the three small boys. Elsewhere in that part of China there was also mayhem. A tyrant had slaughtered the rightful king together with members of his court, usurping the crown and forcing his will on the people. A few private murders like these would not be noticed amid the political upheaval and there was no law that would touch the killers.

Oddly, the bandits themselves had vaguely noted, none of the family had screamed even when they first saw their attackers, nor had even the smallest child cried out, tried to run away or raised an arm in defence against the descending swords. After the initial shock at the bandits' entrance, they died without struggle, with calmness written on their faces.

All five of the victims were very spiritually developed and had recognized the imminence of death. As the darkness had descended and then gradually been lifted by the new bright light, they felt no confusion and did not linger in grieving for themselves or each other.

In the after-life they were greeted joyously and the customary rest and review period began. Soon it was recognized, by themselves above all, that the three small boys had died too early and that they had not developed much further in this lifetime than they had in the lifetime before. Like their mother and father they were devout Buddhists and steadily working towards enlightenment. The spirits that had been the boys decided to test and challenge themselves again and were re-incarnated as the daughters of the wealthy but ruthless king who now ruled their former country. In this new life they would risk being spoiled by luxury and every temptation of material existence. They would also come under the direct influence of a most wicked and impious man.

Only one daughter, the youngest, proved to be equal to the challenge, to be able to retain her principles and to feel inside the cosmic truths she had learned.

For her father the king it had seemed a disaster when yet another little girl was born to his wife. A male heir was badly needed to solidify his hold on the kingdom, to begin a dynasty that would last long into the future. These daughters were useless, he declared to his closest advisers and confidants, among whom his eldest wife was a principal member.

"I would as soon strangle them and try again for sons, but we are growing past the time for such things." He admitted to her, carefully avoiding accusing his wife and partner in ambition of being too old to produce the longed for heir.

"Yes," his queen said. "But all the younger royal wives and concubines have only produced girls, as well." She did not say 'the fault is obviously not mine' but it was the truth and all knew it.

"Trying for sons now would be a waste of time. We have failed."

"That is not true," said another adviser. "You must use what you have and turn it to advantage. One is not able to choose sons. But sons-in-law ..."

"Indeed," said the king with a sly smile, "they could be men whose wealth or lands might expand our influence and power."

"They might also be played against each other until we are old and have selected a successor," the queen pointed out.

"Three is the perfect number. Two might fight too soon or band together. Three will vie against one another," the adviser said. "Each will try to please you, suspect his fellows but fear them, spy and report on them. Three can be used most brilliantly. Of course, two can easily be murdered just before the succession is announced, to avoid civil war and danger to the dynasty."

"It is perfect," the king nodded. "I pity the sovereign with one son. It is an invitation to regicide and patricide, nothing more." He smiled thinly. "Let the princesses be brought up to understand their duty and be best formed to attract worthy, malleable but advantageous suitors. Above all, they must be trained to obey the will of their father and appreciate the power and wealth we hold and must always hold. They must know that nothing is more important. Their loyalty to us and our family's position must be absolute."

Miao Shan was destined to be the problem child in such a clan. From the beginning of her life she demonstrated kindness and consideration for all creatures. She was generous and helpful with her sisters and parents but did not sacrifice the needs of others over theirs. She did not beat servants, inform on them or her sisters, and liked best to eat only plain vegetables and rice, rather than the lavishly prepared food of the court. Once she risked her future value as a lure to useful suitors by getting a scar on her forehead. She had been rescuing a cricket from a preying mantas in the garden and had fallen out of the tree while carrying out this mercy mission and hit her head. Bleeding copiously from the wound, Miao Shan told her attendants that the injury had been well worth the price of saving the life of the cricket.

This incident infuriated her father, embarrassed her mother and nearly got the child's nurses killed. The nurses hardly minded this threat, for they had come to love Miao Shan and although they were sorry she had hurt herself, they admired her courage and her kind intentions. She had been in their care since early childhood and they were the first to be inspired by her spiritual qualities and inner serenity.

As she grew older there would be many other adherents to her way.

Needless to say, none of these people who thought the young princess admirable were of the sort her parents considered desirable, any more than they found Miao Shan's attributes in accord with their own values. The love of servants and peasants, people who were in one's power as a matter of course, was valueless and a waste of effort. Gentleness and a fondness for simplicity were counter-productive in that they did not demonstrate authority, as did ostentation, or the fruits of high position. If these things were not valued, the argument ran, one seemed not to value one's position, and this showed dangerous weakness.

Lectures on this subject were a common thread in the lives of all three girls. Miao Shan's sisters took them to heart, fully enjoying their privileges, the gossip and intrigue of court life, the trappings of wealth, and the thrill of power over others. When they were old enough to marry, the only thing they insisted upon in their husbands that their parents had not put in their own list of priorirties for them was good looks. The king and queen could see the wisdom of this requirement, however. A handsome face was certainly an asset if one was to command respect and loyalty of the aristocratic and middle ranking classes. Heirs were more likely to be forthcoming if the princess found her husband attractive. This attribute was also considered a sign of good breeding.

"Only the helpless marry the ugly and have ugly children," the king pronounced, reassuring his eldest daughter on this point. "Wealth might be first found through marriage to the ugly, naturally, but this is not a necessity for our family. We are rich, powerful and feared for our ferocity. Our neighbours will be only too glad to send not only their most noble princes to us, but their most handsome too, lest we turn them away as unsuitable. As to character, I will mould them myself. You need not concern yourself."

So the first princess did not worry and indeed a husband was found among the princes from nearby, very intimidated, realms. The king and queen decided he was excellent material for their purposes, being good-looking, spoiled, vain and greedy, all qualities which greatly endeared him to them. The princess was far less likely to risk having an affair of the heart (or loins) on the side with this fine specimen available to her. Her parents were mindul that scandal of that sort often caused internecine fighting that could endanger even well established dynasties.

It was decided that the second eldest daughter should be married off promptly the following year, and that just as this second son-in-law was finding his feet, perhaps even getting ideas of his own, the third would arrive.

The king and queen were as fortunate in their choice for their second daughter as they had been first time around. Handsome, devious, shallow, malleable, yet clever, prince number two was a match both for the girl and his brother-in-law. He was a counter-balance and yet a possible future king if, in the end, he proved the more worthy in the eyes of the royal couple.

All was well with the dynastic scheme until the time came for Miao Shan to be married. She flatly refused to entertain the notion. Though respectful to her parents, far more so than her sisters were, she was always thought of as troublesome, difficult and impossible to understand. A foundling or changeling could not have been less like the rest of her family.

All her young life Miao Shan had been dedicated to charity and kind service to others within the limited world of the court. Kindness and consideration, modesty and calm were her most obvious traits. She always put other people's interests before her own, was gentle and helpful to all living things and known by now to have a heart of pure gold.

"I have not been unaware of your nature, as you have grown," her father said when she was called before him to discuss her marriage yet again. "Your qualities, all very well and good in a lowly peasant or official's offspring, are not welcomed in a family trying to hold on to vast wealth, estates, titles and authority we have but recently stol...," the king pretended to cough. "come into. You must mend your ways. You can make up for all the years of disappointment you have thus far given your mother and me by making a suitable match."

"I am sorry that I have disappointed you," Miao Shan said respectfully, her hands clasped before her and her eyes cast down. "That has never been my intention."

"It is simply that you do not value any of the important things in life," her father said.

"I know it seems so to you, father," Miao Shan told him. "But the wealth and glory of this world is only an illusion. It is without permanence and true substance. Why should I pursue such things? You do not share this belief, but please let me go to be a nun and escape the ways of a world I do not fit into. I apologize, father, but no matter what you do or force upon me, I will never think or act differently and," she added with absolute determination, "I will never, ever marry."

"Never marry," cried the outraged king, while beside him his wife nearly swooned. "Never marry!"

"No father, not even to some kind and brilliant doctor who lives to heal the sick and aid the poor, though a weak part of me might like such a union. No, it is my resolve to become a nun and dedicate my life to the Buddha."

"Never marry," the king said, his tone now scornful. "We shall see about that, my girl. Now get out of my sight. You will regret defying me."

Miao Shan went away, followed quickly by her mother, who pleaded with her to change her mind and not so anger and displease her father. No one in the world knew better than she how he might react. Usually, of course, no one agreed more with his methods than did his queen. But danger to a daughter was another matter. Besides, dead girls brought no vital third son-in-law into the kingdom.

At last Miao Shan was persuaded to return to her father's presence, at a time of his choosing, of course. It had been necessary to talk him into another meeting, so perturbed was he with his youngest daughter.

When Miao Shan was once more summoned before the king, it was in front of the entire court. Her mother felt that she was less likely to defy her father there, and might be intimidated by so many witnesses to any of her wilfulness. Let the pious child show publicly whether or not she would obey her parents.

So it was that Miao Shan appeared like a supplicant at the feet of her sovereign, dressed, as was her custom, in very simple clothes, the pyjama-like trousers and lightly quilted jacket of a peasant. All around her stood nobles and courtiers in fine silk robes, jewels and carefully arranged hair styles. None were more ornately or expensively dressed than her sisters, brothers-in-law and parents. They also sported the long nails associated with the mandarins of a later era, denoting the use of servants for even the most intimate of the functions of life.

"Have you reconsidered, child?" her father intoned, speaking now more as a king than a father to the young princess bowing to him. "Will you marry as your parents bid?"

"Yes," Miao Shan said without hesitation. The shock of the seeming ease with which she said the word fluttered around the assembly. "I will do as you bid, you who have long taught me to serve my family and myself first, if you can promise an end to three ills which we all face. That is to say, ills the world, ourselves and our family must endure."

The mistake had been to give Miao Shan a bigger audience, her mother thought at once. The foolish girl could not help but preach and try to sway people's souls to her path. The queen cursed herself.

"What ills are these?" the king huffed, taken aback and curious in spite of himself.

"I will gladly marry, as you wish, if you can guarantee that it will end for the world, or even just for me, the ravages of time. If you can stop the onset of grey hair, a withering, weakening, less energetic body, poor eyesight and hearing and the pains and cares of old age."

"And the second," her father rolled his eyes, slowly getting the drift of what she was saying.

"If you will promise, and keep the promise that even while young, one's body will stay hale and whole, that no evil will ever befall it. Assure me that no illness awaits, no accident, no pestilence or war or storm or foolishness will do anyone harm."

"The third?" the king asked darkly, his eyes narrowing dangerously.

"Tell me truly that death will not overtake loved ones, that it need never be feared for one's self. Say that the sadness of loss and the darkness of uncertainty are eliminated. If these things can be in this world, if by my marrying I can make it so, then I will marry and embrace this existence and do your bidding always."

"And if I cannot promise you these things?" The king's mood changed yet again as he pondered her words. How could you take such nonsense seriously? The girl was a ninny. Perhaps he had spoiled her by not making her enjoy material luxury. Yes, this is where indulging her in silly notions like simple dress and food had led. But why should he blame himself when the nurses and ladies-in-waiting should have done a better job?

"If these things cannot be, father, if my marriage cannot bring them to myself or this world, then let me seek a world in which they are possible. Let me become a nun and devote my life to service and contemplation, to attaining enlightenment and reaching Nirvana."

"Oh," the king groaned and cast his eye around the court. "Go be a nun then," he laughed, partly to hide his uncertainty. With his look he invited all to join him. The uproar of laughter was tremendous but ended abruptly when he spoke again a few moments later.

"See how you like it, my girl. See how you like a life of sacrifice and manual toil. You need to grow up a little. I recall that you were always more backward at each stage of life than your sisters. Go and get this religious rubbish out of your system for good. Soon enough you will beg to come home and then we will find you a patient, or perhaps rather masterful, husband to take you in hand."

Once more he allowed the court to join him in laughter and Miao Shan was led away by attendants to pack for her journey. Through one pretext or another her departure was delayed. The poor girl assumed this was because her parents hoped she might have second thoughts and would not go at all. However, it was for a different reason.

"Go to the head nun," the king commanded one of his officers. "Take your whole troop and intimidate her, let the men leer at the nuns and make it clear that I will be very displeased if she does not do as I order."

"Yes, sire," the officer saluted.

"The nunnery must be a hell for Miao Shan not a sanctuary. She must be put to all the most arduous and unpleasant tasks. No one must show her kindness or encouragement. In every way she must be made unwelcome and convinced that she should come back to where she belongs."

"I will see that this is fully understood, sire," the officer bowed low and backed away from the king's presence, setting off at once with his mounted warriors. The little Nunnery of the White Bird was in for a terrible shock.

Fearing the power and wrath of a king of such deservedly violent repute, the mother superior of the nunnery was duly cowed. Convinced, for everyone's safety, that it was wisest to do just as she was commanded, she summoned the other nuns. Speaking forcefully, still unnerved, as they all were by the visit of the soldiers, she made it clear to everyone that they must cooperate in the plan to drive Miao Shan back to the court, or risk not only her displeasure but the king's fury.

When Miao Shan arrived she was a little taken aback by her reception. Expecting to find devout like-minded sisters who would assist her along the path, she met only with hostility, resentment and rejection. She also found herself in the kitchen working like a slave to prepare meals and clean the place endlessly. To cap it all, any dirty jobs that needed to be done elsewhere were her final tasks before she crawled onto her sleeping mat for the brief repose she was allowed.

Through it all she never complained, even when she realized it was not simply an initiation or weeding out process. She even found time to help others with their work. It was soon observed that the dreadful chores she had to perform had never been done so well, never so thoroughly. The meals were better, too, and soon she became renowned for the salads she prepared.

After seeing her suffering and sacrifice, Heaven itself sent her assistance in her various duties. A dragon helped her dig a well, tigers fetched her firewood and birds brought her fruits and vegetables, while the Spirit of the North Star gave her aid in her kitchen work.

Moved by her devotion and service, inspired by her contacts with the divine, most of the nuns began to love Miao Shan and only a few spiteful ones, who resented her beauty, title and supposedly advantageous background, still treated her badly. Word of all that was happening at the Nunnery of the White Bird was brought to the king's ear and he was maddened with rage.

One night a carefully selected troop of soldiers arrived at the nunnery, surrounded it and set it on fire. Each man had been chosen for his cruelty, ruthlessness, ambition and willingness to follow the most horrible commands to get ahead and gain financial reward. None of them would baulk at their present assignment.

"Cut down anyone else who leaves the building," the leader shouted to remind his men. "But bring me the princess Miao Shan alive."

Terror gripped the nuns as the flames and smoke engulfed the nunnery, and chaos reigned. Everywhere the nuns ran screaming and some tried to escape only to be slaughtered by the waiting soldiers. The ones who had never accepted Miao Shan now began to curse her and insist that this would never have happened if she had stuck to her proper station in life.

Hearing this and seeing the fear in the faces of all the nuns, Miao Shan knelt down to pray.

"The Buddha was a prince when he sought enlightenment," she pleaded. "Surely it was not wrong of me to do so. Please send us help and please spare these good sisters."

Miao Shan's plea was quickly answered. Guided by some unknown divinity, she took a bamboo pin from her hair and pierced the roof of her mouth with it. Next she spat blood in the four directions – north, south, east and west. The blood spray formed a mist that became great dark rain clouds, and as she prayed once more rain began to fall, at first lightly and then quickening in intensity until it became a violent deluge.

Even so big a fire as the one consuming the nunnery could not survive such torrential rain and soon the flames and embers were extinguished. Then Miao Shan surrendered. Somehow, in the excitement and relief of taking her alive, the army commander forgot to have all the other nuns put to the sword. In reality of course, he had been made to forget as part of the answer to Miao Shan's prayer.

The last mile of the way home for Miao Shan was bestrewn with all the comforts she was supposed to have missed while at the nunnery. Music played, delicious foods were cooking, and lovely garments were on display. At the palace more luxury than ever was on show as she was led before her father. None of the sumptuous earthly delights turned Miao Shan's head for an instant, nor did the array of young princes backing her father's throne as he stared at her grim faced.

"Any of these men will I let you choose if you agree to marry at once and forget forever the stupid idea of becoming a nun," he said flatly. "And make no mistake, I command you to marry on pain of death."

"Is it not a crime," her mother put in quickly, "and a sin for a child to disobey her father?"

Miao Shan nodded solemnly.

"Then you must do what is right, mustn't you?"

"Yes," Miao Shan admitted. "I must."

"Then you will obey your father and marry," her mother said delightedly. Why had they not used this tack long before?

"Please forgive me for disobeying you, but I must bow to an even higher authority."

"What authority is that?" the king demanded.

"The highest possible," Miao Shan said. "Let me return to the nunnery and follow my vocation. Let me work towards spiritual perfection and enlightenment. Then, my parents and sisters, I can serve you all so much better. I can help you to that which is real and truly valuable and lasting."

"Silence," the king bellowed. He had had enough. He felt certain that the world was laughing at him. He feared that whispers were already abroad that he was weak, soft and sentimental, unable even to command his own daughter. The danger was far too great. The two sons-in-law might already be plotting. Now he had the perfect opportunity to quash all that, to demonstrate his determination to be obeyed by all in this land, or ruthlessly eliminate anyone who would not do his will. Let it be a lesson to the kingdom. Let the neighbouring countries take note.

"You must die." The king said simply. Turning to the guard commander, he nodded, and Miao Shan was dragged away.

Without delay, though with ample time for a curious and horrified crowd to gather, Miao Shan was taken to the usual place of execution. Here her head was placed on the block and as ordered, wasting no time, the headsman struck. There, however, before the king and the people, the blade of the axe shattered. Infuriated further by this, the king ordered that other weapons be used, so the spears and swords of the soldiers around about were used, but all of them broke too.

So enraged was the king by now, so blind to the portents of divine favour, that he howled at the executioner.

"Strangle her with a silk cord, you fool, or I will disembowel you, after feeding you your roasted children and giving your wife to the soldiery."

Hastily the executioner found a silken cord and pulled it tight around Miao Shan's neck. Though she did not struggle, it seemed to take an age for the girl to expire. When at last she was dead and plainly so, the executioner let go of the cord and her limp body fell to the ground.

A great hush fell over the crowd, the king's party and the guards. The executioner wept silently as a strange stillness settled over the palace and the city. Suddenly it was broken by a huge collective gasp. An instant later there was much confused scrambling and a rapid parting of the crowd of common people in the square around the place of execution. A massive tiger had bounded in amongst them but, attacking no one, it made straight for the body of Miao Shan. Picking it up in its enormous mouth, it ran away like a house cat with a small bird. Dumbfounded, everyone stood staring, unable to move.

While her body was being taken to a forest and put gently down upon a bed of moss, Miao Shan herself awoke in the first level of Buddhist hell. Perhaps she went there because she was feeling so unfulfilled, having failed to do any great works or to find enlightenment, or perhaps she was there because she had not been able to keep anger out of her heart at the moment of death.

Disconcerted by the dull, lifeless silence of the dark place, she was just wondering what to do next when a young man, dressed in robes of luminescent blue, appeared and smiled curiously at her.

"Surely your coming here is some mistake," he told her. "But before you go, those in charge in this region would dearly like to see you. Your reputation for goodness is second to none and your eloquent prayers are very well spoken of at every level of existence. We who work down here see so few good souls, I am afraid, so please come with me."

Miao Shan was taken before the judges of the hells and they asked if they might hear her pray.

"Only if the souls suffering on all the levels of hell are allowed to hear me, too," said Miao Shan. "I would very much like to help them as much as I can."

"I don't see why not," the chief among the judges said.

So it was that all the souls in all the hells heard Miao Shan pray and they were much moved, for evil could not exist when she was near. Indeed she was all for releasing the suffering souls then and there, having them forgiven and helping them forgive themselves, when the judges intervened.

"No, Miao Shan, that cannot be. How could the hells continue thus? They must be places of punishment and justice, where lessons are learned, as on earth. Forgiveness without understanding is not what is needed. What does it teach about cause and effect?"

Finding that her presence disrupted their routine far too much to let her linger and with still much to learn for her own enlightenment, Miao Shan was returned, alive, to her earthly body. At last she was free to perfect herself, to pursue enlightenment, to become a Buddhasattva.

Walking among the mountain on Hsiang Shan, as an aid to contemplation, she was startled to see a handsome fellow staring at her and even more astonished to realize that he was the Ju Lai Buddha.

"How did you come to be in this place?" he asked, looking at the vista before them and the peaks on either side, but meaning far more than that.

"I was born a princess but my father would have me marry when all I desired was to do good, become a nun and seek enlightenment." She then told him what had happened afterwards.

"I am alone now and left to learn and serve as best I can."

"I too am alone," the Ju Lai Buddha said. "Perhaps we ought to get married and live in a wonderful little house together. We could raise a family and grow old in great harmony and bliss among our grandchildren, comfortable and happy. "

"How can you say that? Marry, have a house? Children? How

384

could we ever find the right path in that way? You know we would become earth-bound by such things, such actions, such connections. We would be ..."

"Ah, Miao Shan I was only testing you," the Buddha laughed. "Your devotion is unshakeable. I want you to come to a place that has been prepared for you, where you can work to further perfect yourself. It is on the island of Pu To Shan. The Monastery of the Immortals."

Miao Shan agreed and went there for nine years after which time Heaven itself praised her wisdom and character.

She was given two disciples who would remain with her always. During this time, however, her father and mother had held on to power in their stolen kingdom. They continued to amass power, prestige and possessions. Their other two daughters continued to value nothing more than the pleasures of a pampered life, while the two brothers-in-law eyed one another suspiciously and awaited events.

Perhaps as a punishment even while in the flesh, the king began to suffer a strange illness. Weakened and depressed, his skin covered in running sores, he lay in agony for many months. His daughters found the sight of him disgusting, and it was all his wife could do to be in the same room with him. Ill as he was, however, and obviously at death's door, he lingered, seemingly unable to die.

All the doctors in the land came to treat him and all failed, often inflicting much pain and doing more harm than good. Then one day a mendicant monk arrived apparently from very far away, and he too examined the king.

"I have identified the illness from which his majesty suffers," the monk said after a few days studying him, reading, meditating and discussing his case with his baffled colleagues. "I am pleased to say that it can be cured with ease."

"Magnificent!" cried the queen, much relieved. Already she sensed her daughters and sons-in-law were eyeing the throne and muttering among themselves. She loved her husband, however, and needed him alive and well. Like him, she too had been wondering what had brought such a terrible affliction on them, for she suffered when he did, though she would not have expected such a thing when they were young, even at the height of their lust for each other.

"I am afraid it is not a cure that an apothecary will have to hand," the monk explained.

"What is this treatment?" asked the king. "Will it be painful? What will you do to me? Is it long and difficult?"

"It is simple, quickly done and only involves rubbing you with an ointment made of ingredients that will cure you. It has no other effect."

"It will not burn, or chill me? There is no cutting, no binding, no scrubbing with caustic solutions?"

"No. The application of the ointment only. It is worn only for a few seconds and washed off. Then you are cured. It is simple. The ingredients are very difficult to come by, however."

"What are they?" the queen enquired. "We will pay anything, send anywhere for them."

"It is not a question of payment," the mysterious monk replied, with a shake of his head. "Nor is it a matter of sending far. The necessary things may be found near or far. The basic elements are everywhere about us, but the right ones ..." the mendicant monk shrugged.

"Tell us what we must find," the king said weakly.

"Yes," the queen concurred with urgency.

"You must have the hand and the eye of a human being ..."

"Send to the hall of corrections at once," the queen said to an attendant.

"Sometimes two eyes and two hands ..." the monk went on.

The queen nodded to the pausing attendant, who started out again.

"Wait," the monk commanded sharply. "It cannot be just the hand and eye of anyone. The person whose hand and eye you need must give them willingly."

"Willingly?" the king groaned. "There are no such persons in the hall of corrections, nor in all the kingdom. All the world."

"Some inducement may be found," the queen said thoughtfully. "For the poor, what would one hand and one eye be against ..."

"It may be two," the dying king pointed out.

"Two poor beggars ..." the queen began again, but the monk stopped her short.

"They must be the hands and eyes of the same person, if two are indeed needed."

"Where in all of creation would a man like me find someone like that?" the king howled in agony. "Oh, priest, you mock me in my misery."

"We will search nevertheless," swore the queen. At once the word was put about but, as the king suspected, nowhere was someone willing to become blinded and handless for his sake.

The monk did not go away and saying he would make his own inquiries he risked staying, even though everyone who knew the king supposed he would have the holy man tortured and killed for getting his hopes up and then dashing them. It seemed the old tyrant was too sick to bother, though.

At last the monk announced that he knew of one who would give the king a hand and an eye, two if need be. The king must send to the Monastery of the Immortals, for there was one there who was willing to do this for him and asked nothing in return.

Hardly able to believe this, the queen sent a delegation at once to go and fetch the eye and hand. In the meantime, two assassins fell over each other attempting to slip into his lodging and kill the monk, but he had vanished. It had been Miao Shan in disguise of course, all along. The ambitious brothers-in-law were both disappointed but they hoped to eliminate the monk if he returned to apply the remedy when the ingredients arrived. But the monk was never seen again.

The king's ambassadors duly found themselves at the Monastery of the Immortals and there they were taken to Miao Shan who appeared now as herself. She bowed to them and they to her, impressed by her radiance and calm. With her own fingers she plucked out her left eye and with her own right hand she took an axe and chopped off her left hand. Bleeding profusely she presented them to the king's men.

Rushing back to the ailing monarch, the ambassadors were shocked and profoundly impressed. The ingredients were dried and ground down to a powder and made into a paste as the monk had left instructions for them to do. Mixed with a few more ordinary things, the paste was applied to the king's person and then washed away.

Miraculously half of the king's body was restored to health, the sores vanished and he felt much better. Realizing what was needed the ministers were sent again to the Monastery of the Immortals and again Miao Shan calmly tore out her right eye and stood while her right hand was cut from her.

Again the body parts were dried, ground, mixed and applied and when they were washed away the king was plainly cured, his appetite and colour were back, his skin smooth once more and glowing with health.

"Tell me all about the wonderful man who sacrificed his two hands and eyes that I might be cured," he commanded his ambassadors.

"It was a woman," the senior one said a little awkwardly.

"Well, then, tell me about her. Was she young or old? A nun? A wise woman? What class of person was she? What did she look like?"

"She ..." the minister stuttered. "She looked remarkably like your third daughter, Miao Shan, sire. And she was of the age Miao Shan would be ..." the man trailed off, not finishing as he gaped at the tears in his sovereign's eyes. He had never seen the king cry, even at the height of his illness, even in the depths of despair at ever recovering, even when under the worst of the pain he had endured in battle.

The queen, nearly fainting, sat beside her husband, very pale, tears also running down her cheeks.

"Take us there at once," the king ordered them.

The journey was long and arduous for the old couple. They had much time to think and contemplate their lives, their relationship with their daughters and their treatment of Miao Shan. Far worse than the cold or rugged travel was recalling their past and remembering what they had done to their saintly little girl.

When they finally reached the Monastery of the Immortals the king and queen were conducted in to see Miao Shan, who stood at an altar in a small walled garden. There they beheld her, somehow still bleeding from her wrists, with blackened holes where her eyes had been. On her face was a calm, serene expression.

Recognizing the daughter they had thought was dead, and seeing her condition, her parents abased themselves before Miao Shan, begging for forgiveness. Smiling, she spoke with gentleness and compassion.

A flood of comfort and peace came over the grieving parents, and as she stepped towards them they got to their feet and embraced her warmly.

"I am an evil man for what I have done to you," the king cried. "And for the way I have lived."

"And I am no better," the queen sobbed.

"The sacrifice you have made for me is too much." Miao Shan's father said. "You have suffered always because of me, and now more than ever can be imagined."

"I have suffered nothing," Miao Shan said softly. "And I have done nothing but express a daughter's love. The trials of this human body, the loss of any part of it, are nothing. People are given other bodies, other lives. I have had many. Now, though, I will have a body of light, and live in another world."

"Let us stay here with you and devote ourselves to service and finding the right path," her father pleaded.

"Yes," her mother agreed. "We do not wish to go back to the way we were before."

"You will not," Miao Shan told them. "Return to your kingdom. It is too late to undo what has been done, it must be lived with and corrected by effort and time. Rule with justice, compassion and understanding and serve your people. Encourage righteousness in them by example. Teach them the ways of the Buddha."

Suddenly they saw before them the eyes of their daughter shining brightly upon them, and her hands reached out to comfort them, then to bid farewell. It was not the physical body of Miao Shan they now saw, but slowly moving away from it another body, rising from the physical one, which fell to the floor at their feet. Their eyes were drawn to the glowing form that ascended to the heavens, the music of the spheres resounding beautifully in their ears as Miao Shan disappeared.

Returning to their kingdom, they did as Miao Shan had instructed them to do. They also built a shrine to her where her last earthly form was buried. For the rest of their long lives her parents and her sisters revered her memory and the lesson of her life. Through them many people were set on the true path, and when they died they themselves had learned much and advanced well towards enlightenment.